THE
BIBLE
PROMISE
BOOK®
Devotional

© 2017 by Barbour Publishing, Inc.

Editorial assistance by Ed Strauss.

Print ISBN 978-1-68322-181-4

Published by Barbour Books, an imprint of Barbour Publishing, Inc., P.O. Box 719, Uhrichsville, Ohio 44683, www.barbourbooks.com

Our mission is to publish and distribute inspirational products offering exceptional value and biblical encouragement to the masses.

Member of the
Evangelical Christian
Publishers Association

Printed in the United States of America.

THE
BIBLE
PROMISE
BOOK®

Devotional

—◆—

365 Days of Encouragement
for Your Heart

BARBOUR BOOKS
An Imprint of Barbour Publishing, Inc.

Introduction

For more than three decades, *The Bible Promise Book*® has blessed millions of lives by providing scriptural wisdom and encouragement for dozens of key life topics. This brand-new daily devotional is inspired by this bestselling book and is a rich source of assurance to ground you deeply in God's Word so that you won't be shaken by life's many troubles and storms.

How powerful are God's promises? He told the Israelites, "Set your hearts on all the words which I testify among you today. . . . For it is not a futile thing for you, because it is your life" (Deuteronomy 32:46–47 NKJV). Jesus said, "The words I have spoken to you—they are full of the Spirit and life" (John 6:63 NIV).

The verses in this book can unleash the grace and power of God's Spirit in your daily walk, and with great authority declare your new identity in Christ. You may be pressed and distracted by the troubles of life, constantly reminded of your sins and failures, but never forget—you are a son or daughter of God, washed and forgiven by the blood of Jesus Christ. So He's not giving up on you, no matter how often you fail or how discouraged you become with yourself.

Are you looking for guidance about a specific situation or topic? Check the table of contents for a breakdown of weekly themes. Or you may choose to start at the beginning and read all fifty-two weeks in order. Either way, you will be blessed by new insights into 365 of God's promises to His children.

May this devotional help you be daily encouraged and transformed by God's Holy Spirit. Remember, "His compassions fail not. They are new every morning: great is thy faithfulness" (Lamentations 3:22–23 KJV).

The Editors

Weekly Themes

Day 1

IMPERISHABLE ETERNAL LIFE

*The wages of sin is death; but the gift of God
is eternal life through Jesus Christ our Lord.*

ROMANS 6:23 KJV

———————

Heaven is a place of wonder, breathtaking beauty, and boundless joy that you will enjoy forever. It consists of ever-unfolding panoramas of delight and astonishing vistas where you will enjoy everlasting life, together with your loved ones, the saints of all ages, and God Himself.

You were spiritually dead and destined for hell, but God has given you eternal life through Jesus Christ. What's more, you don't need to maintain possession of this inheritance through your own efforts. Jesus said, "I give them eternal life, and they shall never perish; neither shall anyone snatch them out of My hand" (John 10:28 NKJV).

No worry or fear or sorrow will ever mar your everlasting sojourn in this heavenly country. No sickness or infirmity will cause you to sigh. All the sorrows and pain you've known will be gone. "You will surely forget your trouble, recalling it only as waters gone by" (Job 11:16 NIV).

Heaven is not some stuffy landscape where bored saints dressed in starchy white robes make a discordant noise on harps day in and day out. Heaven is fascinating, interesting, and exciting. It will be far more beautiful than you ever hoped it could be.

WE SHALL BE CHANGED

*We will not all sleep, but we will all be changed,
in a moment, in the twinkling of an eye. . .for the
trumpet will sound, and the dead will be raised
imperishable, and we will be changed.*
1 Corinthians 15:51–52 NASB

When you pass from this life, your spirit is separated
from your mortal body and goes into the presence of
God. But you won't be a disembodied spirit for all
eternity. When Jesus returns in the rapture, if you're still
living, your physical body will be instantly transformed.

If you're no longer alive in that day, your body—
though it's scattered dust and ashes—will be resurrected
and reunited with your spirit.

Your new body will be physical and solid. Though
once weak and aging, it will be gloriously transformed
and made eternally youthful. It will have powers
that you never dreamed of. Your body is presently
perishable, but it will be raised imperishable; it's full of
imperfections, but it will be raised in glory; it is weak,
but it will be raised in power (1 Corinthians 15:42–44).

You can get along fine in heaven as just a spirit,
but you will *need* an amazing new body to live on the
wonderful new earth and all the many other worlds
you will go to.

HOLY NEW JERUSALEM

And I John saw the holy city, new Jerusalem,
coming down from God out of heaven, prepared
as a bride adorned for her husband.

Revelation 21:2 kjv

God said of the Old Testament saints, "But now they desire. . .a heavenly country. Therefore God. . .has prepared a city for them" (Hebrews 11:16 NKJV). And *what* a city! Just as a bride goes to great pains to make herself lovely, so God will spare no effort to make the new Jerusalem beautiful beyond compare.

The heavenly Jerusalem is an enormous city complex fashioned out of unearthly, crystalline gold, vaster than any earthly city. The Bible states that it's over 1,400 miles high, wide, and long. This doesn't necessarily mean that it's a giant cube. Likely it's a towering, many-spired structure.

Believers have been desiring just such a fantastic city for thousands of years. It's therefore the true home of every longing soul, because "the Jerusalem above is free, which is the mother of us all" (Galatians 4:26 NKJV). Right now this amazing city is in the heavens, but in the future it will descend to earth.

This city is where God dwells, where His throne is, and its millions of palaces, boulevards, and parks glow with the glory of the Almighty. It's a real place, and you'll be there soon.

ETERNAL HEAVENLY DWELLINGS

*"There is more than enough room in my Father's
home. If this were not so, would I have told
you that I am going to prepare a place for you?
When everything is ready, I will come and get you,
so that you will always be with me where I am."*

JOHN 14:2–3 NLT

Jesus has gone ahead into the highest heavens, where He sits enthroned upon the right hand of the eternal Father, robed in splendor and magnificent light. He said that He wanted His disciples to be with Him where He was so that you could see Him in all the glory that His Father gave Him (John 17:5, 24).

But Jesus' presence and light fill the *entire* city, not just the throne room (Revelation 21:23). There are many places in this fabulous city where you can "always be with Him where He is." Jesus will also visit you in your heavenly palace—a spacious, mansion-like dwelling. He went ahead to personally prepare your eternal abode. Every detail of your reward will reveal His intricate care and love for you.

The Son of God wants you to always be with Him, forever. That's why He makes this beautiful promise: He's coming back to get you, to take you to His astonishing city, where you will dwell joyfully forevermore.

TREASURE IN HEAVEN

Lay up for yourselves treasures in heaven,
where neither moth nor rust doth corrupt, and
where thieves do not break through nor steal.

MATTHEW 6:20 KJV

Jesus urged believers to diligently store up treasure in heaven, but many Christians don't take it literally. They think it's a metaphor for some transcendent reality. They envision heaven as an enormous cloud bank where believers perpetually drift around strumming harps and singing hymns. They therefore think that the "treasure" Jesus was referring to must refer to abstract quantities like joy and peace.

But the truth is, God has promised you treasure in the afterlife. He said, "Behold, I come quickly; and my reward is with me, to give every man according as his work shall be" (Revelation 22:12 KJV). Consider the heavenly mansion you will live in, the crown you will wear, and the streets of gold you will walk on.

The Bible repeatedly tells you about heavenly rewards to motivate you to do good deeds, and whatever form these rewards take, they're well worth striving for.

You obey Jesus simply because it's the right thing to do, regardless of whether He ever rewards you. Just the privilege of living in the heavenly city would be enough. But be assured, it's God's good pleasure to bless you beyond measure.

A CROWN OF RIGHTEOUSNESS

*In the future there is laid up for me the crown of
righteousness, which the Lord, the righteous Judge,
will award to me on that day; and not only to me,
but also to all who have loved His appearing.*

2 TIMOTHY 4:8 NASB

God has promised to abundantly reward those who
love Him, who believe and follow Him. These heavenly
rewards will take myriad forms, for God will delight in
surprising you with His goodness for all eternity. "In
Your presence is fullness of joy; at Your right hand are
pleasures forevermore" (Psalm 16:11 NKJV).

One of these rewards is the crown of righteousness—
also called the "crown of life." These crowns will be
unique for each believer and will likely reflect your
virtues and the righteous deeds you've done for the
Lord—a permanent glorious declaration of your
accomplishments.

Some people think it odd that believers in heaven
will always wear a crown, but bear in mind that the
Greek word doesn't refer to a heavyset European-type
crown but a light tiara. Since it will glow with radiant
light, it's probably what many people refer to as a halo.

All you need to do is love and obey Jesus. He says,
"Be faithful until death, and I will give you the crown
of life" (Revelation 2:10 NKJV).

Day 7

EXALTED THRONES

"I grant you that you may eat and drink at
My table in My kingdom, and you will sit on
thrones judging the twelve tribes of Israel."
LUKE 22:29–30 NASB

God has promised that faithful believers will rule with
Him in paradise, as well as reign over the nations of
the earth. John promised that "they will be priests of
God and of Christ and will reign with Him" (Revelation
20:6 NASB).

But bear in mind that not all believers will sit on
thrones governing the nations—only the most faithful.
When they stand before God, if they have rendered
extraordinary service, He will say, "Well done, good and
faithful servant; you were faithful over a few things, I
will make you ruler over many things. Enter into the
joy of your lord" (Matthew 25:21 NKJV).

Those who have served well will be set over cities;
those who have given exemplary service will be made
rulers of districts; those who have served most faithfully
will rule over entire nations.

Are you serving Christ now so that He can trust
you with great responsibility? You may be of little
account, unrecognized by the powerful of this world
and passed over by the ambitious, but God knows the
qualities that make a true ruler—humility, compassion,
and integrity.

Day 1

BEARING THE WEIGHT OF SIN

*But he was pierced for our rebellion, crushed
for our sins. He was beaten so we could be
whole. He was whipped so we could be healed.
All of us, like sheep, have strayed away.
We have left God's paths to follow our own.
Yet the LORD laid on him the sins of us all.*

ISAIAH 53:5–6 NLT

Sin, by its nature, is heavy. When your spouse or best friend betrays you, or when someone robs or assaults you, or when somebody lies to you and offends you, you feel the full weight of the other person's sin. It damages your trust, wounds your heart, and leaves lasting effects—sometimes even physically.

Imagine the weight Jesus felt when He was pierced for the sins of the world. He was beaten and whipped for every sin. God laid on Him the sins of the world, and yet He bore it willingly. You groan over the sins of one person because you feel its effects. Jesus spread His arms and endured crucifixion, even stopping to pray for His executioners because they were ignorant (Luke 23:34).

How might visualizing the way Jesus mercifully handled your sin change your attitude about the reality and heaviness of your sin and the sin of others?

REMEMBER NO MORE

For I will be merciful to their unrighteousness,
and their sins and their iniquities
will I remember no more.

HEBREWS 8:12 KJV

———— ✦ ————

Think about the last person who wronged you. Is his or her name firmly in your mind? Who did you talk to about the circumstances that led up to this offending party's infraction? Your best friend? A coworker? Your spouse? Whoever it was, how much time did you spend in that conversation going over every detail?

Was it worth it? No doubt, you probably felt better—at least temporarily. But did it bring you any closer to offering the offending party forgiveness? Or did it drive an even bigger wedge between you?

Praise God, He is merciful to your unrighteousness, and He even forgets your sins—even though He has every reason and every right to remember every single one. Yet, He doesn't hold your sins against you. Nor does He talk to others about them. Instead, His love covers a multitude of sins. As far as the east is from the west, so far has He removed your transgressions from you.

How can you do anything other than imitate His actions? Forgive the offender. Cast his or her sins so far from your mind that you're unable to retrieve them.

CHRIST'S RIGHTEOUSNESS

*Here is a trustworthy saying that deserves full
acceptance: Christ Jesus came into the world
to save sinners—of whom I am the worst.*

1 TIMOTHY 1:15 NIV

A person who is trusting in his own righteousness seeks to be great in the kingdom of God. This is the very thing the disciples did in Matthew 18 when they approached Jesus to ask who was the greatest in the kingdom.

His answer? Only those who take the lowly position of a child. And whoever welcomes such a child in His name. For only children are completely dependent on their parents.

Paul had more reason than most to trust in his own righteousness. He spelled out his reasons in Philippians 3:4–6 (NIV): "If someone else thinks they have reasons to put confidence in the flesh, I have more: circumcised on the eighth day, of the people of Israel, of the tribe of Benjamin, a Hebrew of Hebrews; in regard to the law, a Pharisee; as for zeal, persecuting the church; as for righteousness based on the law, faultless."

And yet, in today's verse, he referred to himself as the worst of sinners. He knew that his righteousness was only filthy rags. How about you? What are you trusting in? Nothing but Christ's righteousness will suffice.

FREED FROM SIN

*Knowing this, that our old man is crucified
with him, that the body of sin might be
destroyed, that henceforth we should not serve
sin. For he that is dead is freed from sin.*
ROMANS 6:6–7 KJV

Your old sinful nature was crucified with Christ for two
reasons, according to the apostle Paul in today's verses:
so your body of sin (in its totality) might be destroyed,
and so you would no longer serve your sinful desires.

You have power from on high living inside you that
allows you to overcome the old man who is still exerting
his influence. That's not to say you will never sin or
that the old, sinful habits have no allure, but you no
longer have to give in to them. Christ has freed you.

Practically speaking, how does your life look
different since you've become a Christian? What sins
that you engaged in before you were redeemed has
Christ enabled you to overcome? Has He calmed your
rage? Tamed your salty tongue? Stopped your gossip?
However, what sins have you carried over to your new
life in Christ? What has prevented you from obeying
Christ, rather than the old man?

Take heart. If you belong to Christ, He is still
working in you to destroy your sinful nature.

THE DELIVERER

Who gave Himself for our sins so that He might rescue us from this present evil age, according to the will of our God and Father.

GALATIANS 1:4 NASB

❖

When you attended a worship service last Sunday, did your mind drift at any point to what you were having for lunch or maybe what you had planned for later in the day? When you last attended a Bible study, did you glance at your watch more than once, wondering when it would be over because you had other things you needed to do?

If so, you aren't alone. The world pulls you away from Christ—even when you are in sanctuaries. The demands of this world and the lusts of your heart are strong, no doubt. But Christ came to rescue you from this present evil age, and He did so according to the will of God the Father.

"Jesus Christ has died to deliver us from this present evil world, not presently to remove his people out of it, but to rescue them from the power of it, to keep them from the evil of it, and in due time to possess them of another and better world." So writes Bible commentator Matthew Henry.

This is God's promise to you: He rescues and delivers.

WALK IN THE LIGHT

*But if we walk in the Light as He Himself is in
the Light, we have fellowship with one another,
and the blood of Jesus His Son
cleanses us from all sin.*

1 JOHN 1:7 NASB

———— ◆ ————

When you're walking in darkness, it's easy to fall for Satan's lie that walking in the light isn't really possible. Nobody's perfect, right? How can engaging in sin really be harmful, given that everybody else is doing it?

The truth is, you *can* walk in the light, as long as you aren't trying to do it in your own strength. And you already know and feel the full effects of your sin, and of those around you, so you know how harmful it is.

Today's verse gives you a hint of what walking in the light entails. When you're doing it, you're in fellowship with other believers. Fellowship involves much more than sitting next to another Christian on Sunday mornings. The Greek word for "fellowship" here means "partnership" and "participation."

Does this sort of spiritual intimacy describe your current relationships with other believers? If not, then step into the light. Join a Bible study. Volunteer for a church mission trip. Begin meeting with the men's or women's church group you've been avoiding.

REASONING WITH THE LORD

*"Come now, let us settle the matter," says
the LORD. "Though your sins are like scarlet,
they shall be as white as snow; though they are
red as crimson, they shall be like wool."*
ISAIAH 1:18 NIV

In the old covenant, God's people purposely separated themselves from Him—fearing the repercussions of their sin. They knew what happened to Nadab and Abihu when they were struck dead after offering unholy fire (Leviticus 10), and what happened to Uzzah when he was struck dead after touching the ark of the covenant (2 Samuel 6).

While sin certainly has its repercussions, today's verse paints a picture of a merciful God—one who asks His people to come to Him so they can reason together regarding their sins. In a sense, He is calling them to a courtroom and asking them to confess their guilt. As long as they do so, He will pardon their sin and make them white as snow.

Have you been hiding from God, fearing how He will react to your sin? You know He can find you anywhere, but maybe you've concluded that if you give up the battle, He'll leave you alone. Today, this very moment, He calls to you and says, "Come now, let us reason together."

Day 1

WHERE IT ALL BEGINS

*Faith shows the reality of what we hope for;
it is the evidence of things we cannot see.*

HEBREWS 11:1 NLT

———◦●◦———

Faith is a term used by many but is often misunderstood. *Faith* isn't a term applied to people who believe God has a *cool factor*. It doesn't apply to the personal motivation to pray to an undetermined deity. It's not wishfully thinking that everything will work out.

For the Christian, faith is a decision about whether you really believe God can do what He's promised. Faith is confidence in God's perfect plan. Faith is knowing that you need rescue and accepting it. Faith is believing God's truth even without proof. Faith is the assurance that God directs your everyday steps and has your best interests in mind.

Faith is more than a "God" acknowledgment in an acceptance speech. It's more than working hard for a spiritual cause. Faith is substantially more than you may give it credit for.

Over the next few days we'll learn that faith believes the impossible and then sees the impossible become possible. Faith leans into God's plan and is supported by God's hand. Faith introduces you to a forever friendship with the Father and delivers the benefits of a sold-out belief in a truth the world needs to discover.

Day 2

STAND FIRM

Be on guard. Stand firm in the faith.
Be courageous. Be strong.
1 CORINTHIANS 16:13 NLT

For every decision you make there will be someone who questions your choice. A decision made by faith withstands these challenges. God knew your worst adversary would try to confuse you and make you think good decisions are bad and bad decisions are best.

The Bible says this adversary comes to "steal and kill and destroy" (John 10:10 NLT). No wonder you're told to "be on guard, be courageous, and be strong." You need all the encouragement you can get, because your adversary works overtime to move you from the narrow path God created to a road leading to destruction. He challenges your faith. He questions whether God can be trusted, if He really cares for you, or even whether God loves you at all.

Because faith is an absolute trust in the God of all gods, you can discover that entertaining the challenges of the adversary increases the chance that you will falter in your faith.

The armor of God is supplied to help you stand firm (Ephesians 6:10–18). Each piece of armor is designed to help you remember who you are in Christ and then to remind your adversary that you never stand alone. Be courageous. Stand firm.

Week 3

FAITH - PART 1

HAVING GOD-TRUST

*Your faith should not be in the wisdom
of men but in the power of God.*

1 CORINTHIANS 2:5 NKJV

Friends disappoint you. Coworkers say things that are untrue. Strangers gossip. Your sense of trust and self-worth are battered with each betrayal. Yet this shouldn't come as a surprise.

Think about it. You place your trust in people who sin (Romans 3:23), your own deceitful heart (Jeremiah 17:9), and aren't even sure what they think about God (Romans 1:25). God calls you to love imperfect people, but your *faith* should be placed in the power of God. He doesn't disappoint, He speaks truth, and He never gossips.

The wisest of men can't measure up to the wisdom of God, but you may treat the opinion of other humans as more valuable than God's instructions for living. Faith is a trust that rests on the certainty that God is the same "yesterday, today, and forever" (Hebrews 13:8 NKJV).

You need friendship with others, so you shouldn't eliminate their companionship. However, there will be moments when someone lets you down, or you disappoint them. No human can save you, restore your past, or ensure your future. This is God's domain. This is God's promise. This is God's gift.

You should accept by faith what only *He* can provide.

Day 4

A GIFT ONLY GOD COULD GIVE

*For it is by grace you have been saved,
through faith—and this is not from
yourselves, it is the gift of God.*

EPHESIANS 2:8 NIV

Consider a paraphrase of today's verse: "God offers to rescue you and make you part of His family. You have to believe you can't rescue yourself and need His help. When you act on that belief, you receive a gift only God can give."

It may sound peculiar, but you have to have faith (believe) that you can't rescue yourself. You may agree that you need faith and need God, but you must be wholeheartedly convinced that on your own you can't do enough good, make up for bad decisions, or rely on your ability to make perfect decisions in the future. You will fail yourself, others, and God.

God's gift is important for two reasons. (1) It takes the pressure off because you accept the perfection of God's Son, Jesus, on your behalf, and (2) it ensures that if you accept His gift you're completely accepted by God.

If you believe you have the ability to live up to God's standard, you also indicate that you don't believe you need to be rescued. Without rescue you can't be part of God's family.

Week 3

♦

FAITH - PART 1

THE FAITH SENSE

For we walk by faith, not by sight.
2 CORINTHIANS 5:7 KJV

If you couldn't see, you'd use other senses to compensate. You'd feel for obstacles, listen for echoes, or smell for the familiar or dangerous. You learn to trust different senses when they're the only way to engage life.

Faith is the primary sense of your spiritual life, but when you come to new life in Christ, your sight is less useful in determining where you go. Faith can be a difficult sense to understand.

You'll try to assign faith to secondary roles in your journey. You might attempt to make faith a feeling, or a statement ("I have faith"), or a physical place of union with Christians (church). While faith can interact with emotion, conversation, and partnership with other followers, it trusts in the One who leads, is certain of the future He's prepared, and is confident in God's plan even when you can't see beyond your next step (Psalm 119:105).

Faith assures you that each *next step* with God is infinitely better than any steps you take on your own. It's not easy to trust what you can't see, but faith isn't just walking forward; it's walking with God. Each new step leads closer to home.

Day 6

IT COMES STANDARD

*It is impossible to please God without faith.
Anyone who wants to come to him must
believe that God exists and that he rewards
those who sincerely seek him.*

HEBREWS 11:6 NLT

When you buy a car, you have certain options to consider. It could be things like heated seats and GPS or something like remote start and rear camera. You could purchase the basic model and it would provide the transportation you need, but the options are what make it feel more like the car was made for you.

When you try to customize your spiritual life, you'll discover that certain things that come standard aren't options to be removed from your new life in Christ. It's impossible to follow Him from a distance. You can't view Christianity like a documentary of what others have experienced. You can't even say you're associated with those who follow and still expect to please God.

If you're going to come to God for life rescue and restoration, you have to be convinced that He exists and He provides spiritual rewards to those who ask for help, seek His wisdom, and knock on doors of spiritual opportunity (Matthew 7:7–12).

You can't remake God in your image. His new life for you requires the transformation of your mind, heart, and soul.

Day 7

GROW DEEP

Now, just as you accepted Christ Jesus as your Lord,
you must continue to follow him. Let your roots
grow down into him, and let your lives be built
on him. Then your faith will grow strong in
the truth you were taught, and you
will overflow with thankfulness.

COLOSSIANS 2:6–7 NLT

God's Word contains word-pictures that help you understand spiritual truth. In today's verses your journey with Jesus is explained through an illustration of seeds and soil inviting you to the garden, field, or flower pot. These images encourage you to consider that something within a seed reacts with nutrient-rich soil to create new life. The roots grow deep into the soil and the seed is transformed into something more (John 12:24).

You also have a front-row refresher to a story of how you choose to build your life. Do you trust your own strength and build on the sands of personal preference, or do you trust God and build your life on the solid rock foundation of One who has all knowledge, power, and wisdom? (See Matthew 7:24–27.)

True faith provides that "Aha!" moment when you realize there's no other answer to life's purpose than trust (faith) in the God who asks you to love, forgive, share, and overflow with thankfulness.

Day 1

HOW TO LOVE GOD

But whoever loves God is known by God.
1 CORINTHIANS 8:3 NIV

————◆————

It's a simple thing to say you love God, but another to reflect that love in the way you live. And there's a big difference between loving God in the best way you know how and loving Him the way He tells you to. You show your love for God two ways: obeying His commands and loving the way He loves. Paul observed that "knowledge puffs up while love builds up. Those who think they know something do not yet know as they ought to know" (1 Corinthians 8:1–2 NIV). In other words, if you think you know everything about love, you've got a lot to learn.

What is it that we're supposed to know? How to love.

You show God you love Him as you love others the way He loves you. God loves you sacrificially, knowing who you are completely, all your pros and cons, and investing His absolute best in your highest good. Something happens when you try to love others like that: you also love God.

As it turns out, you may not know the first thing about love, but God does. When you love Him enough to love others the way He loves you, He will teach you all you need to know.

INCREASING YOUR APPETITE

"Therefore take careful heed to yourselves,
that you love the LORD your God."
JOSHUA 23:11 NKJV

———•◆•———

You can't really love someone you don't know. Until you move beyond your idea of who that person is and see who they really are—in all their complex, imperfect ways—you can't truly love them. The same goes for loving God. The best way to learn to love Him is to get to know Him, and one of the best ways to know Him better is through His Word.

Joshua advised God's people to "meditate in [the Bible] day and night, that you may observe to do according to all that is written in it. For then you will make your way prosperous, and then you will have good success" (Joshua 1:8 NKJV). What you're doing right now—reading a devotional—is a great icebreaker in getting to know God, but you'll whet your appetite even more by spending time reading His Word each day.

Ask Him to show you something about Him as you read, and He will give you wisdom and righteousness (Psalm 119:98, 101), and His words will be "sweeter than honey" (Psalm 119:103 NIV). God's Word is His love letter to you, and you show your love for Him when you read it, think about it, and apply it.

ALL IN

*"You shall love the LORD your God with
all your heart and with all your
soul and with all your might."*

DEUTERONOMY 6:5 NASB

Going all in to love God means learning to love like
He does—no holding back. Jesus said, "If you love
Me, keep My commandments" (John 14:15 NKJV). That
boils down to putting God first and foremost in all
you do, and loving others like you do yourself (Mark
12:29–31). Loving God wholeheartedly will transform
your life—your relationships, your work, your leisure
time, your life goals.

Learning to love God as the first and highest
priority in your life is part of the ongoing process of
the Christian life, your sanctification. Because He is
faithful, you'll get better at it as you go, digging into
His Word to know Him better and acting on what you
uncover there by loving others.

One way to check your love quotient is to ask yourself
what you love more, God or ____? Fill in the blank:
spouse, work, kids, recognition, accomplishment—
because chances are good, you're still learning to love
God more than whatever fills that line. Have faith that
He is worth the effort. Above all else, avoid loving Him
in half measures; God took your worst and gave you
His very best in Jesus.

Day 4

OPEN EYES, FULL HEART, CAN'T LOSE

Give me your heart, my son,
and let your eyes delight in my ways.
PROVERBS 23:26 NASB

———————

Solomon's words to his son mirror what God would say to you as His child. You show Him a great deal of love when you submit to His will for you—trusting that He knows best and wants the best for you. You have faith that His warnings are for your protection and His chastening for your growth. Whether or not you had an earthly father whom you could trust in those ways, God will not let you down.

God's track record is impeccable: He has never broken a promise, never forsaken or forgotten His children, never gone back on His word, never left unfinished anything that He started.

Love God with all the freedom of a child running into loving arms. Enjoy getting to know Him in His Word, and relish the blessings He gives you each day. Let yourself be vulnerable before Him; He knows you better than anyone else ever could, and He cherishes you. The better you know Him, the more you'll love Him, and the more you love Him, the better you'll know Him. That sounds circular, but think of it instead as a spiral, lifting you to a higher and deeper relationship with your heavenly Father.

THE IMAGE OF LOVE

"I have made you known to them, and will continue to make you known in order that the love you have for me may be in them and that I myself may be in them."

JOHN 17:26 NIV

If you've ever wondered what God looks like, just look at Jesus. The Bible avoids any physical descriptions of this carpenter from Nazareth, except in the prophecy that there was "nothing beautiful or majestic about his appearance, nothing to attract us to him" (Isaiah 53:2 NLT).

When Jesus was here the first time, He was just another book judged by its cover: "Can anything good come out of Nazareth?" (John 1:46 NKJV). So His looks matter less than His words, no doubt by design, so you wouldn't get lost in the woods wondering what color His eyes or hair were. So, how did Jesus make God known to you? By His love.

Nowhere is God's love for you clearer than in the person and work of Jesus Christ. Jesus is the image of the invisible God (Colossians 1:15), His promise never to leave you or forsake you (Deuteronomy 31:6) made flesh. This amazing revelation of God's heart makes it possible for you to truly love God, since, as John said, "We love Him because He first loved us" (1 John 4:19 NKJV).

OPEN ARMS

The LORD says, "I will rescue those who love me.
I will protect those who trust in my name.
When they call on me, I will answer;
I will be with them in trouble."
PSALM 91:14–15 NLT

The comfort of God's presence and protection in times of trouble can't be overstated. The peace you have when you have no business being peaceful not only impacts you but others who are left wondering why you're not totally freaking out.

While it's God's pleasure as your heavenly Father to protect and provide for you, especially in the clutch, there are things you can do to show that you appreciate His love and love Him back.

Many assign Psalm 91 to Moses, who was deeply acquainted with God. God even called him a friend (Exodus 33:11)—not because he was perfect but because he poured his heart into everything he did, seeking God's glory.

Moses established conditions for having God as your 911: "If you make the LORD your refuge, if you make the Most High your shelter, no evil will conquer you" (Psalm 91:9 NLT). God will send angels to protect you and give you strength to handle danger in your path (vv. 11–13). You show your love for God by running to Him in hard times, trusting Him with your trouble.

DON'T LOSE HEART

God is not unrighteous to forget your work
and labour of love, which ye have
shewed toward his name.

HEBREWS 6:10 KJV

———◆———

You sometimes hit rough patches in your walk with
God where the way is rocky, slippery, and isolated. It's
especially hard when you're clicking on all cylinders
spiritually—God is regularly showing you new things in
His Word, your prayers seem aligned with His will, and
you discern His hand at work in and through you—but
then, suddenly, it's not clicking. Your prayers seem to
bounce off the ceiling, and when you beg God to show
Himself to you, you see nothing.

After a few panicky moments, it slowly dawns
on you: you're being tested, something you're told
to patiently endure (James 1:12) without losing your
confidence in God (Hebrews 10:35–38). When you shift
from asking "Why, Lord?" to "What are You trying to
accomplish, Lord?" you're on the right track.

Because you have His promise that He will remember
the love you've shown in your time of closeness to
Him and your hard work for Him, you can, without
understanding the specific details of your desert
experience, trust that God hasn't forgotten you. You
will be able to sense His presence again in due time "if
[you] do not lose heart" (Galatians 6:9 NKJV).

AN INCOMPLETE REPENTANCE

Rend your heart and not your garments.
Return to the LORD your God, for he is gracious
and compassionate, slow to anger and abounding
in love, and he relents from sending calamity.

JOEL 2:13 NIV

It was the custom of the day to rip apart one's garments to express deep grief or sorrow. The prophet Joel wasn't telling God's people to discontinue that practice as much as he was telling them to go beyond an external expression of sorrow for sin, all the way to the heart.

Today, Christians no longer tear their clothes in grief, but it's common to pay lip service to sins—often referring to them as mistakes or struggles but stopping short of doing the difficult work of "rending the heart" (ripping the urges from the heart). This makes for an incomplete repentance.

In Psalm 51:17, King David properly acknowledged that God would not despise a broken and contrite heart. Such a heart stops making excuses and looking for loopholes and instead, with God's empowerment, seeks to change from the inside out.

Don't stop short in your repentance. God is slow to anger, and He will be gracious and compassionate when you have done the difficult work of naming your sin and then turning from it to walk in His mercy.

CAUSE FOR CELEBRATION

*"In the same way, I tell you, there is joy
in the presence of the angels of God
over one sinner who repents."*

LUKE 15:10 NASB

———◆———

Twenty years ago, Kansas City police officer Sgt. Jeff Colvin went above and beyond the call of duty for a nine-year-old girl on his beat who grew up in a home filled with drugs and violence.

A television station in Memphis recently reported that Colvin stopped by her house every day to check on her and her two brothers, telling her he was there for them if they needed him. She says he was the only person she trusted as a child, referring to him now as a hero. She tracked her hero down recently and was reunited with him, thanking him for everything he did and surprising him by saying that she is on the road to becoming a police officer because of him.

Reunions are cause for celebration. Luke says every time a sinner repents and is reunited with the Father through the finished work of Christ, there is joy in the presence of the angels.

All of heaven is waiting for your friends and co-workers to turn to Christ. Are you like a Sgt. Colvin to them? Can they turn to you, no matter what, for spiritual truth?

REPENTANCE   ◆   *Week 3*

Day 3

YOU CANNOT HIDE FROM GOD

*Come near to God and he will come near
to you. Wash your hands, you sinners,
and purify your hearts, you double-minded.*

JAMES 4:8 NIV

Man's natural inclination is to run from God after
sinning. Adam and Eve did it in the garden of Eden.
Isaiah 2:6–10 describes the propensity of God's people
to hide in caves, fearing His judgment for their idolatry.
Apparently, even King David considered running from
God but concluded that he couldn't see the point.

"Where can I go from your Spirit?" he asks in Psalm
139:7–10 (NIV). "Where can I flee from your presence?
If I go up to the heavens, you are there; if I make my
bed in the depths, you are there. If I rise on the wings
of the dawn, if I settle on the far side of the sea, even
there your hand will guide me, your right hand will
hold me fast."

James wants you to stop running *from* God and
start running *toward* Him. This is the way of biblical
repentance. As David pointed out, there's no use in
trying to hide from God, anyway. He's omnipresent
and He sees everything. The good news is, He's quick
to settle accounts with those who are quick to confess.

Day 4

WAKE UP!

"Remember, therefore, what you have received and heard; hold it fast, and repent. But if you do not wake up, I will come like a thief, and you will not know at what time I will come to you."

REVELATION 3:3 NIV

Sin dulls the conscience, making it easier to indulge the flesh in ways previously unexplored, with fewer internal warning bells sounding the alarm. If you can get through a day without a warning from the Holy Spirit, then you're already sleeping.

For a time is coming, writes Bible commentator Matthew Henry about this verse, when Christ will come as a thief to strip those who are asleep "of their remaining enjoyments and mercies, not by fraud, but in justice and righteousness." What a dreadful time that will be.

The antidote is your memory. Remember how it used to feel when you heard a sermon that spoke directly to a spiritual need and you responded? Remember how anxious you used to be to rise up early every morning to meet with God in His Word because He felt so near? Remember the sweet fellowship you used to share with other believers? Remember what you have received and heard; obey it and repent, says the apostle John. Turn back to the God who loves you.

REPENTANCE ◆ *Week 5*

TAKE HEART

The Lord is not slack concerning His promise, as
some count slackness, but is longsuffering toward
us, not willing that any should perish but
that all should come to repentance.

2 PETER 3:9 NKJV

If you're a parent, teacher, coach, aunt, or uncle, your patience has been tried by children who are under your authority. They throw temper tantrums. They say selfish things. And they make the same mistakes over and over again, no matter how many times you correct them.

Then, finally, one day they begin to understand the danger they pose to themselves and others, and their practices begin to change. They still make poor choices at times and they still put themselves first on occasion, but you see progress, and it makes it all worth it. You never even considered giving up on them because you cared deeply about seeing their character shaped for the better.

God feels the same way about you. He sends correction your way, and sometimes you view it as a negative—as if He doesn't love you. But nothing could be further from the truth. In fact, if you aren't feeling His loving discipline on occasion, be concerned, because God disciplines those He loves (Hebrews 12:5–6). Take heart! God isn't done with you yet.

Day 6

THE LORD IS NIGH

The LORD is nigh unto them that are of a broken heart; and saveth such as be of a contrite spirit.

PSALM 34:18 KJV

In modern culture, it's difficult to imagine a person having a broken heart over anything other than a relationship that has gone bad or the death of a loved one. But in today's verse, the psalmist promises that God is close—in a special way—to those who are brokenhearted over their sin.

What's the first emotion you typically feel after committing a sin? Is it shame? Remorse? Fear? Nominal conviction? The psalmist's words in today's verse indicate that you ought to feel the effects on a much deeper level. When is the last time your sin wore on you so heavily that the people around you would have said you appeared to be brokenhearted? Have you *ever* felt that way?

God cannot comfort a man who is cavalier about his sin. Therefore, He doesn't draw near to the sinner who is never brokenhearted. Take inventory of your heart today. What ongoing sin is just part of your routine? Consider your sin in light of the cross and the awful penalty that Jesus paid for it. Allow His Spirit to convict you and break your heart.

REPENTANCE ◆ *Week 5*

REPENTANCE IS A COMMAND

"God overlooked people's ignorance about these things in earlier times, but now he commands everyone everywhere to repent of their sins and turn to him."

ACTS 17:30 NLT

————— ◈ —————

The prevailing thought in the West in the twenty-first century is that all religions are created equal and all paths lead to God. There was a time in Israel's history when God overlooked such theological ignorance—a time when priests stood in the gap and made ritualistic sacrifices to atone for the sins of God's people without fully understanding the call to repentance.

But when God came in the flesh, the old covenant came to an end and such ignorance was no longer acceptable in His sight.

In the new covenant, He commands all men everywhere to repent and turn to Him. Inherent in that command is to not turn to any other god. Your call, as a member of His church, is to take that message everywhere you go, even though it's not popular. You'll certainly need to be as wise as a serpent and as gentle as a dove as you do, but you must not fall prey to the misconception that all belief systems are correct. They can't be, for Christ claimed to be the only way to the Father (John 14:6).

FREE GIFT OF ETERNAL LIFE

For the wages of sin is death, but the free gift of
God is eternal life through Christ Jesus our Lord.
ROMANS 6:23 NLT

———————

If you knew that moving ahead with something would lead to certain death, would you still do it? Odds are you didn't even need to think about that for one-tenth of a second before responding with a firm "No!" You'd look for a way to avoid death at all costs, right?

The Bible says that "the wages of sin is death." Every human being is born into sin, and there's nothing you, or anyone else, can do to change that. Sin leads to death 100 percent of the time. However, because of Jesus, there's a promise of hope. Through the sacrifice of His Son on the cross, God provided a way for all people to be free from sin. . .free from death *forever!*

All you need to do is believe. Choose to become a Christ follower. Choose to accept God's free gift of salvation. Choose eternal life! If you haven't already done so, pray this prayer: "Father God, I know I'm a sinner. I believe that Jesus died on the cross for my sins. Please forgive me. Send the Spirit of Jesus into my heart today. Lead me, and I will follow. Amen."

Week 6 ◆ SALVATION

NEW AND IMPROVED

*"This means that anyone who belongs to Christ
has become a new person. The old life
is gone; a new life has begun!"*
2 CORINTHIANS 5:17 NLT

The idea of a do-over, a fresh, new beginning, is quite appealing, isn't it?

With God's promise of salvation, a do-over isn't a far-fetched dream. The wonderful reality for those who make the decision to follow Christ is this: your past may be one giant mess. . .but just ask—just *believe*—and God will wipe the slate clean. He will present you with an opportunity to leave your old self behind and become a brand-new version of yourself!

In your sin, you were dead, separated from God. When you acknowledged your sin and asked God to forgive—and as you trusted Him to come into your life and lead, accepting His gift of eternal life—you became His beautiful child! He looks at you through the clear lens of His matchless grace.

As His child, your life will never again look the same. "Since you have heard about Jesus and have learned the truth. . .throw off your old sinful nature and your former way of life. . . . Put on your new nature, created to be like God—truly righteous and holy" (Ephesians 4:21–24 NLT).

Day 3

HEAVENLY HERITAGE

*Yet to all who did receive him, to those who
believed in his name, he gave the right to become
children of God—children born not of natural
descent, nor of human decision or a
husband's will, but born of God.*

JOHN 1:12–13 NIV

Imagine the perfect earthly father. What kind of characteristics would he exude? For starters, he'd be loving, rich in wisdom, kind, fair, humble, and full of joy. . . He'd be a provider. A source of protection. A calm and steady presence. But even in all of this "perfection," human nature is destined to kick in at some point, and he will let his kids down—in things both large and small.

No matter who your earthly father may be, if you've accepted Christ into your life, God is your heavenly Father. On the day you believed and asked Him to become Lord of your life, you were immediately adopted into His kingdom and became His child.

He is the *only* perfect father. He will always love you *perfectly*. He will always provide for you *perfectly*. He will always protect you *perfectly*. "See what great love the Father has lavished on us, that we should be called children of God! And that is what we are!" (1 John 3:1 NIV).

Praise Him! Thank God today for your heavenly heritage!

SALVATION ◆ *Week 6*

Day 4

ONE WAY

"There is salvation in no one else! God has
given no other name under heaven
by which we must be saved."

ACTS 4:12 NLT

———◆———

When you're traveling, there are often several different roads that will lead you to your final destination. Just google directions to a place you'd like to visit. Be it the beach or a private mountain getaway, chances are you could take a direct route or a more scenic route, if you'd rather enjoy the sights along the way.

But know this: if your final destination is heaven, there are no two ways to get there. Just *one* way. . .just *one* path. . .leads to eternity with the heavenly Father. In John 14:6 (NLT), Jesus said, "I am the way, the truth, and the life. No one can come to the Father except through me."

God gives the promise of eternal life through the sacrifice of His Son on the cross. "He has given us eternal life, and this life is in his Son. Whoever has the Son has life; whoever does not have God's Son does not have life" (1 John 5:11–12 NLT).

"Believe in the Lord Jesus and you will be saved" (Acts 16:31 NLT). If you have faith in the one and only Savior of humankind, your future—your eternal destination—is secure.

FREEDOM!

For everyone has sinned; we all fall short of
God's glorious standard. Yet God, in his grace,
freely makes us right in his sight. He did this
through Christ Jesus when he freed
us from the penalty for our sins.

ROMANS 3:23–24 NLT

———— ◆ ————

"I'm a good person. I volunteer my time to help others less fortunate than myself. I treat others the way I want to be treated. Love others? Sure, I do! And of course, I pray, too!"

No matter how "good" you are, there's *nothing* you can do to earn a place in heaven. There's no way for you to earn your salvation.

Everyone born into this world—every child, mother, father, brother, sister, grandparent, cousin, aunt, and uncle—is sinful. But there's hope. Because of God's amazing love for you and for *all* humankind, He provided a way for your eternal freedom through His amazing grace. The price of your sins was paid in full by Jesus alone.

If you ever feel less than worthy of God's love, or doubt His love for you, remember this: His love for you is perfect. When you talk to Him, when you tell Him you're sorry, He wraps His arms around you and whispers, "I forgive you, child. I love you." Every. Single. Time. That's a promise you can count on.

LOVE'S GREATEST GIFT

*For God so loved the world that he gave his one
and only Son, that whoever believes in him
shall not perish but have eternal life.*

JOHN 3:16 NIV

Do you ever struggle with feelings of being not quite
"enough"? The world carelessly communicates so many
hurtful messages. Messages like. . .

You're not smart enough. You're not rich enough.
You're not talented enough. You're not handsome or
beautiful enough. You're not good enough. You're
simply not. . .*enough.*

God wants you to quit believing the world's lies,
because for Him, you *are* enough. He loves you so
much that He forgives your every sin. He loves you
so much that He listens to your every prayer. He loves
you so much that He sent His only Son, Jesus, to die
for you so you can spend eternity with Him. And the
best thing? Love's greatest gift doesn't cost a thing:
the only requirement is that you believe.

Believe. Place all of your hope, all of your trust,
in the One who loves you more than your mind
could ever fathom. *Believe.* Know there's nothing you
could do to make God love you more and nothing
you could do to make Him love you less. *Believe.*
You are enough!

Day 7

BY GRACE

For by grace are ye saved through faith;
and that not of yourselves: it is the gift of God:
not of works, lest any man should boast.
EPHESIANS 2:8–9 KJV

When it comes to salvation, do you ever feel like you must complete a checklist to secure your spot in Christ's heavenly kingdom?

Do you volunteer at church? Check! Do you tithe 10 percent of your income? Check! Do you spend time in prayer every day? Check! Do you show up for church every time the doors are open? Check!

But the Christian life doesn't consist of an exhausting, never-ending to-do list. Jesus said in Matthew 11:28–30 (NLT), "Come to me, all of you who are weary and carry heavy burdens, and I will give you rest. Take my yoke upon you. Let me teach you, because I am humble and gentle at heart, and you will find rest for your souls. For my yoke is easy to bear, and the burden I give you is light." A personal relationship with Christ leads to a fulfilling life, not a burdensome task list.

Know this: the heavenly Father always lavishes His abundant grace on you. Good works are the *result*, not the reason for your salvation. You provide the faith, and God will do the rest. His grace is all you need.

Day 1

NO MORE FOREVER WOUNDS

*"Forgive us our debts,
as we also have forgiven our debtors."*
MATTHEW 6:12 NIV

———•◦•———

Unforgiveness is like acid to the soul. It's an inhuman IV that drips, burns, and damages the core of who you were meant to be. God never wanted you to endure this pain.

When you refuse to forgive, you're inviting the acid of past offenses to affect your mood, decision-making, and relationships. . .every day. You can wrongly think that withholding forgiveness is your right and that you have the power to make others whole or damaged based entirely on whether you forgive them. *You don't.*

However, you do have the ability to free *yourself* from pain by releasing the offender through forgiveness. That may seem counterintuitive, but the choice is to live with the same wound for the rest of your life *or* discover healing.

You receive forgiveness from God when you accept salvation and restoration from His Son, Jesus. The restoration God offers, however, necessitates you setting aside the anger you may feel for past offenses. Why? That's exactly what He's done for you. You owed God a debt for the things you'd done that offended Him. You couldn't pay, so He paid the price. If you're offended by the actions of others, know that God has a remedy: forgiveness.

FORGIVEN AND FREE

O Lord, you are so good, so ready to forgive,
so full of unfailing love for all who
ask for your help.

PSALM 86:5 NLT

———— ◆ ————

God promised forgiveness. That's good! You *need* to be forgiven. The part where you forgive others? That's a little harder.

The concept of forgiveness isn't exactly foreign. When you were a child, your parents insisted you apologize for something done to a sibling. The sibling was then encouraged to forgive. These early responses weren't always genuine. You didn't want to apologize and you didn't want to forgive. If you forgive, how do you fuel your anger? How do you blackmail the offender? How do you justify withholding love?

God knew forgiveness would make no sense to you, but He forgave you. When He forgives, nothing comes between your relationship with Him. He won't even bring up the past.

It's unnatural to forgive. People want war. They secretly find pleasure in being angry with others. Why? Maybe if they're the *offended* instead of the *offender*, they feel superior. To keep their focus on the sins of others makes them feel better about their personal sin count.

Blaming others has never been part of God's promise. Forgiveness came at a cost, and when Jesus paid the price, you were set free.

THAT THING WE DO

Sensible people control their temper;
they earn respect by overlooking wrongs.
PROVERBS 19:11 NLT

— ◆ —

"I wouldn't have to forgive if other people would just do the right thing." If that sounds like a logical argument, then you should probably clear some things up first. God's Word says in Romans 3:23 (NLT), "Everyone has sinned; we all fall short of God's glorious standard."

To discover a perfect response in every situation, *everyone* would need to live up to God's standard. *They can't.* You wouldn't need to offer forgiveness if no one sinned. *They will.*

Overlooking wrongs is an important concept. It doesn't mean the offense wasn't painful. It doesn't mean you have to immediately offer the same level of trust to that person. It doesn't ignore the offense. Forgiveness simply removes the power of the offense to hurt you.

As long as you live, and because you're human, you *will* make mistakes. Since you make mistakes then you should remember that every other human will do the same. Everyone sins. All people fail to live up to God's perfect standard. That's why Proverbs 19 says controlling anger is something sensible people do.

If someone's offended you, you must remember that you've offended others, too. That's what humans do. To forgive? That's what Christ followers do. That's what God did for you.

Day 4

A WORLD WITHOUT COMPASSION

Be kind and compassionate to one another,
forgiving each other, just as in
Christ God forgave you.
EPHESIANS 4:32 NIV

Imagine a world without forgiveness. The ancient feud between the Hatfields and McCoys seems tame by comparison. Wars would be the norm, not the exception. Everyone would push for a vendetta against others. There would be no kindness. There would be no compassion. There would be no trust.

In this alternate world you would exist without empathy for others, without meaningful relationships, and without hope for something better tomorrow.

Followed to its natural conclusion, payback would be required for every offense, hatred for every slight, and revenge for each infraction. Yet, there's a wise God who instructed you to do something unnatural—forgive. This forgiveness is to be marked by kindness, compassion, and relationship. This forgiveness gives the world hope, urges peace, and inspires friendship.

Your motivation for offering the gift of forgiveness to others is your gratitude for the gift of forgiveness you've received from your great God.

People who forgive tend to be the ones you remember most fondly. Why? They care about you. That compassion shows up in their willingness to follow God's example—forgive when forgiveness is needed, show compassion when help's needed, and offer kindness when friendship's simply a dream.

Day 5

NOT YOUR ENEMY

*Don't repay evil for evil. Don't retaliate with insults
when people insult you. Instead, pay them back
with a blessing. That is what God has called
you to do, and he will grant you his blessing.*

1 PETER 3:9 NLT

———————

Laws determine a punishment for every offense. There are consequences for every choice to sin. Galatians 6:7 (NKJV) says, "Whatever a man sows, that he will also reap."

Forgiveness isn't a free pass. It doesn't excuse bad behavior. It doesn't act as if the offense didn't matter. Forgiveness allows the offended party to acknowledge the pain, set aside revenge, and reengage life without the baggage of bitterness.

The Bible urges you to repay evil with a blessing. This is another difficult concept within the role of forgiveness. You offended God with your sin, and the *Offended* (God) forgives and extends blessings to the *offender* (you).

Think about it this way: How do you argue with someone who refuses to argue? You try to make them mad, but they refuse to fight. At some point you move on. It's hard to fight with someone who won't play the part of an enemy.

Adding a blessing to forgiveness suggests you don't plan on being an enemy. God's blessings in the midst of forgiveness assure you *He* is not your enemy.

THE FORGIVENESS CARD

*Then Peter came and said to Him, "Lord, how often
shall my brother sin against me and I forgive
him? Up to seven times?" Jesus said to him,
"I do not say to you, up to seven times,
but up to seventy times seven."*
MATTHEW 18:21–22 NASB

FORGIVENESS ◆ Week 7

God never asks you to do something He wouldn't do
Himself. If He asks you to love, it's because He loves. If
He asks you to forgive, it's because He forgives.

Humans tend to think there's a limit to things
like patience, kindness, and forgiveness. Maybe that's
why Peter wanted a defined ending point to the
responsibility to forgive. Whatever *forgiveness limit*
Peter had in mind was probably lower than seven, but
that was the number he suggested.

Jesus had other ideas. He came up with the figure
of 490 times. Most scholars believe the number was
simply high enough that people would stop counting
each offense and understand forgiveness should have
no limit.

Did God restrict Himself to the number of times
He'd forgive you? He's the God of second chances, and
He asks *you* to give second chances. You don't get to tell
other people, "Looks like you just got your last punch
on the forgiveness card. Congratulations, you blew it."

God has promised forgiveness, and He commands
you to forgive.

Day 7

DO WHAT HE DOES

*"And whenever you stand praying, if you have
anything against anyone, forgive him, that your
Father in heaven may also forgive you your
trespasses. But if you do not forgive, neither will
your Father in heaven forgive your trespasses."*
MARK 11:25–26 NKJV

The message of today's verses is pretty straightforward:
It's hard to expect forgiveness when you refuse to
forgive. To be clear, God is able to offer forgiveness
because His Son, Jesus, paid the price for your sin. To
accept Jesus' payment is to embrace forgiveness, not
just as something you receive, but something you give.

To follow Jesus means to do what He does. Sure,
you'll forgive imperfectly, but it should be the goal of
your life to reflect His character in how you deal with
others. Forgiveness is an act of love, and Jesus said the
greatest commandments were to love God and then
love everyone else (Matthew 22:36–40).

You might marvel at God's promised gifts and want
to receive them for yourself, but the same gifts you
receive are the very gifts God wants you to share with
others. When you don't share, it's as if you're saying
you want preferential treatment and would like to play
by a different set of rules.

God said, "Forgive." What's your response?

Day 1

THE GIFT OF MERCY

*Be ye therefore merciful,
as your Father also is merciful.*
LUKE 6:36 KJV

Did you ever play Mercy as a kid? It's a rather silly and painful game, locking hands and fingers with your opponent and testing strength and endurance by bending until one person gives up in pain, crying, "Mercy!"—or maybe "Uncle!"

Thankfully, God's mercy is nothing like this foolish children's game. You can find examples and descriptions of it all throughout His Word. Only Jesus can offer the mercy that saves people from sin, as described in 1 Peter 1:3 (NIV): "Praise be to the God and Father of our Lord Jesus Christ! In his great mercy he has given us new birth into a living hope through the resurrection of Jesus Christ from the dead." And in Ephesians 2:4–5 (NKJV): "But God, who is rich in mercy, because of His great love with which He loved us, even when we were dead in trespasses, made us alive together with Christ (by grace you have been saved)."

Christians are called to be grateful for mercy and offer it to others, mimicking the way God expresses it and grants it so freely. This week, may you discover more about mercy and what a gift it is to both receive and give it.

Day 2

MERCY FOR ALL

Even though I was once a blasphemer and
a persecutor and a violent man, I was shown
mercy because I acted in ignorance and unbelief.
The grace of our Lord was poured out on me
abundantly, along with the faith and love that are
in Christ Jesus. Here is a trustworthy saying that
deserves full acceptance: Christ Jesus came into the
world to save sinners—of whom I am the worst.
1 TIMOTHY 1:13–15 NIV

As the apostle Paul so clearly communicates in this scripture passage, God's mercy is available to *all* people, even the very worst of sinners—even the kind who kill and persecute others and blaspheme God Himself. That was Paul once upon a time. But he was shown mercy by a merciful God, "so that in [him], the worst of sinners, Christ Jesus might display his immense patience as an example for those who would believe in him and receive eternal life" (1 Timothy 1:16 NIV).

Oh, what hope is in that scripture! Such confident assurance for absolutely anyone, no matter what kind of sin they might be entrenched in! No darkness is black enough to blot out the saving light of God's mercy through Jesus Christ, a beacon calling sinners to repentance and full acceptance by God.

PLENTEOUS MERCY

For thou, Lord, art good, and ready to forgive;
and plenteous in mercy unto all
them that call upon thee.

PSALM 86:5 KJV

━━━━━━◆━━━━━━

"*Plenteous* in mercy," the psalmist in the KJV Bible says. What a good thought! To mimic the Lord's mercy, believers must be ready to forgive and have an abundance of mercy to share.

Are you quick to forgive and offer mercy? It's difficult at times, for sure, especially if the offense is serious. But your heavenly Father never weighs the offense to decide whether to give or withhold His mercy from you. No, He's constantly ready, wanting you to come to Him at any and all times to make things right in your relationship with Him.

Because He so mercifully and readily forgives, you are called to do the same. And the more you give mercy, the more you receive. Matthew 5:7 (NKJV) says, "Blessed are the merciful, for they shall obtain mercy."

Those who don't offer mercy and forgiveness, however, are in grave danger, for if "you forgive those who sin against you, your heavenly Father will forgive you. But if you refuse to forgive others, your Father will not forgive your sins" (Matthew 6:14–15 NLT).

Day 4

SLOW TO ANGER

*But You, O Lord, are a God merciful
and gracious, slow to anger and abundant
in lovingkindness and truth.*
PSALM 86:15 NASB

God's character reveals that being slow to anger goes hand in hand with being merciful. What a blessing that He's not quick to get mad but is abundant in lovingkindness. If God were easily angered, imagine how upset He would constantly be with you and your sins.

When a difficult situation arises or someone frustrates or wrongs you, take a deep breath (literally), count to ten, or whatever you need to do to hinder the anger rising in you. Ecclesiastes 7:9 (NIV) says, "Do not be quickly provoked in your spirit, for anger resides in the lap of fools." And James 1:19–20 (NIV) says, "My dear brothers and sisters, take note of this: everyone should be quick to listen, slow to speak and slow to become angry, because human anger does not produce the righteousness that God desires."

As you work to control anger, think about mistakes you have made and be grateful that God has been slow to anger with you. Pray and thank God, and then extend that same kind of mercy to others, remembering that Proverbs 19:11 (NASB) says, "A man's discretion makes him slow to anger, and it is his glory to overlook a transgression."

Day 5

TENDER MERCIES

*The LORD is good to all: and his tender
mercies are over all his works.*

PSALM 145:9 KJV

———— • ❦ • ————

Everything God does is full of His tender mercy and goodness. That might seem hard to understand in a world so broken and painful. Yes, it's impossible to fully figure out on this side of heaven, but it's a promise from God's Word, and it's worthy of your trust.

Evil is hard at work here on earth, but that never means God is unseeing or uncaring. His tender mercies will prevail over all things in the long run, and you must keep on trusting Him to sustain you through the good and bad. Lamentations 3:19–23 (NLT) says, "The thought of my suffering and homelessness is bitter beyond words. I will never forget this awful time, as I grieve over my loss. Yet I still dare to hope when I remember this: The faithful love of the LORD never ends! His mercies never cease. Great is his faithfulness; his mercies begin afresh each morning."

Your hope is in heaven. There you'll find perfect eternal life with your Savior, where He'll wipe away every tear (Revelation 21:4). There's nothing more merciful than the God who has prepared such an eternal home for you. And in the meantime, He offers fresh new mercies with each new dawn. Praise Him!

Day 6

BECAUSE OF HIS MERCY

*He saved us, not because of the righteous things
we had done, but because of his mercy. He washed
away our sins, giving us a new birth and new
life through the Holy Spirit. He generously poured
out the Spirit upon us through Jesus Christ our
Savior. Because of his grace he made us right
in his sight and gave us confidence that
we will inherit eternal life.*

TITUS 3:5–7 NLT

No one can earn God's mercy. No amount of good deeds can make up for the fact that your sin separates you from Him. Only because of God's character and His great love and mercy for you does He provide a way to make things right, through the blood of the Lamb, Jesus Christ. And there are no works required to *keep* mercy either.

True believers will do good works and share love and offer mercy to others, but not because they feel obligated; such works are a spontaneous result of sincere faith and the Holy Spirit's work in their lives. Works are never required to gain the great mercy of salvation. "For it is by grace you have been saved, through faith—and this is not from yourselves, it is the gift of God—not by works, so that no one can boast" (Ephesians 2:8–9 NIV).

Day 7

LIMITLESS MERCY

*Surely goodness and mercy shall follow me
all the days of my life: and I will dwell
in the house of the LORD for ever.*

PSALM 23:6 KJV

God's mercy is limitless; it follows those who fear Him all the days of their lives and it spreads to their children and grandchildren and generations more. Luke 1:50 (NIV) says, "His mercy extends to those who fear him, from generation to generation."

What are you doing to teach the children in your life about God's love and mercy? Are you encouraging them to be authentic and sincere in their faith, receiving and giving mercy and growing more mature each day in their walk with Jesus? It matters, not only for their current lives and relationships but for their long-term future and their children's and grandchildren's futures as well.

Deuteronomy 6:4–8 (NLT) urges, "Listen, O Israel! The LORD is our God, the LORD alone. And you must love the LORD your God with all your heart, all your soul, and all your strength. And you must commit yourselves wholeheartedly to these commands that I am giving you today. Repeat them again and again to your children. Talk about them when you are at home and when you are on the road, when you are going to bed and when you are getting up."

FEAR GOD

*"Do not be afraid of those who kill the body but
cannot kill the soul. Rather, be afraid of the One
who can destroy both soul and body in hell."*
MATTHEW 10:28 NIV

Many people believe that since "God is love" and "there
is no fear in love" (1 John 4:8, 18 KJV), that the Bible's
admonitions to "fear God" must be somehow wrong.
Statements like, "God is greatly to be feared" (Psalm
89:7 KJV) are, at the very least, considered outdated.

People have problems with Jesus' command to fear
God "who can destroy both soul and body in hell"
because they believe that a loving God would never
punish people in the afterlife. But the God of love
is also the God of justice and righteousness, and He
must judge evil.

Part of the confusion over the word *fear* is resolved
by Bible versions such as the NIV, which frequently
translates "fear" as "revere." When it states that you are
to fear God, the Bible means you are to greatly honor
and respect God.

Fearing God is not a negative thing. The Bible says,
"The fear of the LORD is pure" (Psalm 19:9 NIV). Revering
and fearing God motivates you to do good, knowing
that "we will all stand before God's judgment seat"
(Romans 14:10 NIV) to account for our deeds.

THE FOUNDATION OF KNOWLEDGE

Fear of the Lord is the foundation of true knowledge, but fools despise wisdom and discipline.
PROVERBS 1:7 NLT

Many people are very learned in a worldly way and have a reputation for being wise and knowledgeable, but this isn't true knowledge. It's often mere head-stuffing with facts and figures.

You also have to consider the *effect* of such vaunted knowledge. Paul declared, "We know that 'We all possess knowledge.' But knowledge puffs up while love builds up" (1 Corinthians 8:1 NIV). Worldly knowledge is like a bullfrog, vainly puffed up beyond its true size, boasting that it's greater than it really is. It's proud and showing off.

Whereas knowledge founded upon the fear of God actually does something constructive and helps others. The "fear of the Lord is the foundation of true knowledge." If you fear God, the most immediate effect is that you obey Him, and His greatest commands are for you to love God and the people He created. This kind of knowledge will move you to do good to others.

Something else: "The fear of the Lord is to hate evil" (Proverbs 8:13 NASB). Love what is good and hate what is evil, and you'll be motivated to do good with the knowledge you possess. Now, that's *true* knowledge!

Day 3

BENEFITS OF FEARING GOD

The angel of the Lord encamps around those
who fear him, and he delivers them.

PSALM 34:7 NIV

⸻ ◆ ⸻

There are distinct benefits for fearing God. One is that if you fear God, you won't need to fear the devil. The reason is that if you have a healthy fear of God, you'll draw near to Him and will focus on obeying Him. These things bring you close to His all-powerful presence and cause Him to bless and protect you.

"The angel of the Lord encamps around those who fear him, and he delivers them." The Angel of the Lord isn't just one of the many angels of God. This title refers to the very presence and person of God Himself.

"He who dwells in the secret place of the Most High shall abide under the shadow of the Almighty. I will say of the Lord, 'He is my refuge'" (Psalm 91:1–2 NKJV). Fearing God causes you to dwell under His protective shadow.

There is a similar promise elsewhere in Psalms: "He will fulfil the desire of them that fear him: he also will hear their cry, and will save them" (Psalm 145:19 KJV). God will not only protect you but will hear your prayers and give you the things you truly need. It pays to fear God!

Day 4

HAVING THINGS GO WELL

"Oh that they had such a heart in them, that they
would fear Me and keep all My commandments
always, that it may be well with them
and with their sons forever!"

DEUTERONOMY 5:29 NASB

God wants things to go well for you. He promises that if you're faithful to Him, revere Him, and keep His commands, things *will* go well with you. In the verse above, you can hear God yearning for His people to love Him. Know that God longs to bless you. He has promised, "Draw near to God and He will draw near to you" (James 4:8 NASB).

When you realize that God is all-powerful and that you're immeasurably weaker than He is, it causes you to experience a godly fear. This kind of fear is healthy. Realizing that God is eternal and that you, by comparison, are mere dust in the wind gives you a humble attitude. Such humility is the beginning of true worship and brings you many blessings.

The prophet Samuel told the Israelites, "Be sure to fear the LORD and faithfully serve him. Think of all the wonderful things he has done for you" (1 Samuel 12:24 NLT). Sit down and count your blessings. God has been good to you. And He isn't done yet! He wishes to bless you even more.

Day 5

MOTIVATED BY GODLY FEAR

*Because we have these promises, dear friends,
let us cleanse ourselves from everything that can
defile our body or spirit. And let us work toward
complete holiness because we fear God.*

2 CORINTHIANS 7:1 NLT

———•———

God has given many promises in His Word which,
empowered by His Spirit, can transform you into
the image of His Son (2 Corinthians 3:18). But being
changed from your present imperfect state into the
image of Jesus Christ means letting go of your faults
and habits, and this often isn't easy to do.

You have to be highly motivated to change. Only
if you sincerely fear God will you be compelled to
cleanse yourself from everything that displeases Him,
that defiles your body or your spirit.

The Bible urges you to "work out your own salvation
with fear and trembling" (Philippians 2:12 NKJV), but
it's also clear that you can't do good works to *earn*
your salvation (Ephesians 2:8–9). So what does this
command mean? It means to continually implore
God to change you and, though you're already saved,
to complete the process of renewal.

Jesus described this ongoing work of transformation
when He stated that the kingdom of God was like yeast
being worked through an entire lump of dough until
it was all leavened (Matthew 13:33).

BEYOND FEARING GOD

Let us. . .offer to God an acceptable service with
reverence and awe; for our God is a consuming fire.
HEBREWS 12:28–29 NASB

———————•◆•———————

As important as it is to fear God, fear and awe in
themselves aren't enough. After all, even the demons
believe in the existence of one supreme, all-powerful
Being of absolute good and shudder with terror (James
2:19). They know that He's a consuming fire. Their
problem is that they're set in rebellion against God,
hate Him, and have no intention of repenting.

Hebrews 11:6 (NIV) says about God, "Anyone who
comes to him must believe that he exists." That's the
first step. The second step is to be aware of your sinful
nature and believe that God will one day judge you.
This causes you to revere and fear Him (Acts 24:25).

The third step is to "love the LORD your God with
all your heart and with all your soul and with all your
strength" (Deuteronomy 6:5 NIV). As Jesus said, if you
love Him you will automatically obey Him. "Whoever
has my commands and keeps them is the one who
loves me" (John 14:21 NIV). Only then will you offer
to God an acceptable service with reverence and awe.

The fear of God should motivate you to love Him
and obey Him.

FEARING GOD ◆ *Week 9*

IN CONCLUSION

Now all has been heard; here is the conclusion of
the matter: Fear God and keep his commandments,
for this is the duty of all mankind.

ECCLESIASTES 12:13 NIV

Many Christians are stuck in one of two extremes: either they have a dread of God that eats away at them—giving them stomach ulcers and insomnia—or else they think He's a jolly Santa Claus and have no fear of Him at all.

In the first camp, people have "a certain fearful looking for of judgment and fiery indignation" (Hebrews 10:27 KJV) that destroys them from the inside. They're consumed by the negative image of a judgmental God. In the second camp, they've latched onto an unrealistic image of a God of endless grace who never judges sin.

God is not defined by human doctrines. He lives in eternity, complete and perfect, and is both a God of infinite love (1 John 4:8) and a God who sits in judgment of sin. While His mighty hand graciously upholds your weak spirit (Psalm 37:24; 63:8), for the disobedient it is "a fearful thing to fall into the hands of the living God" (Hebrews 10:31 KJV).

Learn to have a balanced view of God. Fear and love Him, and you'll keep His commandments—and all will be well with your soul.

Day 1

THE RIGHTEOUS ARE SATISFIED

*"Blessed are those who hunger and thirst for
righteousness, for they shall be satisfied."*
MATTHEW 5:6 NASB

Righteousness has a bad name today. Those who
aren't pursuing it often criticize those who are—falsely
believing that Christians think they are better than
everybody else. This is simply not the case for the true
Christ follower. In reality, those who are truly seeking
the narrow path have a real understanding of how
sinful they are. As a result, they constantly exchange
their sin for Christ's righteousness.

If you're seeking righteousness through your own
merits, rather than through the finished work of
Christ, you'll never achieve it. *Beatitudes* means "a
state of supreme happiness," and in them, Jesus says
that those who hunger and thirst for righteousness are
blessed and satisfied. Notice the need for the *pursuit* of
righteousness—for this brings blessings and satisfaction.

Pursuing righteousness doesn't come naturally,
though, even for Christians. Your hunger and thirst
must be stirred up on a regular basis by attending
worship services, reading your Bible, fellowshipping
with other believers, and prayer. If you neglect these,
you'll seek your own righteousness by default, thinking
more highly of yourself than you ought, and your
spiritual life will become dry.

Day 2

SURRENDER YOUR KINGDOM

*"Seek the Kingdom of God above all else,
and live righteously, and he will give
you everything you need."*
MATTHEW 6:33 NLT

Near the end of Jesus' temptation, Satan made one final attempt to get Him to stumble. He took Jesus to the peak of a high mountain and showed Him all the kingdoms of the world. "'I will give it all to you,' [Satan] said, 'if you will kneel down and worship me'" (Matthew 4:9 NLT).

But Jesus didn't buy it, telling Satan to flee.

That doesn't stop Satan from trying to get you to focus on ruling your own little kingdom in search of your perceived needs, though, rather than seeking the kingdom of God. How do you know if you've fallen for his ploy?

Earthly kings are authoritarian, refusing to bow the knee to anyone or anything, short of being conquered. They are the final authority on all matters—the top of the appeals chain. Does this resemble your life? Are you unwilling to submit to authority? If so, be careful, because you're on shaky ground.

The paradox of the Christian life is that you lay down your life to live. You stop pursuing your kingdom in favor of a superior one—one that ultimately will provide everything you need.

THE DIVINE NATURE

*Whereby are given unto us exceeding great
and precious promises: that by these ye might be
partakers of the divine nature, having escaped
the corruption that is in the world through lust.*

2 PETER 1:4 KJV

———— • ⬥ • ————

Peter wrote his two epistles to persecuted Christians
who were scattered across Asia Minor. As difficult as
it would have been for them, Peter wanted them to
remember to be partakers of the divine nature, rather
than giving in to the lusts of the world. But he didn't
leave them wondering how.

He reminded them that they had been given the
great and precious promises of God. Those promises
were the means to the divine nature. In Matthew
Henry's *Commentary on the Whole Bible*, he states:
"Those who receive the promises of the gospel partake
of the divine nature. They are renewed in the spirit
of their mind, after the image of God, in knowledge,
righteousness, and holiness; their hearts are set for
God and his service; they have a divine temper and
disposition of soul."

How are the promises of the Gospel shaping you
today? Are you jotting them on index cards and
referencing them? Are you talking about them in
Bible studies? Are you texting them to your friends?

Day 4

IT'S NEVER TOO LATE

*Do you not know that the unrighteous will not
inherit the kingdom of God? Do not be deceived.
Neither fornicators, nor idolaters, nor adulterers,
nor homosexuals, nor sodomites.*

1 CORINTHIANS 6:9 NKJV

Have you ever looked at a list of sins such as this in
scripture and wondered how you could possibly inherit
the kingdom of God? In one sense or another, you're
guilty of one or more of these evils. At the very least,
it's hard to deny what John Calvin said about the
human heart: "Man's nature, so to speak, is a perpetual
factory of idols."

So what's a Christian to do with such a promise?

Note that this list of sins contains no mention
of repentance. A person who openly embraces one
of these lifestyles with no struggle or regard for God
and His ways is already condemned. This isn't to say
a Christian can't fall, but he will always get back up
if he is regenerate.

Consider your behaviors in light of the list in 1
Corinthians 6:9. Have you given yourself over to any
of these sins? Have you given up the fight? It's never
too late to repent. Seek the strong support of a believer
who is in the habit of mortifying the flesh.

ABIDING WITH GOD

Lord, who shall abide in thy tabernacle?
who shall dwell in thy holy hill? He that
walketh uprightly, and worketh righteousness,
and speaketh the truth in his heart.

PSALM 15:1–2 KJV

The psalmist here asks a two-fold question, and it's the most important question any person can ask himself: Who can dwell in God's tabernacle (meaning an earthly dwelling place where God's presence is represented, such as the church)? And who can dwell in His holy hill (heaven)?

The answer to both questions is the same: those who walk (live) uprightly, work righteousness (perform deeds of righteousness), and speak the truth to themselves.

If you're living uprightly, working righteousness, and speaking truth to yourself, you'll have much less time to dabble or immerse yourself in sin and falsehoods. But this sort of lifestyle doesn't happen on its own. It can only be lived intentionally, with your heart and mind firmly fixed on truth. How are you doing in all three areas? If you see some deficiencies, don't ignore them.

Instead, look at the list and work backward. Speak truth to yourself by making God's Word a bigger priority. From there, you'll want to perform righteous deeds. And then, as God's Spirit flows through you, He will empower you to live righteously.

Day 6

HOLD THE LINE

*"Blessed are those who are persecuted because of
righteousness, for theirs is the kingdom of heaven."*
MATTHEW 5:10 NIV

———— • ◆ • ————

Pressure reveals what you truly believe. Nobody
knows that more than Christians who are persecuted
around the world because of their righteousness—their
unwavering refusal to bow the knee to false doctrines
or false messiahs. Jesus says they are blessed, though,
because theirs is the kingdom of heaven.

For the first time, the West is becoming intolerant
toward Christianity and those who embrace it as truth.
The unregenerate see it as an archaic system driven by
hate. Societal laws that were once rooted in biblical
truth are being overturned. And if you're vocal about
certain Christian beliefs, you can expect to pay a price.
It might cost you your job, your reputation, and one
day, maybe even your freedom.

Working to maintain religious freedom is a must,
but if the day comes when that battle is lost, are you
prepared to face the pressure cooker of persecution?
Will you stand strong, while still speaking about
the love of Christ for sinners? Will you accept the
consequences? Will you keep the big picture (heaven)
in mind?

Jesus will call you one of the blessed if you just
hold the line.

Week 10 ◆ RIGHTEOUSNESS

TELL THE TRUTH

*A righteous man hateth lying: but a wicked man
is loathsome, and cometh to shame.*
PROVERBS 13:5 KJV

You don't hear the phrase "little white lies" much
anymore, but a generation ago, people used it to justify
one action or another, or simply to be polite. Today,
people—including Christians—are quicker to simply
lie without even trying to justify it. But a man who
is walking in the truth, a righteous man, hates lying.

Lying is a grievous sin with alarming consequences.
Revelation 21:27 (KJV) says, "And there shall in no wise
enter into [heaven] any thing that defileth, neither
whatsoever worketh abomination, or maketh a lie:
but they which are written in the Lamb's book of life."

How quick are you to lie to your boss, your spouse,
or your friends when one of them asks you a question
you'd rather not answer because you know he or she
wouldn't like what you have to say? How quick are you
to embellish your accomplishments to make yourself
seem more qualified?

When you read a scripture verse such as Proverbs
13:5, does it prick your conscience? If so, take heart.
Deep down, the Holy Spirit is telling you that something
is off. Repent and resolve to tell the truth.

Day 1

THE RIGHT FIT

*Evening, and morning, and at noon, will I pray,
and cry aloud: and he shall hear my voice.*

PSALM 55:17 KJV

———— ·◆· ————

The psalmist David prayed to God three times a day. Think about the last time you talked to God. Was it this morning? . . . Last night? . . . Last week? . . . Last month? . . . Do you even remember when you last prayed? Many of you would be ashamed to admit that it was much too long ago.

Life gets in the way. Every day seems like a repeat of the same drudgery: rush to work, rush home, rush through supper, rush through laundry, bills, homework. . .rush to bed. It's difficult managing life as is, without adding more to your to-do list. So where does your one-on-one time with the heavenly Creator fit into your daily routine?

The good news is that prayer can fit in anywhere, anytime. Morning. Noon. Night. God will hear you. He will give you His undivided attention. "This is the confidence we have in approaching God: that if we ask anything according to his will, he hears us" (1 John 5:14 NIV).

You, too, can pray as David prayed. God never tires of hearing your voice. Whatever is on your heart, share it with Him today.

Day 2

PERSEVERE IN PRAYER

Rejoice in our confident hope.
Be patient in trouble, and keep on praying.
ROMANS 12:12 NLT

One peek at the daily news and it's difficult to remain hopeful. Troubling events take place every day in every corner of the world, and it seems there's no end in sight.

But God promises that, amid the world's turmoil, you can remain confident as you keep an eye toward heaven. Whether you're inundated with news of terrorist attacks, natural disasters, or crime in your hometown, you can rejoice in the hope that you have through Jesus Christ.

Rather than throwing your hands up in defeat, God's Word tells you to patiently endure tough times and to persevere in prayer. While the state of the world is in decline, and it seems as though your prayers for peace aren't being answered, you can have complete assurance—the hope!—of eternal life: "For the wages of sin is death; but the gift of God is eternal life through Jesus Christ our Lord" (Romans 6:23 KJV).

You can *know* with 100 percent assurance that perfect peace is the ultimate hope for your future: "He will wipe every tear from their eyes, and there will be no more death or sorrow or crying or pain. All these things are gone forever" (Revelation 21:4 NLT). You need only wait on God.

WITH BOLDNESS!

Let us therefore come boldly unto the throne
of grace, that we may obtain mercy,
and find grace to help in time of need.
HEBREWS 4:16 KJV

—— • ◉ • ——

When you enter the Lord's presence, do you go boldly?
Or do you make a tip-toe-like entrance?

Your heavenly Father wants you to approach
Him with confidence. Unafraid, you may reveal your
heart—your fears, your flaws, your frustrations—to Him.
Whatever it is you're feeling, share it *boldly*. He is a
mighty God. He can take it!

Nothing in this life depends on you, but rather on
Him. God is merciful. A sufficient sacrifice was made
on your behalf when He sent His Son, Jesus, to die
on the cross. "If we confess our sins, he is faithful and
just to forgive us our sins, and to cleanse us from all
unrighteousness" (1 John 1:9 KJV). He is faithful. He is
just. He is a forgiver of sins.

And your loving heavenly Father always has your
best interests in mind. "'For I know the plans I have
for you,' declares the LORD, 'plans to prosper you and
not to harm you, plans to give you hope and a future'"
(Jeremiah 29:11 NIV). He looks upon you with holy
favor because you belong to Him. You are His beloved
child! Go boldly!

A WORD OF HOPE

*Then you will call upon Me and go and pray
to Me, and I will listen to you. And you will
seek Me and find Me, when you search
for Me with all your heart.*

JEREMIAH 29:12–13 NKJV

———— ✦ ————

Have you ever felt like God is so very far away? That every time you call on His name, your prayer falls on deaf ears? That your mistakes, your imperfections, your unlovable qualities have put miles and miles of distance between your heart and His?

Here's a word of hope: *nothing* can change the fact that you are His beloved child. He loves you in all of your imperfection. Because of His boundless love, you can call on Him anytime, day or night, and He will hear you. There are no miles of separation. No difficult travels are required to gain His ear.

What can separate you from His love? *Nothing!* "Neither death nor life, neither angels nor demons, neither our fears for today nor our worries about tomorrow—not even the powers of hell can separate us from God's love. No power in the sky above or in the earth below—indeed, nothing in all creation will ever be able to separate us from the love of God that is revealed in Christ Jesus our Lord" (Romans 8:38–39 NLT).

IN ALL CIRCUMSTANCES

*Is any among you afflicted? let him pray.
Is any merry? let him sing psalms. Is any sick
among you? let him call for the elders of the
church; and let them pray over him, anointing him
with oil in the name of the Lord: and the prayer
of faith shall save the sick, and the Lord shall
raise him up; and if he have committed
sins, they shall be forgiven him.*

JAMES 5:13–15 KJV

———•❖•———

When life is going as planned and you're healthy, happy, content, and energized, pray!

When life is handing you one difficulty after another and you're sick, sad, dissatisfied, and weary, pray!

In *all* circumstances, where should you go but to God? He wants you to approach Him first—before your spouse, before your best friend, before your parents (Proverbs 3:6). Every. Single. Time.

God's Word says that the prayers of the righteous are powerful: "The earnest prayer of a righteous person has great power and produces wonderful results" (James 5:16 NLT). Don't you want powerful, wonderful results from your conversations with the Almighty?

The expression that is always fitting for both sorrow and joy is worship, and prayer is an important element of worship. In the words of hymn writer Joseph M. Scriven, "What a privilege to carry everything to God in prayer!"

BECAUSE HE IS GOOD

*Oh, that men would give thanks to the LORD
for His goodness, and for His wonderful
works to the children of men!*
PSALM 107:15 NKJV

———•◦•———

When you last sent a prayer heavenward, did your words include thanks to your heavenly Creator? Or were they laden with requests for Him to fulfill your every want and need?

There's certainly nothing wrong with asking God to meet your needs. In fact, you *should* ask Him for those things. "If you. . .know how to give good gifts to your children, how much more will your Father in heaven give the Holy Spirit to those who ask Him!" (Luke 11:13 NKJV).

There's nothing wrong with asking Him for your wants either. "Take delight in the LORD, and he will give you the desires of your heart" (Psalm 37:4 NIV). If you're in need of a new job, include that request in your prayers. If you'd like a new car, by all means mention that, too. However, don't forget to pray with a thankful heart.

God is gracious and merciful. He forgives. He delivers. He loves. Reflect upon His goodness, and you'll be certain to include a "Thank You, Father!" in your daily prayers. "Give thanks to the LORD, for he is good; his love endures forever" (Psalm 107:1 NIV). Pray today. . .and give thanks!

THE PRAYERS OF YOUR HEART

*Because he bends down to listen,
I will pray as long as I have breath!*
PSALM 116:2 NLT

———— • ◆ • ————

Need some motivation to help jump-start your prayer life? This verse from Psalm 116 is it. The psalmist says, "Because he bends down to listen. . . ." Imagine your loving heavenly Father bending low to better hear your voice. He's listening intently to every word coming out of your mouth. No smartphone distracts Him. Because He's omnipotent, no other voices drown you out. He listens intently to the prayers of your heart.

Now think about that one friend who listens to you best. Does that certain someone always give you their undivided attention? Or do distractions sometimes creep up in the middle of your conversations? A text that can't be ignored? . . . A phone call that has to be taken *right this very minute*? . . . No matter how loyal the listener, human minds are often preoccupied, and therefore, ears are missing out on what you're trying to communicate.

Your heavenly Creator misses *not one single word*. What better reason to continue praying to Him each and every day of your life.

Do as the psalmist says, and pray as long as you have breath. Talk to the One who listens to you best.

NO LONGER ORPHANS

*Behold, what manner of love the Father hath
bestowed upon us, that we should be
called the sons of God.*

1 JOHN 3:1 KJV

———— • ◆ • ————

Ask people if God exists and some will say that *if*
He exists He's cold and uncaring. Some picture Him
as an old man who strikes fear into the hearts of
humanity. He's often viewed as cruel. Yet today's verse
tells something different.

The writer wanted you to stop and pay attention
to a profound love sent from God to mankind. The
gift of love was paired with the gift of grace. How
do you know this? God's Word says the love of God
was so profound that you became something more
than a follower, adherent, disciple, or student. You
became a *child* of God who is loved by your Father
and given all the rights of a family member. You aren't
an acquaintance, part of His extended network, or an
employee. You're family. By God's love you were offered
the grace to become a son or daughter.

God's love didn't just provide rescue. It moved you
from an orphan without a home to a family member
with *anytime* access to God.

This is a big deal! Many have never accepted the
lavish love God has for them. Maybe they can see it
in you.

WITHOUT GOD'S LOVE

God commendeth his love toward us, in that,
while we were yet sinners, Christ died for us.
ROMANS 5:8 KJV

Mankind broke God's law repeatedly. God's commands were ignored daily. His plans went unrecognized globally. And in the midst of man's disregard, God developed a plan that defied all expectations. When you distanced yourself from His wisdom, rejected His claim on your life, and acted as if He didn't matter, and when your sin defined your choices, God sent His Son to pay the full price for your rebellion.

Why did He do this? He loved you. How did He demonstrate His love? By removing every barrier to relationship with Him. If it weren't for God's greatest sacrifice, you'd be perpetually separated from Him.

God's love is as much a choice for Him as it is for you. Without God's choice to love, you'd be expected to personally accept the wages of sin, death (Romans 3:23). God hates sin but loves the people He created. In the midst of humanity's rebellion, Christ died so you could live, forgiven and free.

God's love provides the example you need to love others and return His love. A catastrophic future was radically altered because God loves you. Discover this most incredible reason for joy. Share it.

Day 3

RETURNING GOD'S LOVE

*It is written: "Eye has not seen, nor ear heard,
nor have entered into the heart of man the things
which God has prepared for those who love Him."*
1 CORINTHIANS 2:9 NKJV

————•◆•————

God's love is promised and available to all who trust
(have faith) in the perfect sacrifice of the sinless Jesus
Christ. Your sins can only be removed through an act
of faith. The greatest ideas you have of what God's love
is like will always be too small. How do you know
this? Stop for a moment and read the verse again.
Take your time.

Welcome back. Let's share the verse another way:
"No story has fully expressed it, no song has adequately
conveyed it, and our minds can only begin to imagine
the planned blessings God lavishes on those who love
Him."

God loves you intensely, and richly blesses you if
you love Him in return. His blessings always outshine
money because while you can buy a house, God can
bless you with a home (there's a difference). Money is
useful when you need things that don't last. However,
when you want things that are everlasting, look first
to your relationship with God.

He's better than your best dream and greater than
your greatest hope. Accept His blessings by offering
your love to the God who loved you first.

Week 12 ♦ GOD'S LOVE – PART 1

Day 4

NOTHING

*I am convinced that nothing can ever separate
us from God's love. Neither death nor life,
neither angels nor demons, neither our fears for
today nor our worries about tomorrow—not even
the powers of hell can separate us from God's love.
No power in the sky above or in the earth below—
indeed, nothing in all creation will ever be able
to separate us from the love of God that
is revealed in Christ Jesus our Lord.*

ROMANS 8:38–39 NLT

God's love is real. No one can match it, take it away,
or make God stop loving you.

You can reject Him. You can stiff-arm God. You can
try to run away from Him. In the end, God isn't moved
in His opinion of you. He has, does, and always will
love you. Only you have the power to separate yourself
from Him by *never* accepting His love. Even that won't
stop Him from offering His love.

As a believer you can be sure that nothing can ever
separate (remove) you from His love—when you die,
while you live, the meddling of spiritual beings, fear,
worry, or physical objects. Nothing separates God's
children from the love of God. Let that sink in and
then look at the verse again. *Nothing* can *ever* separate
you from God's love.

Day 5

COMPLETELY DRENCHED

Hope does not put us to shame, because God's love has been poured out into our hearts through the Holy Spirit, who has been given to us.
ROMANS 5:5 NIV

———•◦•———

We're told that hope anchors the soul (Hebrews 6:19). Hope holds your spiritual life in place in a societal stream bent on the mad rush, the latest trend, and the mocking insistence that God is dead.

Like most things, shame is a choice. When your hope is in the love of God, there's no shame in embracing it. It should be a primary source of joy.

Like a cloudburst in a drought, a blanket on a cold night, or snow on Christmas morning, God's love completely envelopes the core of what makes you "you." There's no part left out of His loving touch, and God's living water saturates. . .daily.

For the first time in this look at God's love, please discover your Helper, Guide, and Counselor, the Holy Spirit. It's His job to drench you in the love of God.

God is rich in love, and He shares the source of that richness with you. It's a promise, a gift, and the perfect environment for life change. Bring it on, accept its fullness, and let it spill over into your life. You need it. He gives it. Accept it.

Day 6

RETURN ON INVESTMENT

*"I will heal their waywardness and love them freely,
for my anger has turned away from them."*

HOSEA 14:4 NIV

You've probably heard the term *return on investment* (ROI). Most people use the term when talking about financial investments. If applied to your spiritual life, two very different outcomes to investment strategies emerge.

One strategy occurs when *you* invest love in the God who designed you and gave you life. The return on your investment is forgiveness, eternal life, the guidance of His Spirit, and His ability to work all things together for the good "of those who love him, who have been called according to his purpose" (Romans 8:28 NIV).

A second strategy occurs when *God* invests love in you. His ROI is less assured. You could choose to follow, be transformed through obedience, and become close to God; or you could ignore His love, turn from His rescue plan for your life, and act as if you never knew about His plans.

God always invests love in others. Do you? He cares for all people. Do you play favorites? He has a plan for each life. Can you help someone follow it?

When you invest in love, it's returned. You make investments. Some investments don't seem like much, but God offers you incredible investment opportunities. Choose wisely.

TAKE HIS HAND

*"I am the Lord your God who takes hold of your
right hand and says to you, Do not fear;
I will help you."*
ISAIAH 41:13 NIV

Visit any mall or shopping center. If a child is walking
with her parents, there's a good chance she's holding
hands. Kids instinctively reach for Mom's hand when
they're nervous or just want assurance that everything
is going to be all right.

This gesture that delivers confidence to a child and
delight to parents is how God deals with you. He uses
that word-picture to describe His care and promise to
be present during life's most stressful moments.

If you think of the worst life issue you've ever
experienced, you should add the word-picture of God
holding your hand through it. Imagine His words,
"Do not fear; I will help you." When you deal with
others who are going through similar pain and need
assurance, remember today's verse and share this
reassuring picture.

There's no truth to the statement "God helps those
who help themselves." It's not in the Bible. You should
work hard, do your best, and complete tasks. However,
He Himself holds your right hand, so your future is
never left to blind chance. He's with you in every
moment of joy and instance of sorrow. Take His hand.
Feel accepted.

Day 1

THE UNBREAKABLE TETHER

"The Lord is my portion," says my soul, "therefore I have hope in Him." The Lord is good to those who wait for Him, to the person who seeks Him.

<small>LAMENTATIONS 3:24–25 NASB</small>

———◆———

For the child of God, hope is a rich inheritance, a priceless, limitless resource that lights the darkest night and kindles the dullest ember. To belong to God is to have hope on speed dial, a prayer or scripture away, a ready connection with your sovereign Savior who purchased hope for you on the cross.

Sometimes, though, the only way to appreciate what you've been given is to think of what life would be like without it. To lose hope, then, is to pull anchor in a storm, to be untethered from the very idea that tomorrow might be better than today. Hopeless people give up on relationships because they've gotten stuck in fight-or-flight mode. They give up on getting help, because how could anything ever be good again?

As a Christian, though, God tenderly holds you in the palm of His hand: "The Lord directs the steps of the godly. . . . Though they stumble, they will never fall, for the Lord holds them by the hand" (Psalm 37:23–24 NLT). Nothing can separate you from His love (Romans 8:38–39) or the hope you have in Christ.

Day 2

A DIFFERENT GRIEF

*Dear brothers and sisters, we want you to know
what will happen to the believers who have died
so you will not grieve like people who have no
hope. . . . When Jesus returns, God will bring
back with him the believers who have died.*

1 THESSALONIANS 4:13–14 NLT

It's hard to keep an eternal perspective when you're
waist deep in grief. Sometimes the sorrow barely
covers your toes, and other times it's up your nose
and stinging your eyes. Forget heaven, you just want
to get to the next moment. But here's the thing: you
will get to the next moment, and the next. The world
should have stopped spinning, but it just keeps on
keeping on.

As annoying as that is, it's also pretty astonishing,
because while grief or sickness or getting fired has put
a pin in your life, God is holding your place. He will
comfort you when your thoughts have all gone black,
and when you're ready to take a next step, He will be
right there on the path ahead of you.

And in the end, your Father is holding your place
in heaven, the place He made specifically for you, a
place of reunion and rejoicing. Death stinks, but it
really has lost its sting because of the wonder of Jesus'
resurrection.

PROGRESSION AND PROCESS

We glory in tribulations also: knowing that
tribulation worketh patience; and patience,
experience; and experience, hope:
and hope maketh not ashamed.

ROMANS 5:3–5 KJV

The Christian life starts in the most hopeful way, riding the crest of a wave of joyful expectation. You thought that shifting your eternal destination from hell to heaven surely meant sunny skies and smooth sailing from here on out. Not quite. While the glory that awaits you is worth celebrating, you have just begun a process that will consume the rest of your time on earth—sanctification.

Your response to everything you go through from then on will either make you more like Jesus or less like Him. And you'll be doing it with a target painted on your back, a mark for Satan's wiles and society's scorn, even as you fight the battle of the flesh. Would it be easier if you hadn't responded to Christ's call on your heart? Maybe—but only in this life. Eternity is a lot longer than the seventy or so years you might get here, so it's worth the preparation.

That preparation, though, will come through tribulation, patience, and experience. Take encouragement from the progress and the process, because the hope that results is ironclad, unassailable by the very gates of hell. You are Christ's, and the ultimate victory is yours.

HOPE'S SPOKESPERSON

*"I have the same hope in God as these men. . .
that there will be a resurrection of both
the righteous and the wicked."*

ACTS 24:15 NIV

The world's evil knows few bounds, and it can be a satisfying thought to know that God will righteously judge each unrepentant terrorist and child molester. But hell is only an appeasing thought if you think you could never possibly feel its flames—that your goodness and decency are enough to keep you in the clear. A redeemed soul recognizes each evil act for what it truly represents: an assault on the hope of knowing God's love and grace through Christ. Never forget who the real enemy is.

Evil should be a stench to you the way it is to God, but will you breathe through it and remember a lost and dying world? Jesus broke through death and hell to build a bridge back to God, and He calls you to show the way, to be this world's salt and light—its preservative against decay and its hope in the darkness.

You are truth's ambassador and hope's spokesperson. The stakes are eternal, and you know the only way out of this mess. You know God's heart: John 3:16. Focus your prayers today on as many being covered by the blood of Christ as possible.

Day 5

RECONNECT AND REJOICE

*For in this hope we were saved. But hope that is
seen is no hope at all. Who hopes for what they
already have? But if we hope for what we do
not yet have, we wait for it patiently.*
ROMANS 8:24–25 NIV

———— • ❖ • ————

Sometimes, hope seems to slip away so secretly that
you don't even know it's gone. Nothing disastrous has
struck; everything's cruising along, but you look around
and feel like you took a wrong turn somewhere. Maybe
you thought you'd be further along in your career or
in a relationship, or that you would have done more
with your life—traveling, maybe, or even ministering.

The fact that you can't be fully satisfied in this life
suggests that this life isn't meant to fully satisfy you.
Life's importance isn't the end products of your work
or relationships but what you learn about God, others,
and yourself along the way. Only God can grasp the
full scope of every little thing you think, say, and do,
but you have His promise that He is working it all
together for your good (Romans 8:28).

When you lose sight of God's path, reconnect
with Him—through prayer, His Word, and Christian
fellowship. Be reassured that all the things you can't
see are clear as day to the One who directs your steps.

A DAILY GETAWAY PLAN

*Thou art my hiding place
and my shield: I hope in thy word.*
PSALM 119:114 KJV

If you've recently had the chance for a quick getaway, you know what a blessing it can be to take in a new setting, to get a break from the busyness of the everyday hustle and bustle. Sometimes, the refreshment can last you quite awhile; other times it evaporates on the drive home.

Most times, even getting away for a weekend just can't be done. The question becomes, *How can I be refreshed in the middle of all that I have to do* today? David offered a solution: God's Word. You may not be able to go out of town or even go camping, but scripture can be your hiding place, a refuge of hope and rejuvenation when life is spinning madly around you.

Reading the Bible enables you to look beyond your circumstances and rest. "Blessed is the man who trusts in the LORD, and whose hope is the LORD" (Jeremiah 17:7 NKJV). After all, no matter where you are, your "soul finds rest in God" (Psalm 62:1 NIV), and "those who hope in the LORD will renew their strength" (Isaiah 40:31 NIV). A spa day or fishing trip is great, but God's Word gives deep refreshing no matter where you are.

THE WONDER OF HOPE

Who, contrary to hope, in hope believed, so that he became the father of many nations, according to what was spoken, "So shall your descendants be."
ROMANS 4:18 NKJV

———————

Hope is a contrary thing. It flies in the face of common sense. What Abraham did, for example, makes no sense—uprooting his family, taking them from their ancestral homeland to some place he'd never heard of or seen, all on the say-so of an unknown Deity who came and told him to get going, that He had big plans for him. And yet, something about God gave Abraham hope that all His promises would come true.

The power of hope lies in belief, or, more specifically, the one in whom belief is placed. To hope in God is to believe in someone you can't see now but will someday. And when you do, everything you hoped would be true about Him will be dwarfed by His reality. Everything about Him—His love, His warmth, His wonder—will be more than you could ever imagine.

After all, if Paul said all the troubles of this life, which overwhelm you, are but momentary things compared with heaven's glories (2 Corinthians 4:17), how great must heaven be? And how much greater the one who makes it *heaven*—God Himself? Hope in Him is well-placed.

WHY LOVE?

We love, because He first loved us.
1 JOHN 4:19 NASB

———•◆•———

It's interesting that God created some animals to be mostly loners. Examples are bears, koalas, and sea turtles. Sometimes a solitary life seems appealing, doesn't it? Wouldn't it be a peaceful existence to just do your own thing without answering to or dealing with anyone? No cooperation or communication required. Yet what a lonely life, too—void of relationships, connection, and love.

God created solitary animals in their unique ways, but He created humans entirely different. He created people in His image, to be more like Him. And that's exactly why people *do* have love for others. "We love, because He first loved us." It's as simple and profound and beautiful as that.

God is love itself as the whole chapter of 1 John 4 explains. Apart from Him, it's impossible to know what real love is. And because He created you and showed His love for you—especially through the sacrifice of His Son, Jesus Christ—people are consequently wired to want to imitate Him in sharing love and being part of loving relationships with others.

Day 2

NO GREATER GOAL

And now these three remain: faith, hope and love.
But the greatest of these is love.
1 CORINTHIANS 13:13 NIV

Faith, hope, and love are vitally important virtues for Christians. Without them, there is no Christian life. They're fundamental to your walk with God through your Savior, Jesus Christ. Yet the Bible promises that one of these virtues stands out above the others—and without it the others are empty. That virtue is *love.*

Love is the greatest virtue of all. As a Christian, you must cling to it and constantly convey it to people around you. Why? Because as the first part of 1 Corinthians 13 explains, love is what gives your words weight, your life significance, and your motives meaning. Anything said or accomplished without love is absolutely worthless.

Jesus said, "Your love for one another will prove to the world that you are my disciples" (John 13:35 NLT). Cultivating and sharing *faith* and *hope* certainly are important. But *love* is the greatest and most essential virtue for pointing others to Jesus Christ as Savior and encouraging them to surrender their lives and follow Him. Christians must cultivate and share it above all. There is no greater goal than to win others over to Jesus with your love.

Day 3

REAL LOVE

*Beloved, let us love one another, for love is from
God; and everyone who loves is born of God
and knows God. The one who does not love
does not know God, for God is love.*

1 JOHN 4:7–8 NASB

———◦◦◦———

The world pretends to know what real love is. Secular
culture has all kinds of ideas—some harmless, some
not far off the mark, and some that are deceiving and
dangerous. The basic reason humans are even looking
for love is because God Himself is love and He instituted
it among them when He created them in His image.

Authentic love is simply impossible to know without
first knowing who God is and how He demonstrates
His love to you. It's described so well in this passage:
"God showed how much he loved us by sending his
one and only Son into the world so that we might
have eternal life through him. This is real love—not
that we loved God, but that he loved us and sent his
Son as a sacrifice to take away our sins. Dear friends,
since God loved us that much, we surely ought to love
each other. No one has ever seen God. But if we love
each other, God lives in us, and his love is brought to
full expression in us" (1 John 4:9–12 NLT).

ACTIVE LOVE

*We know what real love is because Jesus gave up
his life for us. So we also ought to give up our lives
for our brothers and sisters. If someone has enough
money to live well and sees a brother or sister
in need but shows no compassion—how can
God's love be in that person?*

1 JOHN 3:16–17 NLT

———— ·◆· ————

Telling children they're loved but never playing with
them or providing for them proves those loving words
empty and gives them a false idea of love. The same kind
of thing goes for relationships with spouses, extended
family, and friends. Loving words in relationships are
nice, of course, but they're hollow if not accompanied
by action. Real love is active. Real love is sacrificial.

Christians who tell the world that they love others
without actively helping brothers and sisters around
them who are in need give a false idea of the love of
the Savior. Jesus gave up His very life, and He calls His
people to sacrifice in order to lovingly meet others'
needs as well. First John 3 continues by saying, "Dear
children, let's not merely say that we love each other;
let us show the truth by our actions" (v. 18 NLT).

CONFIDENT LOVE

*Our actions will show that we belong to the truth,
so we will be confident when we stand before God.
Even if we feel guilty, God is greater than our
feelings, and he knows everything. Dear friends,
if we don't feel guilty, we can come to God with
bold confidence. And we will receive from him
whatever we ask because we obey him and
do the things that please him. And this is his
commandment: We must believe in the name
of his Son, Jesus Christ, and love one
another, just as he commanded us.*

1 JOHN 3:19–23 NLT

It can be intimidating, even terrifying, to think of standing before almighty God, the Creator of all the universe. Yet scripture promises that because of Jesus, Christians are made right with God (Romans 3), so you have no need to fear.

Believers will surely bow the knee (Philippians 2:10) in humility, respect, and awe before the King of all kings, but those who love God and obey His commands have no need to cower in fear. The passage above explains that believing Jesus and offering love to one another are what give Christians not just a little bit of assurance but *bold* confidence before their holy heavenly Father.

So, trusting in your Savior, go and boldly share His love, knowing that one day soon you can confidently stand before the one true God!

HELP FOR LOVING OTHERS

But concerning brotherly love you have no need
that I should write to you, for you yourselves
are taught by God to love one another.

1 THESSALONIANS 4:9 NKJV

Christians don't need instruction from other people on how to love, when God Himself is the very best teacher of love. He *is* love itself, after all!

Simply ask God for His help to love others. Do you have people in your life who are difficult to deal with, yet you know God is calling you to show them kindness and compassion? You don't have to take the time to read a pile of books on how to treat others well; simply ask God Himself day by day—sometimes moment by moment—to show you how to act and what to do for others, to give you the opportunities and the right words to say to share His love and point others to Him. Philippians 2:13 (NLT) promises that "God is working in you, giving you the desire and the power to do what pleases him."

Of Corrie ten Boom's many famous words, one quote stands out at this point. She prayed, "Dear Jesus. . .how foolish of me to have called for human help when You are here." A hearty "Amen!" to that.

LOVE ABOVE YOURSELF

Be devoted to one another in love.
Honor one another above yourselves.
ROMANS 12:10 NIV

Secular culture has taken self-help to a cringe-worthy level for Christians. Of course, it makes worldly sense that a person must be healthy, happy, and well himself *first* for him to be able to help anyone else. Yet what does the Bible say about worldly wisdom? Read 1 Corinthians 3:18–19. Not to mention, how is the propensity for self-first kind of thinking consistent with the scriptures that say Christians should rejoice in suffering and trials? (See Romans 5, James 1, 1 Peter 4, 2 Timothy 3, and 2 Corinthians 4.)

Many times, the Bible talks about laying your life and selfish desires down and lifting others up. Take Philippians 2:3–4 (NIV) for example: "Do nothing out of selfish ambition or vain conceit. Rather, in humility value others above yourselves, not looking to your own interests but each of you to the interests of the others."

Loving others means sacrificing your own desires in order to help meet their needs (despite whatever trials and suffering you might be enduring yourself), just like Christ sacrificed to meet the world's greatest need—and thus saved mankind from sin. Thankfully, God doesn't expect this kind of sacrificial love from your own ability. He urges His people to depend on Him for endless power and strength.

GOD CARES FOR YOU

*Give all your worries and cares to God,
for he cares about you.*
1 PETER 5:7 NLT

————

You may feel like a hopeless mess, with a discouraged spirit, staggering through life burdened with countless cares and problems, isolated from friends and loved ones. You may seriously wonder if God even remembers you or cares about you. If so, where is He when you need Him most?

But be assured that God hasn't forgotten you—and He *does* care. His eyes are continually upon your plight, and He hears all your groanings. He understands your frustration when your anguished prayers seem to be going unanswered, but He is working to *answer* your prayers, even if—from your perspective—He seems to be moving glacially slow.

Don't try to carry all your problems and concerns by yourself. Certainly, do your best to deal with situations you face, but you must also realize that one of the best things you can do is cry out to Him for *His* help in dealing with problems. Having done all that you can, give them into God's powerful hands and trust Him to work things out.

When you do that, He will send peace into your heart and comfort you, assuring you that everything will work out. . .even when the situation seems hopeless.

Week 15 ◆ COMFORT

Day 2

THE COMFORTING SAVIOR

The Spirit of the Lord GOD. . .*hath anointed me
to preach good tidings unto the meek; he hath sent
me to bind up the brokenhearted. . .
to comfort all that mourn.*
ISAIAH 61:1–2 KJV

In Luke 4:17–21, Jesus declared that this Old Testament
passage was written specifically for Him and fulfilled
by Him. It therefore describes what Jesus is like, giving
you a look into His heart and the overwhelming love
He had—and has—for people around Him.

Isaiah's prophecy went on to say that the Messiah
would "provide for those who grieve in Zion—to bestow
on them a crown of beauty instead of ashes, the oil of
joy instead of mourning, and a garment of praise instead
of a spirit of despair" (Isaiah 61:3 NIV). The people were
despairing, figuratively smearing their faces with ashes
in their deep mourning, but Jesus came along, anointed
their heads with the oil of joy, and dispelled despair.

God's Holy Spirit anointed Jesus "to comfort all that
mourn," so you should picture Him as gentle, caring,
and continually seeking to cheer people up. If you can
understand and believe this one facet of Jesus' heart,
you will have grasped His most basic thought toward
you. No wonder He was constantly talking about His
disciples experiencing joy!

Day 3

PROTECTED AND COMFORTED

Even when I walk through the darkest valley,
I will not be afraid, for you are close beside me.
Your rod and your staff protect and comfort me.

PSALM 23:4 NLT

David declared that the Lord's staff protected and comforted him, even when making his way through the darkest valleys. A shepherd used his staff as a deadly weapon against fierce animals, and knowing that their guardian was always looking out for them was a source of great comfort to the flock.

Jesus is the Good Shepherd, and He has promised to always be close to you, never to abandon you. But perhaps you worry that although He's been with you *this* far, He will eventually grow tired of you and bail out—most likely during your time of greatest need. But elsewhere He promised, "Surely I am with you always, to the very end of the age" (Matthew 28:20 NIV). He's with you *always*. He will never desert you.

You will be required to cross many dark valleys during your sojourn on this earth. May you find deep comfort in the fact that the Son of God will be with you every step of the way. And when you cross the final "valley of the shadow of death" (v. 4 KJV), He will usher you into the loving presence of His Father forever.

Day 4

GOD WILL CONSOLE YOU

When anxiety was great within me,
your consolation brought me joy.
PSALM 94:19 NIV

Have you ever felt great anxiety? It can be a terrifying experience. When you're facing unrelenting stress or are under serious spiritual attack, anxiety can seem like a great wave rising, powerful enough to rip your boat completely from its moorings. In that moment, you feel as if it's all over. Fear and despair are flooding your mind and about to drive you over the edge, and you don't feel you have the strength to resist.

An unknown psalmist was suffering terrible anxiety and cried out in anguish, "Who will rise up for me against the wicked?" He then flung himself upon God, declaring, "Unless the LORD had given me help, I would soon have dwelt in the silence of death" (v. 17). He knew that God was His *only* hope and was desperate for His help.

You, too, can cling to God when waves of anxiety strike with punishing force. God is your Rock. He will not be moved, and if you trust Him, you won't be moved either. He will come to your defense. He will protect you and comfort you, and in the place where you suffered great anxiety, He will surprise you with peace and joy.

GOD COMFORTS THE MOURNING

"God blesses those who mourn,
for they will be comforted."
MATTHEW 5:4 NLT

———— • ◆ • ————

You typically think of a mourner as someone grieving the death of a loved one, and that's a large part of the picture. But people mourn many things—the death of a dream, the end of a relationship, financial loss, wasted years, or failing health. When you're mourning, there seems to be no reason to have hope, no reason to be happy.

You trudge through life empty, drained of goals and purpose. You're in survival mode, droning along on autopilot. But time after time, God reaches out to tenderly comfort you, to breathe hope into you again. He pierces the clouds of despair, and a single, faint shard of light illuminates your darkness. At first, you're often almost too despondent to be cheered by it. But slowly the clouds part, the light returns, gathering in brightness and strength, and finally hope rises and you can see your way again.

It will be like that at the end of this weary, trouble-filled life. The glorious light of heaven will surround you and sweep you up into its embrace in a fantastic rush of beauty and love, dispelling all your sorrows and heartaches. And your heavenly Father will draw you close, wipe away your tears, and comfort you.

Week 15 ◆ COMFORT

THE TRUEST COMFORTER

*I will pray the Father, and he shall give
you another Comforter, that he may
abide with you for ever.*

JOHN 14:16 KJV

———— • ◆ • ————

After Job suffered great calamities, his three closest friends came "to mourn with him and to comfort him" (Job 2:11 KJV). Unfortunately, they soon forgot their initial mission and began calling his every motive into question and condemning him—so much so that Job lamented, "Miserable comforters are ye all" (Job 16:2 KJV).

There's *another* Comforter, however, who never condemns you or tears you down but always seeks to take your side to comfort and restore you. He may frankly point out areas you need to change in, and urge you to turn to God, but He loves you deeply and always seeks your good. And He constantly assures you that you are God's beloved, saved child (Romans 8:15–16). This wonderful Comforter is, of course, the Holy Spirit.

The Greek word *parakletos* translated "Comforter" in this verse means "one called alongside." It's someone who pleads another's cause, or who helps them by comforting or defending them. The Holy Spirit feels deeply for you. He "prays for [you] with groanings that cannot be expressed in words" (Romans 8:26 NLT). You can be assured that this Comforter is *truly* on your side.

THE GOD OF ALL COMFORT

Blessed be. . .the Father of mercies and God of all
comfort, who comforts us in all our tribulation,
that we may be able to comfort those who are
in any trouble, with the comfort with which
we ourselves are comforted by God.

2 CORINTHIANS 1:3–4 NKJV

This scripture is a beautiful promise to cling to in time of need. God is truly the "God of all comfort" who "comforts us in *all* our tribulation." Whatever you're going through, your heavenly Father personally feels your pain and empathizes with you. When describing the afflictions of His people, scripture assures you, "In all their suffering he also suffered" (Isaiah 63:9 NLT).

And there is a second part to this promise. In the same epistle, Paul wrote, "God, who comforts the downcast, comforted us by the coming of Titus" (2 Corinthians 7:6 NKJV). First of all, Paul states the profound promise that "God. . .comforts the downcast," whoever they are and whatever they're going through.

But God has more than just your benefit in mind. After you've been touched and strengthened, He wants you to be moved by the same compassion that moves Him, to reach out to others and console them. You are to encourage others with the comfort with which you yourself are comforted by God.

Day 1

ASK, SEEK, KNOCK

"So I say to you: Ask and it will be given to you;
seek and you will find; knock and the
door will be opened to you."
LUKE 11:9 NIV

When it comes to the promises of God, there are three key ways to watch them spring to action: Ask. Seek. Knock. It's impossible to see miracles come to pass in your life if you don't ask for them, so start by asking. Sure, God can read your mind. But speaking your request aloud bolsters your faith and reminds you that He is able. So, raise your voice. Speak it aloud. Watch your faith increase.

Next, seek God's will. Just because you ask for something doesn't mean it's God's best for you. When you seek Him with your whole heart, when His desire becomes more important than your desire, you'll be on the right path. He will reveal His good and perfect will to you, and it will be just what you need at this point in your life.

Finally, knock. Don't give up, even if the door doesn't open right away. Be like that persistent widow in Jesus' parable (Luke 18:1–8). Become a nuisance if you have to, but don't stop. Keep on knocking. Keep on seeking. Keep on asking. The Lord loves your persistence.

Day 2

FIRST THINGS FIRST

*But seek ye first the kingdom of God,
and his righteousness; and all these
things shall be added unto you.*
MATTHEW 6:33 KJV

———— • ◆ • ————

Life is filled with exciting things, all vying for your
attention. From the minute you wake up in the
morning, distractions abound. E-mails. Social media.
Text messages. Phone calls. Bills. Spouse. Kids. Job. Car
issues. Mortgage payments. On and on the list goes.

In the midst of the chaos it's easy to forget that you
should be seeking God first. Before your feet hit the
ground, begin to thank Him for the new day ahead
of you. While you're brushing your teeth, praise Him
for the opportunities He's about to give. While you're
driving the kids to school, and as they head off to class,
pray for God's best. Or as you drive to work, begin to
speak His promises over your life.

In other words, give the choicest part of your day—
the untainted first few minutes and hours—to the One
who knows and loves you best. He's got your interests
at heart. If you seek Him first, all of those other things
on your to-do list will fall into perfect alignment.

THE KINGDOM OF GOD

But rather seek ye the kingdom of God;
and all these things shall be added unto you.
LUKE 12:31 KJV

Week 16 ♦ SEEKING GOD

What comes to mind when you hear the words *kingdom of God*? Many people think of heaven, a place of eternal bliss. They think of white, fluffy clouds and pearly gates. Others think of a fairy tale kingdom, with castles and knights, kings and queens. Some people believe it's a literal place; others argue that it's symbolic.

If you really want to know where the kingdom of God exists, take a look inside yourself. Jesus said that the kingdom of God is within you (Luke 17:21). When you "seek first the kingdom" (Matthew 6:33 NKJV), what you're really saying is, "God, I want Your will, Your kingdom, to take first place in my life, my family, my career, my friendships."

You're also saying, "I trust that all things (all of Your promises) will be added unto me when I seek Your kingdom first."

Why would your heavenly Father remind you that putting His kingdom first is key? Because His plans are far superior to your own. He's got amazing things in store for you. Those promises will come to pass in ways you never even imagined. So, hold on for the ride! "All these things" are about to be *added* unto you!

Day 4

A HAPPY HEART

*Glory in His holy name; let the hearts
of those rejoice who seek the LORD!*
1 CHRONICLES 16:10 NKJV

In this crazy, mixed-up world today, folks are looking to many different things to bring joy. Everywhere you look, promises abound! Television commercials. Magazine ads. Billboards. They all guarantee happiness and fulfillment.

However, you've learned the secret, one that doesn't require a slogan or advertisement: *nothing* can make you as happy as the kind of eternal joy that radiates from a heart fully linked with the Lord.

No matter how many cars you own, no matter how many vacations you go on, no matter how expensive the home you live in, you'll never truly be happy until you've accepted Jesus Christ as your Lord and Savior. Once you've crossed that threshold, a whole new world awaits.

When you put Him in His proper place—on the throne of your heart—you'll experience life-altering joy and enjoy peace as never before. His promises become real. Tangible. His Word springs to life. You begin to seek His perfect will for every area of your life because you know you'll find contentment and peace. And where peace reigns, joy abounds.

So, go on! Glory in His name. Let your heart rejoice as you continue to seek His good and perfect will.

Day 5

WITH ALL DILIGENCE

*At night my soul longs for You, indeed, my spirit
within me seeks You diligently; for when the earth
experiences Your judgments the inhabitants
of the world learn righteousness.*

ISAIAH 26:9 NASB

Think back to your school days. Were you a diligent
student or one who procrastinated? If you gave yourself
over to your studies, if you pursued every task with
diligence, then the payoff came with better grades. (How
fun to show *that* report card to your parents!) But if
you waited until the last minute to do your homework
or to study for a test, you paid the price with lower
grades. (Hiding that report card never worked, did it?
Mom always found out.)

That's how it is with the things of God, too. When
you become lackadaisical, when you forget to study
His Word and pray, your faith begins to shrink. But
when you seek Him with all due diligence, you grow
stronger day by day.

Diligence is a critical part of your faith walk. It
bolsters your confidence so that you can stand in
faith, believing God in good times *and* bad. Sure, there
will be days when you don't feel like sticking close to
God. Yes, there will be times that you grow weary. But
diligence always has a payoff.

Day 6

FINDERS KEEPERS

"But from there you will search again for the LORD
your God. And if you search for him with all
your heart and soul, you will find him."

DEUTERONOMY 4:29 NLT

Perhaps you grew up hearing the phrase "Finders, keepers! Losers, weepers!" It's a familiar expression, albeit painful to the loser.

There's one area of your life where this phrase makes perfect sense: in your spiritual walk. When you seek God, when you spend time asking Him for His thoughts, His plans, His desires over your situation, you'll be a winner in the end. His faithfulness will astound you. The answered promises will invigorate you.

But when you rush ahead of God, convinced you have a better way, you'll end up on the losing end every time. In other words, you'll be disappointed and wonder why He didn't come through for you. . .never realizing you didn't give Him a chance to do so.

Here's the key: don't be in a hurry. It's more important to be in sync with your heavenly Father than to strike out on your own and end up crashing and burning. Pace yourself. Then brace yourself for a great outcome. You'll be a finder who gets to keep the prize.

THEN WILL I HEAR

*"Then if my people who are called by my name
will humble themselves and pray and seek my
face and turn from their wicked ways, I will hear
from heaven and will forgive their
sins and restore their land."*

2 CHRONICLES 7:14 NLT

Have you ever been around a person who needed a hearing aid but refused to wear one? Chances are, you spent a lot of time with your voice raised. You probably ended up repeating phrases a lot, too.

Aren't you glad that God doesn't need a hearing aid? Yet there are occasions when He seems to hear your requests louder and clearer than usual. There are times when the Lord calls you to seasons of specialized prayer for your family, your community, and your nation. He asks you to humble yourself and pray. When you're obedient—when you do what He asks— it's as if the volume on His "heavenly hearing aid" is turned way up! God is tuned in to your requests; He hears them with such clarity that He's compelled to move on your behalf by restoring and healing your land.

So, what are you waiting for? Today the Lord is calling you to bow down, to turn from anything holding you back, and to seek His face.

BUILDING ON THE ROCK

*"Therefore whoever hears these sayings of Mine,
and does them, I will liken him to a wise man
who built his house on the rock: and the rain
descended, the floods came, and the winds blew
and beat on that house; and it did not fall,
for it was founded on the rock."*

MATTHEW 7:24–25 NKJV

When Jesus spoke the words in today's verses, He had just finished teaching about not judging others, the importance of diligent prayer, the Golden Rule, the narrow gate that leads to life, a tree being known by its fruit, and the separation that occurs between Christ and people who practice lawlessness.

Whoever hears these sayings of Jesus and *does* them will be considered wise by Jesus Himself. As such, that person will be able to withstand the disasters of life because he or she built upon a solid rock—that is, on Jesus Himself. Some of what He said are hard sayings, and all of them involve forsaking the flesh. But wisdom knows that this difficult battle won't last forever.

How are you doing when it comes to these sayings by Jesus? Are you resisting the flesh in favor of the narrow gate? What practical steps can you take today that will help you walk in wisdom going forward?

Day 2

WISDOM FROM ON HIGH

Be wise now therefore, O ye kings:
be instructed, ye judges of the earth.
PSALM 2:10 KJV

⸺ ⬧ ⸺

Scandals are nothing new. They've occurred in every generation and at every level of society. But the twenty-four-hour news cycle probably makes everybody more aware of them now as they occur than they were of past indiscretions. At the heart of many scandals is the person's belief that they're above the law.

That's what was going on in Psalm 2:2–3 (KJV). It says, "The kings of the earth set themselves, and the rulers take counsel together, against the LORD, and against his anointed, saying, Let us break their bands asunder, and cast away their cords from us."

The psalmist says that even kings and judges of the earth are to receive instruction and therefore to become wise. The next verse (Psalm 2:11) explains where such instruction and wisdom should come from, saying leaders are to serve the Lord with fear and to rejoice with trembling.

How are you doing in the leadership position(s) you find yourself in at work or school, in the community, at church, or in your home? Do you rule with an iron fist or with an open palm? Are you in it for your glory and for your gain or for God's?

SPEAKING WORDS OF LIFE

*My son, pay attention to what I say; turn your
ear to my words. Do not let them out of your sight,
keep them within your heart; for they are life to
those who find them and health to one's whole body.*
PROVERBS 4:20–22 NIV

For better or worse, children remember what they are
taught by their parents—both by word and by deed.
If somebody were to ask you your philosophy about
child rearing, showing emotion, or your work ethic,
you might start with these words: "Well, I was raised
to believe. . ."

But the philosophies you picked up during your
childhood run even deeper than that. If you were raised
in a family in which there was constant unrest in the
home due to addiction, infidelity, abuse, or anger, then
you may have either adopted those problems or you
tend to keep people at arm's length trying to avoid
such troubles.

Whatever the case, you have a chance to speak life
into the next generation. Root yourself deeply in God's
Word so you can pass that wisdom on to your children
and grandchildren. In so doing, you'll be practicing
Proverbs 22:6 (NIV): "Start children off on the way they
should go, and even when they are old they will not
turn from it."

Day 4

THE WISE WILL SHINE

*And they that be wise shall shine as the brightness
of the firmament; and they that turn many to
righteousness as the stars for ever and ever.*
DANIEL 12:3 KJV

All of heaven takes note when God's people are under
persecution. Daniel 12:1 speaks about such a time when
Michael the Archangel will "stand up" (perhaps literally,
but certainly symbolically) for the children of God to
work for their deliverance. During that time, Daniel
says some shall awake to everlasting life, while others
to shame and everlasting contempt (v. 2).

Those who are abiding in Christ by feasting on His
Word, staying in communion with Him, submitting
to the Holy Spirit, fellowshipping with the saints, and
living wisely during such difficult times will shine
as the brightness of the firmament, turning many to
everlasting life. That means it's possible, even under
the hottest persecution, to shine for Christ. As you
do so, people will notice—much like you can't help
but notice the stars right now, even if you're not into
astronomy. Their beauty causes you to look.

Do your neighbors currently see your light? How
about your friends, coworkers, and family? Your job
isn't to convince them to come to the light. It's to shine
so they're attracted to the light.

Day 5

HEAVENLY CONVERSATIONS

*However, we speak wisdom among those who are
mature, yet not the wisdom of this age, nor of
the rulers of this age, who are coming to nothing.
But we speak the wisdom of God in a mystery,
the hidden wisdom which God ordained before
the ages for our glory, which none of the rulers
of this age knew; for had they known,
they would not have crucified
the Lord of glory.*

1 CORINTHIANS 2:6–8 NKJV

———•◉•———

Earlier in this epistle, Paul said the message of the
cross is foolishness to those who are perishing, but
to those who are being saved it is the power of God
(1 Corinthians 1:18). Later, in 2 Corinthians 4:3, Paul
alluded to the fact that the Gospel is veiled to those
who are perishing. Even the rulers of this age can't
understand it apart from the Holy Spirit.

"It is not the wisdom of politicians, nor philosophers,
nor rabbis (1 Corinthians 2:6), nor such as they teach
nor such as they relish; but the wisdom of God in a
mystery, the hidden wisdom of God," writes Matthew
Henry in his commentary.

Colossians 1:26 says this mystery has been revealed
to the saints. Therefore, the conversations among God's
people are to be on a higher plane. What a privilege
to speak wisdom to one another!

GOD'S FAITHFULNESS

Those who are wise will take all this to heart; they will see in our history the faithful love of the LORD.
PSALM 107:43 NLT

------●------

The writer of this psalm takes inventory of the Lord's faithfulness for the purposes of giving people even more reason to praise Him.

Some were homeless, and others were hungry and thirsty. They cried out, and God rescued them (vv. 4–6). Some were depressed and their misery led them to rebel against God. When God weighed them down with hard labor, they cried out, and He saved them (vv. 10–13). Some were fools on the verge of death. They cried out for deliverance, and God healed them (vv. 17–20). Some traveled abroad to earn a living but encountered stormy seas. They cried out in their distress, and God saved them (vv. 23–29).

The Lord not only rescues and delivers His people in the short-term as they cry out to Him, but He also brings them to settle in cities (v. 36), blesses them with large families and heads of livestock (v. 38), and pours contempt on princes who oppress them (vv. 39–40). How can God's people do anything other than praise Him?

How has God been faithful to you and your family when you've cried out to Him? Praise Him for it!

Day 7

CULTIVATING WISDOM

*For wisdom is protection just as money is protection,
but the advantage of knowledge is that wisdom
preserves the lives of its possessors.*

ECCLESIASTES 7:12 NASB

You lock your doors before you go to sleep every night.
You lock your car door, even when you're driving. You're
careful about where you walk and the time of day you
do it. And, whenever possible, you try to build up cash
reserves as a hedge of protection for unexpected expenses.

As important as these measures are, Solomon advises
that you also invest in wisdom because it, too, is a
form of protection. You know this to be true. You
teach your children to not play in the street, to avoid
hot ovens, and to wear a helmet when they climb on
their bicycles. They don't fully understand why, but
you teach them as they grow and mature. Eventually,
they realize the wisdom of such things.

Elsewhere, Solomon says wisdom is a tree of life
to those who take hold of her (Proverbs 3:18). In John
6:63 (NASB), Jesus says: "It is the Spirit who gives life;
the flesh profits nothing; the words that I have spoken
to you are spirit and are life."

How are you currently cultivating wisdom? Are
you paying as much attention to it as to building
your nest egg?

LOOKING FOR PURPOSE?

Let us hear the conclusion of the whole matter:
Fear God, and keep his commandments:
for this is the whole duty of man.
ECCLESIASTES 12:13 KJV

Isn't everyone looking for purpose in life? And the Bible has the simple yet profound, perfect answer—the *only* answer that they will genuinely find fulfilling, if only they will believe it and test it! Yet so many people try anything *but* the Bible for answers; they keep striving and toiling. . .and coming up empty.

Humanity's purpose in life is to fear (or respect) God and obey His commandments. This is the "whole duty" of man, says Solomon. The only authentic fulfillment people can ever find is to do what their Creator intended specifically for them, to obey Him in the things He designed and prepared. Ephesians 2:10 (NIV) says, "For we are God's handiwork, created in Christ Jesus to do good works, which God prepared in advance for us to do."

The greatest commandments are to love God with all your heart, soul, mind, and strength and to love your neighbor as yourself (Matthew 22:35–40). Such obedience will cause everything else to fall in place, not always for an easy life but for a *good* life filled with purpose and satisfaction and sweet relationship with the Creator.

Day 2

AUTHENTIC OBEDIENCE

"Not everyone who calls out to me, 'Lord! Lord!'
will enter the Kingdom of Heaven. Only those
who actually do the will of my Father
in heaven will enter."

MATTHEW 7:21 NLT

The tongue can easily boast about obedience to God. There are all kinds of people today and throughout history pretending to obey the Bible and lauding themselves as true followers of Christ. But in the end, actions speak louder than words.

The Bible warns, "Watch out for false prophets. They come to you in sheep's clothing, but inwardly they are ferocious wolves. By their fruit you will recognize them. Do people pick grapes from thornbushes, or figs from thistles? Likewise, every good tree bears good fruit, but a bad tree bears bad fruit. A good tree cannot bear bad fruit, and a bad tree cannot bear good fruit. Every tree that does not bear good fruit is cut down and thrown into the fire. Thus, by their fruit you will recognize them" (Matthew 7:15–20 NIV).

Good fruit will result from obedience to God's commandments. The true Christian life is not made up of empty words that are easy to say but rather challenging and rewarding obedience to God's good way in His Word—the best way to live.

Day 3

OBEDIENCE EQUALS PROSPERITY

"If you are willing and obedient,
you will eat the good things of the land."
ISAIAH 1:19 NIV

The Bible promises that obedience equals prosperity. Consider the verse above and also these: "Blessed are those who fear the LORD, who find great delight in his commands. Their children will be mighty in the land; the generation of the upright will be blessed. Wealth and riches are in their houses, and their righteousness endures forever" (Psalm 112:1–3 NIV). "When the LORD takes pleasure in anyone's way, he causes their enemies to make peace with them" (Proverbs 16:7 NIV).

The caveat is, sometimes the world's idea of prosperity confuses believers. Obedience to God does not necessarily mean riches and fun and constant good health and perpetually happy/peaceful relationships here on earth. It certainly can mean those things for this temporary life, but ultimately it means all these things and more in your *eternal* paradise home that God is creating.

It also means God's guidance and peace for any hard thing here in this sinful world as you obey His commands, no matter what the circumstances or how you're tempted to ignore them. Obedience to God means His constant, loving presence in your life because "the one who keeps His commandments abides in Him, and He in him" (1 John 3:24 NASB). There is no better prosperity than that!

Day 4

DON'T DREAD DISCIPLINE

*Since we respected our earthly fathers who
disciplined us, shouldn't we submit even
more to the discipline of the Father
of our spirits, and live forever?*

HEBREWS 12:9 NLT

If you were blessed with a loving father to obey, you realized he was worthy of respect. In fact, you probably realized as you became an adult that his discipline was to protect you, train you, and mature you. If imperfect human fathers are capable of that, how much more so is the perfect heavenly Father?

And just like a good earthly dad disciplines his children, the heavenly Abba disciplines those He loves. Proverbs 3:11–12 (NLT) says, "My child, don't reject the LORD's discipline, and don't be upset when he corrects you. For the LORD corrects those he loves, just as a father corrects a child in whom he delights."

A vital aspect of being obedient to God and His commands is being subject to His discipline when you need it. God uses your mistakes and His correction to train and mature you. It produces the fruit in your life that advances His kingdom and brings Him glory. Remember, "No discipline is enjoyable while it is happening—it's painful! But afterward there will be a peaceful harvest of right living for those who are trained in this way" (Hebrews 12:11 NLT).

Day 5

A REAL SERVANT OF CHRIST

*So then, my beloved, just as you have always
obeyed, not as in my presence only, but now
much more in my absence, work out your
salvation with fear and trembling.*
PHILIPPIANS 2:12 NASB

Did you ever have a classmate in school who acted perfectly obedient and sweet in front of the teacher, but whenever the teacher turned away or recess time rolled around, this classmate broke every rule but still cunningly managed to keep out of trouble?

God doesn't want the kind of obedience that is just for show or for selfish gain. He wants obedience that comes from a willing heart—a heart that loves Him and His Word and wants to produce the good fruit He has planned for those who follow Him. He wants obedience that seeks to please Him alone, no matter what people around you think or say. A question to ask yourself regularly in your walk with Jesus is the one Paul asks in Galatians: "Am I now trying to win the approval of human beings, or of God? Or am I trying to please people? If I were still trying to please people, I would not be a servant of Christ" (Galatians 1:10 NIV).

Be a genuine servant of Christ first and foremost, and then let Him help you serve others as He directs.

DO THE WORD

"So if you ignore the least commandment and teach others to do the same, you will be called the least in the Kingdom of Heaven. But anyone who obeys God's laws and teaches them will be called great in the Kingdom of Heaven."

MATTHEW 5:19 NLT

⸺ ⸱◈⸱ ⸺

Believers will be held accountable for their response to God's commandments. It's easy to hear them and pay lip service to them. It's easy to attend church once in a while or even weekly and nod in agreement and sing praise and shake the pastor's hand at the end. It's easy to say that God is real and Jesus died on the cross. It's easy to make an appearance of being a Christian and leave it at that, never truly obeying God and serving Him wholeheartedly. Matthew 5:19 has a strong warning for this, especially for those believers who, by their example, teach others to disobey God.

James 1:22 (NLT) says, "But don't just listen to God's word. You must do what it says. Otherwise, you are only fooling yourselves." And Romans 2:13 (NLT) says, "For merely listening to the law doesn't make us right with God. It is obeying the law that makes us right in his sight."

God's Word is living and active (Hebrews 4:12), never just something to hear, but rather something to *do*.

Day 7

OBEY AND ABIDE

*"If you keep My commandments, you will abide
in My love; just as I have kept My Father's
commandments and abide in His love."*
JOHN 15:10 NASB

When people choose to live outside of God's commands,
they then often complain that God would never want
a relationship with the likes of them, or they complain
about once upon a time feeling close to Him but how
they now feel far away. When someone feels distant from
God or grumbles that a relationship is impossible, it's
never because God has changed or become unreachable.
In Malachi 3:6 (NASB), God promises, "For I, the LORD,
do not change." And James 1:17 (NLT) says, "He never
changes or casts a shifting shadow."

It's difficult to remain close to God in a fallen world.
It takes determination and persistence to maintain
close communion with your heavenly Father when
the world constantly distracts you and Satan seeks
to devour you (1 Peter 5:8). The solution is simple to
explain—just keep God's commandments—yet difficult
at times. It takes day-to-day diligence. However, you're
never without God's help in doing so. Pray constantly,
holding fast to His Word, asking for help to obey, and
you'll surely abide in His everlasting love.

Day 1

A GIFT GOD WANTS

*Let us draw near with a sincere heart in full
assurance of faith, having our hearts sprinkled
clean from an evil conscience and our bodies
washed with pure water.*

HEBREWS 10:22 NASB

You have the ability to give God something that
He's always wanted—your trust. He saves and wants
you to trust that He saves completely. He gives and
wants you to trust He'll give perfectly. He restores
and wants you to trust that you're being made into
a new creation.

Sin minimizes your ability to trust because sin
always gives first place to what *you* want. Grace
enhances your ability to trust because God's gifts are
focused on your well-being while your focus shifts to
God and away from self (because God is taking care
of you). Faith is the key that unlocks grace, brings you
into relationship with Him, and allows Him to begin
restoring what sin has broken.

Faith is an offering of trust to God. It's a choice
to believe the difficult. It's a decision to embrace the
glorious impossible. It's easy to overlook, seems like a
peculiar gift, and defies logic. Yet if you're ever to be
made whole, it's trust (faith) that gives permission to
the Restorer.

Trust, together with obedience, make the perfect gift
for the God who's given you everything else.

A MIRACLE'S WITNESS

I have been crucified with Christ; and it is no
longer I who live, but Christ lives in me; and the
life which I now live in the flesh I live by
faith in the Son of God, who loved me
and gave Himself up for me.

GALATIANS 2:20 NASB

The Bible provides amazing benefits. You can read about the life of Christ, have a front row seat to lessons Jesus taught, and witness the emotion of the final moments of His human existence. You can understand the sacrifice and how that gift offers forgiveness and eternal life.

It was in a reflective moment that the apostle Paul declared himself a follower of Christ. The apostle decided that he wouldn't live his life for himself, but he would put self aside in order to totally identify with the Author of life.

When you do this, you recognize Jesus as the Son of God and realize that His sacrifice was accepted by God as payment for sin. You then live a life subject to God's plan and willingly submitted to His authority. Faith is the starting point of transformation, the declaration that you're a servant of God and a work under divine construction.

Without this transforming faith you can never truly accept the daily miracles God performs on your behalf.

THE SIZE OF YOUR FAITH

Jesus overheard them and said to Jairus,
"Don't be afraid. Just have faith."

MARK 5:36 NLT

———◆———

Was it a parlor trick, a cruel joke, or the mutterings of a madman? Jesus was asked to make a trip to heal the daughter of Jairus. Before He arrived, the young girl died. However, in the midst of those who'd gathered to grieve, Jesus told the parents, "Don't be afraid. Just have faith."

Had they ever witnessed someone raised from the dead? Death was something from which no one returned. Any hope they once held was dashed to the wastelands of internal grief and the external tears of mourning.

Yet faith suggested assurance and hope. How could this family possess what was gone? Faith spoke of impossibilities becoming living realities. They had heard the *Jesus stories*, trusted the object of those stories, and they invited Him, the Story Creator, into their home. In the most unlikely of circumstances, a young girl was brought back to life because the Son of God served the God of the impossible and performed a miracle.

Do you have a dream for your life and then conclude, "That could never happen"? If God's will and your plans connect, then you can expect the miraculous.

Don't let limited faith hinder God's next great gift.

Week 19 ◆ FAITH – PART 2

Day 4

BOLD AND BOLDER

He said to the woman,
Thy faith hath saved thee; go in peace.
LUKE 7:50 KJV

Jesus arrived at the home of a religious leader. Simon made sure all preparations had been made. Or had he? Food? Check. Drinks? Check. Common hospitality? Ah, the missing piece.

She hadn't forgotten, and her hospitality was lavish. After a day of walking, Jesus' feet were tired and dirty. She arrived at the meal uninvited, but Jesus welcomed her. She wept and washed His feet with her tears. She kissed His feet and anointed them with expensive perfume. She was a sinner who understood that she needed rescue.

Simon was upset with the intrusion but received a lesson in the value of forgiveness. Jesus contrasted Simon's hospitality with the gift of the sinner. Even though Simon was a religious leader, he was also a sinner, and the anointing Jesus received was something Simon needed to witness. The faith of this one sinner has given hope to countless others from the first tear, drop of perfume, and radical act of worship.

An act of trust, acceptance, and conviction brought this woman to the feet of forgiveness and rescue. She wasn't afraid of what others would think; she was bold in her commitment, and she's remembered for her faith. What will *you* be remembered for?

FAITH AND GLORY

*Jesus saith unto her, Said I not unto
thee, that, if thou wouldest believe,
thou shouldest see the glory of God?*

JOHN 11:40 KJV

———••••———

Jesus received the first-century equivalent of a telegram.
A friend was sick. Could He come? Would He heal? The
request was simple and Jesus was willing, but He wasn't
ready to visit. He had *God appointments* elsewhere, and
His visit would be delayed. While Jesus was elsewhere,
however, His friend Lazarus died.

When Jesus arrived, His friend had been in the
tomb for four days. Jesus was greeted with a statement
from his sister that ultimately led Jesus to weep. Martha
said, "If You had been here, my brother would not have
died" (John 11:21 NKJV).

A crowd gathered. Many had witnessed the miracles
Jesus had performed. Most had heard His teaching.
Some were convinced Jesus could have healed Lazarus,
but hadn't He arrived too late? The crowd waited to
discover the answer.

Martha continued, "Even now I know that whatever
You ask of God, God will give You" (v. 22). This was a
faith response inviting profound trust to meet God's
provision.

Jesus prayed to His Father for help. *He helped.* Jesus
called His friend to come out of the grave. *He did.* Jesus
pinpointed the need for faith. *They believed.* . .and saw
God's glorious miracle.

A TIME TO FOLLOW

*By faith Abraham obeyed when he was called
to go out to the place which he would receive
as an inheritance. And he went out,
not knowing where he was going.*
HEBREWS 11:8 NKJV

He'd lived many years in the same place, Haran. It was familiar. It was home. Abraham had no children, but he had a promise. When God told this man it was time to move, he must have felt a little apprehensive. Leave all that was familiar? Leave his family and relatives? Start over again at his age? So many questions.

But Abraham obeyed. He followed God to a new land. He had a determined faith that if God led then He would provide everything he and his wife needed. *God did.* In this new country Abraham and Sarah welcomed a son, built a life together, and witnessed the miracles of their Maker.

The Bible is filled with stories of people who expressed a total faith in God's plan for their lives. They had faith in a promise. They believed that what God said was what He would do. God called those who had such faith righteous.

Trust God. He never calls in sick, He works the night shift, and His love is beyond comprehension. If He says to follow, trust His leadership.

THE FAITH OF AN ANALYST

Jesus said to him, "Thomas, because you have seen Me, you have believed. Blessed are those who have not seen and yet have believed."

JOHN 20:29 NKJV

Thomas was an analyst. He paid attention to facts. He was the resident skeptic among Jesus' disciples. He spoke his mind. He wanted proof. Thomas was a lot like you.

It's easy to trust what your eyes see, ears hear, and hands touch. This is observable, scientific, and logical. Jesus was quick to point out that the logical approach missed out on the wisdom of God. When Thomas insisted that seeing was believing, Jesus said people were more blessed when they believed first. Without faith (a complete trust in God) they would always consider the possibility that God wasn't trustworthy. If you require that God prove Himself in every circumstance, you make Him small.

When you question every decision God makes, you may be unintentionally saying that He isn't all-powerful, all-wise, and all-knowing.

When you *can't* trust others, you *can* have complete confidence in God. When people let you down, He can lift you up. When you can't see the future, you can believe in the One who created time. When you don't have answers, you can have faith in the One who calls Himself Truth.

Believe. . .and see.

GUIDING LIGHT

*Your word is a lamp to my feet
and a light to my path.*
PSALM 119:105 NASB

 SCRIPTURE ✦ *Week 20*

Picture yourself on a dark and winding path. There are no visible markers, so you're unsure of each step. To make things more challenging, the pathway is rough, filled with potholes. You ease your way along, praying that you won't take a tumble or make a wrong turn.

Think of your journey with the Lord in a similar light. When you don't take the time to study the Word of God, you find yourself on unsure footing, and when you don't have the illumination of scripture to guide your way, you're sure to stumble. Every fall leads to another spiritual bump or bruise.

There are so many amazing promises in the Bible, and they're there for the taking. But you have to open God's Word, study it, and apply what you've read to your daily life. When you take the time to do that, the promises spring to life. The road is made clear. The potholes are easier to navigate. Best of all, your faith is bolstered. You have the tenacity to keep going, even when you don't feel like it.

So, what are you waiting for? Open that Bible and get ready for an adventure!

Day 2

THE TREASURE TROVE

*Let the word of Christ dwell in you richly in all
wisdom, teaching and admonishing one another
in psalms and hymns and spiritual songs,
singing with grace in your hearts to the Lord.*

COLOSSIANS 3:16 NKJV

Wouldn't it be wonderful to stumble across a treasure chest? Even before prying it open, your imagination would kick in. What will you find inside? Jewels? Gold coins? Family heirlooms? The possibilities are endless.

Now think about the Word of God. It's much like that treasure box, only it contains riches that can't be tallied in earthly dollars and cents. When you allow the words from the Bible to penetrate your heart, you find that they're like priceless jewels, worth more than diamonds and rubies.

The promises you find in the Word of God are treasures, and you can freely claim them. You can cash them in at any time. Best of all, the scriptures penetrate your heart and bring more changes than you'll ever understand. They "dwell in you richly."

You won't ever have to go looking for buried treasure. It's with you, wherever you go. And this is a gift you can share with everyone you come in contact with. Now, that's a real gift!

AFFIXED AND ADHERED

*Fix these words of mine in your hearts and minds;
tie them as symbols on your hands and bind them
on your foreheads. Teach them to your children,
talking about them when you sit at home and
when you walk along the road, when
you lie down and when you get up.*

DEUTERONOMY 11:18–19 NIV

If you've ever used superglue, you know how powerful
it can be. Talk about a long-lasting adhesive! Perhaps
you've inadvertently glued your fingers together, or
maybe you pasted two items together accidentally.
There's no turning back when you use superglue. Once
those items are stuck, they're stuck!

That's how the promises in the Word of God are,
too. When you fix them to your heart and mind, they're
permanent. They're superglued. Those promises become
so much a part of you that you couldn't imagine living
without them. Because of this, you naturally share them
with everyone you come in contact with.

So, crack open your Bible today. Read it with new
eyes—eyes wide open to the fact that the scriptures can
and will have a lasting impact. God's promises will be
stuck to you like glue.

ALIVE AND POWERFUL

For the word of God is living and powerful,
and sharper than any two-edged sword,
piercing even to the division of soul and spirit,
and of joints and marrow, and is a discerner
of the thoughts and intents of the heart.

HEBREWS 4:12 NKJV

———— ◆ ————

There's something incredibly moving about watching the human heartbeat on a hospital monitor. It confirms what you already know, that the person is alive and ticking. And the up and down motion of the graph brings hope.

Try to picture a similar monitor springing to life every time you open the Word of God. Maybe you're going through a rough time financially. You turn to a verse about the Lord's provision. The monitor kicks in. *Tick, tick, tick.* Perhaps you're walking through a deep valley, and you stumble across a scripture about hope. *Tick, tick, tick.* Maybe you've just lost a loved one and you read a verse that brings tremendous comfort. *Tick, tick, tick.*

The monitor sends a visible reminder that those words you've just read are more than words: they're life. Today, as you study the promises in the Word of God, remember this: they're alive and have the power to transform your life.

Day 5

A HOLY BOOMERANG

*So shall my word be that goeth forth out of
my mouth: it shall not return unto me void,
but it shall accomplish that which I please,
and it shall prosper in the thing whereto I sent it.*

ISAIAH 55:11 KJV

———◆———

It's great fun to play with a boomerang! You watch it whirl through the air, headed away from you, and then look on, mesmerized, as it turns back toward you. It's remarkable, if you think about it. That boomerang always wants to head back home again, to return to the one who sent it.

The same is true with the Word of God. When you study the scriptures and then speak them over your situation, you're sending them out to the great beyond. But they always come back home again, taking root in your heart.

So, speak the scriptures. Yes, speak them aloud. If you're going through a crisis, choose a verse that lifts your spirit. Speak the words over your situation and believe in your heart that they won't return void. Then watch as they rebound with life and energy, much like that boomerang, ready to do their work in your situation.

Remarkable! What great power is in the promises of God!

HE'S STILL SPEAKING

*God, after He spoke long ago to the fathers in
the prophets in many portions and in many ways,
in these last days has spoken to us in His
Son, whom He appointed heir of all things,
through whom also He made the world.*

HEBREWS 1:1–2 NASB

———•———

How wonderful it must have been to sit at the feet of
Jesus, gleaning from Him, witnessing miracles, seeing
lives transformed. Can you imagine walking with Him,
talking with Him, listening to Him pray for those in
need? What a glorious experience to hear that voice,
up close and personal. The disciples must have been
in awe every step of the way.

We have the same opportunity. Did you know you,
too, can hear His voice? When you open your Bible and
read the scriptures, they come alive. The words jump
off the page in much the same way that they radiated
from the lips of your Savior two thousand years ago.
They have just as much power, just as much energy.

It brings God pleasure to speak to His children. And
what a creative God He is! First, He speaks through
the prophets. Then, in person through His Son. Now,
through the voice of His Spirit and through His Word.
He's speaking, even now. Are you listening?

DOERS OF THE WORD

*"This Book of the Law shall not depart from your
mouth, but you shall meditate in it day and night,
that you may observe to do according to all that
is written in it. For then you will make your way
prosperous, and then you will have good success."*

JOSHUA 1:8 NKJV

Remember that time you committed to lose weight?
You had every intention of going to the gym several
times a week to work out. Oh, you started off well, but
after a while your *want-to* faded. It's one thing to say
you're going to do something; it's another to actually
follow through on it.

The same is true when it comes to reading the
Word of God and standing on its promises. You can
read all day long, but if you never apply what you've
read, then you're a hearer only. The Lord longs for you
to be a doer of the Word.

Sure, it takes work. Yes, you have to recommit daily.
But, oh, the joy of watching His promises fulfilled in
your life! You'll bear witness to miracles when you
commit to studying the Word.

So, grab your Bible. Meditate on what you're reading.
Become like a sponge, happily soaking up the truth of
what you're reading. Then, spring into action. Become
a doer of the Word.

INFUSING OTHERS
WITH COURAGE

Strengthen the weak hands, and make firm the
feeble knees. Say to those who are fearful-hearted,
"Be strong, do not fear! Behold, your God will come
with vengeance. . .He will come and save you."
ISAIAH 35:3–4 NKJV

———•◦•———

To encourage someone means to infuse them with courage, and the above passage from Isaiah explains how to do this. When you see someone wearily stumbling under a heavy load of affliction, grief, or confusion, you are to come alongside them to strengthen their weary hands. You are to seek ways to make their failing knees firm so they don't collapse in the way.

One way you do this is by saying, "Be strong, do not fear!" Remind them that God will surely come and save them. If they lose hope that He's with them, it's all over. So give them renewed hope that He cares for them and will help them.

The patriarch Job had a lifelong habit of encouraging people. As one of his friends stated, "Your words have upheld him who was stumbling, and you have strengthened the feeble knees" (Job 4:4 NKJV). Again, note that he "made firm" their knees, a crucial point that was about to buckle under the strain.

If you "en-*courage*" someone, create courage in them, you're doing a very great thing.

CONFIRMING AND STRENGTHENING

*Confirming the souls of the disciples, and exhorting
them to continue in the faith, and that we
must through much tribulation enter
into the kingdom of God.*

ACTS 14:22 KJV

It's a very beautiful and powerful thing to encourage others. After Paul and Barnabas had established new Christian communities in several Roman cities, they returned to those cities to strengthen the believers. They encouraged them so that they'd have the tenacity to stick to their professions of faith.

Barnabas's actual name was Joses, but the apostles named him "Barnabas" which means "Son of Encouragement" (Acts 4:36 NKJV). Barnabas was a positive and compassionate soul, always encouraging others. When the early church first heard about Gentiles becoming Christians, they sent out Barnabas to see what was happening. And he "encouraged them all that with purpose of heart they should continue with the Lord" (Acts 11:23 NKJV).

We need more Christians with a Barnabas anointing. To be this way, you need to first of all care deeply about others. Timothy was also like this. Paul said, "I have no one else like Timothy, who genuinely cares about your welfare." He said, "I hope to send Timothy to you soon for a visit. Then he can cheer me up by telling me how you are getting along" (Philippians 2:19–20 NLT).

ENCOURAGE ONE ANOTHER

*Therefore encourage one another and build each
other up, just as in fact you are doing.*
1 Thessalonians 5:11 NIV

———•◆•———

What are some of the most important reasons that
Christians are to meet together, whether weekly on
Sunday or on other days of the week? You might
think the main reasons are to hear biblical teaching
and to sing worship songs—and no doubt these are
important—but the Bible actually emphasizes another
issue.

Paul wrote, "Let us not neglect our meeting together,
as some people do, but encourage one another"
(Hebrews 10:25 NLT). The main reason for meeting is
to *encourage* each other. Paul wrote the Christians of
Rome, "I long to see you so that. . .you and I may be
mutually encouraged by each other's faith" (Romans
1:11–12 NIV).

In the first verse above, Paul urged the believers
in Thessalonica to "encourage one another and build
each other up." These two things are almost identical.
To encourage someone is to buttress them so that they
don't collapse. To build them up is to go beyond mere
survival repairs.

Believers build up and strengthen others in the faith
when they encourage those going through difficult
times to keep their eyes on God. You often accomplish
this by quoting them promises from God's Word.

GOD STRENGTHENS YOU

*He giveth power to the faint; and to them
that have no might he increaseth strength.*
ISAIAH 40:29 KJV

God constantly whispers words of comfort with His Spirit. In Isaiah's day, He said, "This is the resting place, let the weary rest"; and, "This is the place of repose" (Isaiah 28:12 NIV). But God's people, then as today, often didn't listen. They continued on their weary way, trudging under the weight of heavy burdens.

Jesus still says, "Come to me, all you who are weary and burdened, and I will give you rest. Take my yoke upon you and learn from me. . .and you will find rest for your souls" (Matthew 11:28–29 NIV). Often, to build up your strength again, you simply need to rest. This is true with your physical body, and it's surely true of your spirit as well.

Find new strength today by resting close to God's heart. "He who dwells in the secret place of the Most High" (Psalm 91:1 NKJV) will not only find divine protection but renewed spiritual strength.

"Now may our Lord Jesus Christ himself and God our Father, who loved us and by his grace gave us eternal comfort and a wonderful hope, comfort you and strengthen you" (2 Thessalonians 2:16–17 NLT).

ENCOURAGEMENT ◆ *Week 21*

Day 5

A FATHER'S ENCOURAGEMENT

*We treated each of you as a father treats his own
children. We pleaded with you, encouraged you,
and urged you to live your lives in a way
that God would consider worthy.*

1 THESSALONIANS 2:11–12 NLT

⎯⎯ ◆ ⎯⎯

Paul reminded the Christians of Thessalonica how
he had conducted himself when he had been with
them, treating each one of them as a father treated
his own small children. Rather than scolding them,
browbeating them, or shaming them into submission,
Paul had focused on positive methods.

He had pleaded with them and urged them to live
godly lives, and woven throughout all his entreaties
were strong threads of compassion and encouragement.
In so doing, Paul was reflecting the heart of the heavenly
Father. "As a father has compassion on his children,
so the LORD has compassion on those who fear him"
(Psalm 103:13 NIV).

God is always merciful and encouraging and wants
you to relate to others the same way. Ask Him to
transform you into His image. His goal is to help you to
grow up into a mature man or woman of God, gentle,
patient, and long-suffering.

Draw close to God and walk in the Spirit of Christ,
and you'll become a positive, encouraging person, a
joy to be around.

Day 6

THE GIFT OF ENCOURAGEMENT

"The Lord God has given Me the tongue of the learned, that I should know how to speak a word in season to him who is weary."

ISAIAH 50:4 NKJV

———•◆•———

You can claim this promise when you're aware that those around you are discouraged but you don't know how to cheer them up. People you meet are often hurting, and you want to say the right thing at the right time but may be at a loss for words.

At such times, you need God to inspire you what to say. Jesus promised that you could count on your heavenly Father to put His words in your mouth, so that "it will not be you speaking, but the Spirit of your Father speaking through you" (Matthew 10:20 NIV).

You may not have done an in-depth study of God's Word, but He's able to give you the tongue of the learned so that you'll know what to say regardless. "The Holy Spirit. . .will teach you all things" (John 14:26 NKJV).

You can encourage others when they're anxious as well. "Worry weighs a person down; an encouraging word cheers a person up" (Proverbs 12:25 NLT). But as with any kind of encouragement, you need to speak it out loud for it to do any good. So don't be shy. Speak up.

BRINGING OTHERS RELIEF

"I also could speak like you, if you were in my place. . . . But my mouth would encourage you; comfort from my lips would bring you relief."

JOB 16:4–5 NIV

If you have a heart filled with compassion and love, they will naturally flow out of you to others. It's written of the patriarch Joseph, "And he comforted them, and spake kindly unto them" (Genesis 50:21 KJV). This was to his *brothers* who could hardly speak a civil word to him, who had betrayed him, and who sold him as a slave to the Midianites.

Often, the true test of your Christianity is seeing whether you will do good to those who have wronged you, and forgive them and love them. According to many people's way of thinking, after Job's fickle friends falsely accused him, he would've been perfectly within his rights to speak the same way back to them when they ran into trouble.

Many people relish getting in hurtful digs to their foes when they're down. But Job told his friends that this just wasn't his style. He assured them that if they were ever in pain, he would encourage them and bring them relief from their discouragement. He would seek to alleviate their grief. May you have the same attitude as he had.

MADE TO REJOICE

Rejoice in the Lord always; again I will say, rejoice!
PHILIPPIANS 4:4 NASB

———•◆•———

There is something wonderful and mysterious about Christian joy. It's both emotion and deeply rooted truth, both a command from God and a blessing to be received. To rejoice is to be happy because of who God is and what He has done, but it's different than the transient happiness that accompanies life's ups and downs. In fact, joy often results from tribulation, a by-product of the hope that God works out for you as you persevere through hardship (Romans 5:4).

Jesus covered joy's full scope in His teachings: "These things I have spoken to you, that My joy may remain in you, and that your joy may be full" (John 15:11 NKJV). He spoke words of instruction and caution, humbling words full of promise and hope—and His desire seems to be that, as you follow and obey Him, He rejoices in you, which is certainly cause for you to rejoice.

Rejoicing, then, is also both action and response. God rejoices when you abide in Him, bearing fruit by His power and grace (John 15:4), and you rejoice when you are of service to Him. To be joyful is to be actively obedient to God, even as you enjoy the peace and blessing of just belonging to Him.

JOY ◆ Week 22

Day 2

BY HOOK OR BY CROOK

Evil people are trapped by sin,
but the righteous escape, shouting for joy.
PROVERBS 29:6 NLT

———— ·•· ————

When was the last time you rejoiced in your salvation? Some have more obvious reasons to give thanks and celebrate, simply because big sin makes for a big testimony. And while that is certainly something worth celebrating, remember that small sin still separates believers from their heavenly Father and still carries eternal consequences.

So, you have cause to rejoice because you have escaped sin's trap. If there weren't bright lights or angelic choruses accompanying the moment you received Christ, that doesn't make it any less a break from hell's clutches.

Take a moment to consider what Christ delivered you from. It might be a barn burner of a story, involving drugs, sex, and rock 'n' roll, or it might be a quiet tale of a merciful release from pride, cynicism, and self-sufficiency. Now, consider (and pray for) those still caught in a web of their deception. Give thanks for your next breath, because it's the respiration of a freed child of God, given a gracious peace that the world can neither give nor remove (John 14:27).

No matter how you came to Christ, you came, and however you made it into His safe embrace, it's worth rejoicing!

DON'T HOLD BACK

Be glad in the LORD and rejoice, you righteous;
and shout for joy, all you upright in heart!
PSALM 32:11 NKJV

———◆———

What makes you celebrate? Even if you're a typically under-control, what-would-they-say-at-the-club kind of individual, there's something in your heart of hearts that you know would get you fired up—that would elicit a tiny fist pump and an under-your-breath "Yes!" For others, celebration is a way of life; you've got a dance for filling up the gas tank for under thirty bucks and a ten-part handshake for two-for-one burger night.

Either way, how does your rejoicing translate when it's time to worship? You might attend the kind of church where outward expressions of joy are frowned upon as drawing attention to oneself—and that's certainly something to be wary of, since God is the one who should be getting the attention.

Maybe you save it for when you get home, but here's the bigger question: Why raise arms, clap, or shout for a touchdown or a guitar solo when you don't do it for God? Surely it's not because you think those things are more worthy of praise than He is. David is telling you to let loose, at least a little, when it comes to giving God His due and thanking Him for all He has done for you.

Day 4

JOY BOTH NEAR AND FAR

*As sorrowful, yet always rejoicing; as poor,
yet making many rich; as having nothing,
and yet possessing all things.*

2 CORINTHIANS 6:10 KJV

The scope of God's work in your life and in the world is overwhelming, something Paul captured in this list of paradoxes. By the world's standards, to be sorrowful and rejoice at the same time is contradictory, but under the banner of God's love and work in and through you, they represent the short and long view of life.

For instance, you can grieve the loss of a loved brother or sister in Christ wholeheartedly, weeping with those who weep, but even in that sad season, you can still have joy, knowing that you will see them again, happy and whole, in heaven.

Christian joy is a multifaceted gift. On one hand, it's supernatural, given by the Holy Spirit and founded on the grace that secured your salvation. At the same time, it's emotional, a heartfelt response to God and what He has done for you.

God enriches your spiritual poverty with His most lavish gift, the constant presence of His Spirit, and redeems the perishable possessions of this world with life eternal. His love for you never changes, and that's a good reason to rejoice.

Day 5

A NO-GOOD DAY CAN'T COMPETE WITH A REALLY GOOD GOD

Frustration is better than laughter,
because a sad face is good for the heart.
ECCLESIASTES 7:3 NIV

———— • ◆ • ————

Some days are not tailor-made for rejoicing. Some of the worst ones sneak up on you like the proverbial thief in the night. You couldn't possibly anticipate all the things that end up going badly, and you're left wondering what good could come from such a tornado of troubles. Your bones feel dried up, melted like wax, withered like grass, or any of those intense metaphors David came up with when he had a bad day.

Those days, you have to give it time. And then, when you can manage it, let God know what a crummy day you've had. He knows, but tell Him anyway. He can handle your frustration and hard questions; He's heard it all before. More often than not, once you've let it all out, you can look past it.

It becomes easier to remember how the Creator of the universe is your Dad, how He lets you vent because you need to, how your problems shrink in His hands. Somewhere in there, you make your way back to joy, not because your day wasn't so bad after all (it was a *terrible* day, wasn't it?), but because your God is so good.

JOY ◆ Week 22

SORROW'S SOLACE

A cheerful heart is good medicine,
but a crushed spirit dries up the bones.
PROVERBS 17:22 NIV

If someone were to come up to you on a rough day and offer a handy little slogan like, "A cheerful heart is good medicine," you might be tempted to offer a decidedly un-Christian response in a stream of typographical symbols. Later, though, after a nice long walk or hot bath, consider looking more closely at the word *cheerful:* in the original Hebrew, it means "joyful." And *joyful* is a whole different matter.

Joy does come in happy times, but often, it comes disguised as sorrow. When you first read Paul's statement "We also glory in tribulations" (Romans 5:3 NKJV), it seems like a really holy but wholly unrealistic response to hardship. But look at what's sandwiched around it: rejoicing in "the hope of the glory of God" (v. 2) and "knowing that tribulation produces perseverance; and perseverance, character; and character, hope" (vv. 3–4).

Astonishing, isn't it? You can have joy when life's going great because you have peace with God through Jesus, and you can have joy when life stinks because God uses trials to build Christlike character in you and pour out His love on you. Sometimes God's good medicine doesn't taste good, but it does the trick.

FULL ACCESS

*"Until now you have not asked for anything
in my name. Ask and you will receive,
and your joy will be complete."*
JOHN 16:24 NIV

As Jesus prepared His disciples for His departure, He encouraged them with a remarkable promise: they were now to ask God directly for whatever they needed, and when they asked in Jesus' name, they would receive it. And the reason they were to ask? So that they could be full of *joy*.

Joy is an essential part of the work God is doing in your life. Because it comes from Him, the world can't produce or replicate it. When you think of prayer as a way of making your joy complete, rejoicing becomes part of the proof that there is more of Jesus in you and less of you. That doesn't mean that you go around acting happy just to impress others with your spiritual depth; that move is straight out of the Pharisee playbook.

Rather, you seek God more and more, through prayer, by His Word, in fellowship, and through sharing your gifts in ministry and investing in others' best interests. As you fill yourself with more of the things that are dear to His heart, rivers of living water will flow from you (John 7:38) and you will rejoice in being a conduit of God's blessing.

Day 1

WORLDLY PEACE VS. GOD'S PEACE

*And the peace of God, which passeth all
understanding, shall keep your hearts
and minds through Christ Jesus.*

PHILIPPIANS 4:7 KJV

———— ··◈·· ————

What do you consider your most peaceful place? A
serene beach with salty breezes and the soothing sounds
of the ocean? A scenic mountainside with crisp air
and near silence? A relaxing time on a porch swing,
or even just wrapped in a cozy blanket in your own
living room? Whatever the places and circumstances
that bring you a sense of peace, they don't compare to
the peace of God that passes all understanding.

Worldly peace is temporary and conditional, based
on circumstances and feelings. The peace of God is
constant; it keeps (guards) your heart and mind,
protecting them from the worries of the world.

The scripture prior to the one above says that prayer
and thanksgiving are the way to get the peace of God.
If you aren't feeling the constant, unexplainable peace
that God offers, ask yourself: "How are my prayer life
and my time in the Word?" You can't receive anything
from Someone you're ignoring. Draw near to God
this moment and during this week as you read about
peace. Then stay in constant communication with
your heavenly Father who loves you dearly and wants
you to experience His wonderful peace!

BECAUSE YOU TRUST IN HIM

*I pray that God, the source of hope, will fill you
completely with joy and peace because you trust
in him. Then you will overflow with confident
hope through the power of the Holy Spirit.*

ROMANS 15:13 NLT

This verse says, "Because you trust in him. . . ." But *do*
you? It's a good question to ask yourself, especially
if you're lacking peace or having doubts about your
faith. Remind yourself why you trust the Lord. Think
of all the reasons to believe that His Word is true,
that the salvation He offers through the death and
resurrection of Jesus is real, and that He constantly
works in and through His people, drawing sinners to
Him and building His eternal kingdom. Meditate on
the ways God has revealed Himself to you in the past,
has provided for you, and has answered your prayers.

If you're still struggling, then simply go outside and
look at His creation, for "since the creation of the world
God's invisible qualities—his eternal power and divine
nature—have been clearly seen, being understood from
what has been made" (Romans 1:20 NIV).

"Because you trust in him" you can be completely
filled with joy and peace. The one true everlasting God
of all peace is worthy of your total trust!

PEACE AMONG BELIEVERS

Behold, how good and how pleasant it is
for brethren to dwell together in unity!
PSALM 133:1 KJV

———•◆•———

It's incredible to think of the peace there will be in heaven—no more wars, terrorism, or violence of any kind. And do you ever think how incredible it will be to simply have peace and no more dissension among believers—to live in perfect, sinless relationship and fellowship with each other and our Creator? Amazing!

Psalm 133:1 says how good it is for believers to live together in unity. Sadly, in today's fallen world, disagreement and division even in the church are common, often giving a poor testimony to unbelieving bystanders. God will ultimately judge everyone's heart and motives, but each of us are to do our part to seek unity as brothers and sisters in Jesus Christ.

Until you reach your heavenly home, you must do as Paul urged: "Make every effort to keep the unity of the Spirit through the bond of peace. There is one body and one Spirit, just as you were called to one hope when you were called; one Lord, one faith, one baptism; one God and Father of all, who is over all and through all and in all" (Ephesians 4:3–6 NIV).

Week 23 ◆ PEACE

Day 4

PEACE TOWARD UNBELIEVERS

*"The one who desires life, to love and see good days,
must keep his tongue from evil and his lips from
speaking deceit. He must turn away from evil
and do good; he must seek peace and pursue it."*

1 PETER 3:10–11 NASB

Unbelievers are watching how you act and react. As today's scripture indicates, hopefully they see you keeping your lips from lying. Hopefully, they see you turning from evil and toward good, and seeking peace and pursuing it. You can't do any of these perfectly on your own, of course, but with your Savior's help you can show unbelievers what it means to depend upon the God of grace. You can show them what it means to strive to live a life that's pleasing to Him—full of the peace that comes from Him and that extends to others around you.

First Peter 2:11–12 (NLT) advises believers to keep peace in the world and toward unbelievers in this way: "Dear friends, I warn you as 'temporary residents and foreigners' to keep away from worldly desires that wage war against your very souls. Be careful to live properly among your unbelieving neighbors. Then even if they accuse you of doing wrong, they will see your honorable behavior, and they will give honor to God when he judges the world."

Week 23 ◆ PEACE

Day 5

PEACE IN THE MIDST OF FEAR

For God has not given us a spirit of fear,
but of power and of love and of a sound mind.
2 TIMOTHY 1:7 NKJV

If you let it, the world can seem scarier day after day. Alarming news is thrown at you from every angle and every media source—everything from natural disasters to terrorist attacks. Sin and evil are running rampant and, worse, are often widely celebrated.

From a natural perspective, it certainly seems that you have reason to fear. But despite all this, you can have tremendous hope! You have a God who is bigger and stronger than the worst kind of evil, and who shelters you under His wings (Psalm 91:4). This same God will one day eradicate all evil.

Until that day, He's called you to accomplish good things which He prepared for you to do despite everything that's happening around you. And He hasn't left you alone. He's given you His Holy Spirit, not a spirit of fear, but His own Spirit "of power and of love and of a sound mind."

You never have to fear *any* kind of evil. You can have abiding peace in the midst of a scary world, because "if God is for us, who can ever be against us?" (Romans 8:31 NLT).

Day 6

FIGHT FOR PEACE

*You will keep in perfect peace those whose minds
are steadfast, because they trust in you.*
ISAIAH 26:3 NIV

———— •◆• ————

When your mind is full of worry and anxious thoughts, the very best thing you can do is to fill it with God's Word, which can powerfully fight the anxiety threatening to overcome you. God's Word is the "sword of the Spirit" (Ephesians 6:17 NIV) and is "sharper than any double-edged sword" (Hebrews 4:12 NIV). It's ready to do battle to win peace for you! When worry is attacking you, it's effective to repeatedly pray verses like Isaiah 26:3. Here are more scriptures to commit to memory and have at the ready:

"The Lord is near. Do not be anxious about anything, but in every situation, by prayer and petition, with thanksgiving, present your requests to God" (Philippians 4:5–6 NIV).

"Cast all your anxiety on him because he cares for you" (1 Peter 5:7 NIV).

"In peace I will lie down and sleep, for you alone, LORD, make me dwell in safety" (Psalm 4:8 NIV).

"So do not fear, for I am with you; do not be dismayed, for I am your God. I will strengthen you and help you; I will uphold you with my righteous right hand" (Isaiah 41:10 NIV).

PEACE OF MIND AND HEART

"I am leaving you with a gift—peace of mind and heart. And the peace I give is a gift the world cannot give. So don't be troubled or afraid."

JOHN 14:27 NLT

———◆———

In the time leading up to Jesus' crucifixion, His disciples were confused as to how everything would play out, but He explained to them that He wouldn't be leaving them alone. He was sending the Counselor, the Holy Spirit, to guide them and be God's presence among them—not in quite the same way that Jesus had walked among people but to indwell all believers and spread the Gospel far and wide. Jesus also promised a gift that the world couldn't give them, a gift of peace to their minds and hearts, a gift that would keep them from being troubled or afraid.

The Holy Spirit wasn't just for the believers of bygone days. No, He's *your* Counselor, too, God's very presence working within you. The gift of peace of mind and heart is for you as well. Receive it. Know that the Holy Spirit is with you and that Jesus' peace is constantly available to you. Ask Him to fill you and strengthen you with it. He is very happy to oblige.

GENTLY HARSH?

*"Take My yoke upon you and learn from Me,
for I am gentle and humble in heart, and you
will find rest for your souls."*
MATTHEW 11:29 NASB

Jesus promised to be your teacher—not drill instructor. Jesus promised you could learn from Him—not be belittled for what you don't know. Jesus promised a gentle approach—not harsh criticism.

Gentleness should be liberally applied to your relationships. Harshness invites the fighting stance of defensiveness. Any benefits harsh knowledge might offer are dismissed as rude and insensitive. There may be a time for strong words and confrontation, but even these difficult moments can be marked with a gentleness that provides evidence of compassion.

This biblical approach to relationships can be hard in a culture dominated by sarcasm, rude comments, and disrespect. You must remember you're called to respond differently than the culture around you. One of those differences is to be gentle when it would be much easier to interact in ways that burn bridges of friendship, boardwalks of opportunity, and platforms of love.

It's easy to apply crushing words to those who fail you. God's grace never does this. If the God you learn from is gentle, then your interactions should benefit from following His example.

GENTLENESS ♦ *Week 24*

Day 2

A STRONG GENTLENESS

*The meek will inherit the land
and enjoy peace and prosperity.*

Psalm 37:11 niv

Meekness is described as strength balanced by gentleness. Meekness is the picture of a perfect leading man. He's strong, but gentle when he needs to be. He doesn't let emotions dictate his response. He overlooks offenses, but stands up when he needs to. He's not bent on proving himself, but in standing up for the defenseless.

Many great heroes and heroines could be described as meek. They stood up for injustice, but sought peaceful solutions over aggression. They related to others in such a way that their example changed hostile hearts and minds. To be gentle is not to be weak—it is to be in control of a power that could destroy, choosing a path of restoration.

When Jesus is referred to as *meek and mild*, it's not an insult. It doesn't mean He had no backbone. It doesn't mean He was weak.

Jesus fasted forty days in the desert, was betrayed by one of His disciples, and endured the verbal abuse of those who would crucify Him. In the end, He was meek enough to say in His final breaths, "Father, forgive them" (Luke 23:34 kjv).

You would find it hard to come to God if you felt intimidated. Perhaps that's why He chose gentleness.

A FRUIT STAND

But the fruit of the Spirit is love, joy, peace,
long-suffering, gentleness, goodness, faith.
GALATIANS 5:22 KJV

Jesus is described as a vine and Christians are referred to as branches attached to the vine (John 15:5). Jesus states that Christians will be known by their fruitfulness (Matthew 7:16). If you ever wonder what kind of fruit others should be able to identify in your life, the leading verse above names each fruit one by one.

The spiritual fruit you're to grow includes "love, joy, peace, long-suffering, gentleness, goodness, faith." You might sometimes act as if you get to pick and choose which fruit you allow to grow, but Galatians 5 is pretty clear that the fruit comes from God's Spirit, so they're *all* supposed to grow. You're to bear *each* fruit. It won't happen overnight. You need to grow. Make no mistake, God wants you to thrive, and the fruit is the evidence of your growth.

You might agree that fruit like love, joy, peace, and faith are pretty important, but you might be more reluctant to claim the fruit of long-suffering (patience), gentleness, and goodness. God never made such distinctions. He wants each fruit to be evident in your life. He wants others to recognize them. He wants you to accept the value of His fruit.

Day 4

STOP THE HYPOCRISY

*The wisdom from above is first pure, then peaceable,
gentle, reasonable, full of mercy and good fruits,
unwavering, without hypocrisy.*

JAMES 3:17 NASB

———————

Gentleness is a by-product of wisdom. Wisdom also delivers the qualities of purity, peace, and a personality that's easy to get along with. Wisdom shows mercy and relies on a sure and steady moral compass. Wisdom is a good thing and a *God gift*.

It's possible to fake these qualities for a limited time. You might behave pretty godly in the right crowd for a while. The switch of peace, knob of mercy, and touchscreen of purity can read "All systems go," but in your own strength and with enough time you'll fail to continue acting out these traits. God calls this *hypocrisy*.

You don't like to have others see you as a failure so you try to impress them, only to be caught in the state of being human. Far better to let God's Spirit develop these traits so you don't have to claim to be wise. You *will* be.

Gentleness shouldn't be a by-product of personal effort. Gentleness lives in peace, seeks out the reasonable, and chooses mercy. Gentleness shows that God's wisdom still finds a home in the heart of the faithful—and He's still working on you.

SUSTAINED IN HUMILITY

*The Lord sustains the humble
but casts the wicked to the ground.*

Psalm 147:6 niv

Someone is weak. They're injured. They won't get very far without help. So they rest their arm around another. They are helped to move from one location to the next.

"The Lord sustains the humble" is a promise that provides incredible benefits. Gentleness is a key element of humility. It offers an honest assessment of who you are. . .and who God is. Only those who recognize they need help will actually ask for it. They are the people God desires to help. Why? He doesn't ask you to come to Him in perfect condition. Because you sin, you can't expect perfection from your own efforts.

When you admit that you can't do it all, when you understand you need help, and when you ask God for assistance, you've discovered humility. In that moment, God takes the opportunity to help.

How can you learn to rely on God when you constantly do everything yourself? Trusting in your efforts, decisions, and strength doesn't provide any room for God to work on your behalf. When you believe you can do it all, you don't allow God to do anything. Falling is always the result of refusing God's help.

Day 6

GENTLENESS: A NEW NORMAL

*Remind the believers to submit to the government
and its officers. They should be obedient, always
ready to do what is good. They must not slander
anyone and must avoid quarreling. Instead,
they should be gentle and show true
humility to everyone.*

TITUS 3:1–2 NLT

———— •◆• ————

Christ followers should be shaped by something remarkably foreign to what is considered normal. While you can fight for your rights, it shouldn't be at the expense of relationship. Your words and actions should reflect biblical gentleness.

This may be in conflict with the way you're conditioned to think of your government. You may have firm opinions. You have a resolute grip on who you're for and what you're against. You believe debating with those who disagree with you is just the trait of good citizenship.

Today's verses instruct you to humbly submit to the government and those who lead. Arguing means you lose the ability to carry on a meaningful conversation. Defensiveness follows quarrels, and relational distance seems measurable.

Gentleness doesn't remove conviction from your mind or diminish the power of your vote, but it does help you remember that God's in control and His love for others is infinitely greater than your political analysis.

Prescription: Apply generous amounts of gentleness to what you say and do. This results in improved friendship.

AN INTENTIONALLY GENTLE RESPONSE

My beloved brethren, let every man be swift to hear,
slow to speak, slow to wrath; for the wrath of man
does not produce the righteousness of God.

JAMES 1:19–20 NKJV

———— ⋅ ❖ ⋅ ————

God promised to deal gently with you through His love, mercy, and grace. He asks you to follow His lead by showing the same gentleness to others. Today's verse points directly to the reason it's so important.

If you don't aim for gentleness in your relationships, you may tend to respond with wrath. Coming from the desperately wicked heart of man (Jeremiah 17:9), wrath leads to violations of God's laws. You can't demonstrate love in the midst of wrath. When your decisions are defined by rage, there are additional actions that lead to a poor outcome. Bitterness, clamor, slander, and malice (Ephesians 4:31–32) bubble to the surface and spill out on unsuspecting victims.

God was very clear: "The wrath of man does not produce the righteousness of God." Why? It keeps forgiveness at arm's length, refuses correction, and impairs godly wisdom.

You should listen more, speak thoughtfully, and never base your actions exclusively on emotions. Unlike wrath, gentleness leads with compassion, inspires with kindness, and befriends with mercy. Making gentleness an intentional response is a choice you never have to regret.

Day 1

BE SLOW TO WRATH

So then, my beloved brethren, let every man be swift to hear, slow to speak, slow to wrath; for the wrath of man does not produce the righteousness of God.

JAMES 1:19–20 NKJV

———— ◆ ————

Anger is not, in itself, a negative thing. It's right and important to be angry at injustice and wickedness. But if you're too easily aroused to anger and if you don't control it, this tendency will wreak havoc in your life and relationships.

Long experience with a quick, hot temper may have convinced you that you simply can't control your angry outbursts, but James says, "Let every man be. . .slow to wrath." The ability to control your temper is not just something that a *few* people can master. It's something God expects of "*every* man." So you can control it.

Several other scriptures point out that one of the most important Christian virtues is self-control (Galatians 5:23; 2 Peter 1:6), which means the ability to choose what is right and to stick to it, even if strong emotions are surging inside. This, again, is something that God expects of every believer.

It might not come easily. It will probably take concerted and persistent effort, but keep at it, stay determined, and with God's help, you *can* control your temper. That's a promise.

BETTER THAN THE MIGHTY

*He who is slow to anger is better than
the mighty, and he who rules his spirit,
than he who captures a city.*

PROVERBS 16:32 NASB

Solomon made a profound observation: he pointed out that, as most people in his day were aware, certain outstanding warriors could do astonishing feats when waging warfare. Then he stated that if you refrained from being easily aroused to anger, you were doing even better than these super soldiers.

Likewise, a highly disciplined siege army could—with carefully executed planning and great daring—conquer a heavily fortified city, but if you ruled over your own temper, you'd accomplished even more than them.

If you work out a plan and have the guts to stick to that plan, you can succeed. A plan can be as basic as knowing what kinds of things trigger you and thinking of methods ahead of time to defuse your anger in such situations instead of being simply swept along by strong emotions.

You may have an ongoing problem with your temper, and mastering it may be almost more than you can hope for at this time, but don't give up. Proverbs 20:18 (NKJV) states, "Plans are established by counsel; by wise counsel wage war." This works for besieging a city and for conquering your anger.

Day 3

TURNING AWAY WRATH

A soft answer turns away wrath,
but a harsh word stirs up anger.
PROVERBS 15:1 NKJV

———•◆•———

At times, you may have to tell someone things they don't want to hear, and that may cause them to become upset, but if you use consideration and wisdom, you can defuse much of their anger.

If someone lashes out at you or verbally assaults you, the temptation will be strong to answer back in a belligerent tone of voice. Don't. You'll only stir up their anger. Respond in a calm, nonthreatening tone and choose your words carefully.

If you're insecure, you may insist that you're not going to put up with verbal abuse from anyone—and immediately give people both barrels in return. But the mature refuse to respond in anger. You let it pass. "Sensible people control their temper; they earn respect by overlooking wrongs" (Proverbs 19:11 NLT).

Have empathy. Think how you would feel if *you* were in their situation. "So in everything, do to others what you would have them do to you" (Matthew 7:12 NIV). You would prefer being handled with love and respect, so treat others that way. If you put forth an effort to treat others gently, it can make a huge difference in them and calm the whole situation down.

CONTROLLING YOUR TONGUE

Do everything without complaining and arguing.
PHILIPPIANS 2:14 NLT

———◆———

It's easy to recognize a blatant verbal outburst as anger. But it's often harder to put a finger on subtly expressed anger, the kind that escapes your lips as sullen grumbling or a constantly contentious attitude. You may even *deny* that you have issues, though it's obvious to those around you that something has ticked you off or is eating away at you.

Paul said, "Do everything without complaining and arguing." You may find that much easier said than done. Bellyaching and snapping back at others may be such an ingrained habit that they seem like a part of your nature and personality.

You can't simply put a Band-Aid on a festering wound and try to keep your mouth shut. You have to deal with the underlying issues. That means admitting that you *are* angry, then facing the "root of bitterness" (Hebrews 12:15 KJV) that's the source of your anger. And then you must forgive and let go of the offense.

When you've done this, you'll finally get a handle on the slow-burning anger that's been expressing itself in complaining and arguing. And you can overcome it. God's Word commands, "Do *everything* without complaining and arguing," so He will give you the grace to do precisely that.

LET GOD GET MAD

*Never take your own revenge, beloved, but leave
room for the wrath of God, for it is written,
"Vengeance is Mine, I will repay," says the Lord.*
ROMANS 12:19 NASB

The Bible says to never seek your own revenge but to step back completely out of the picture and let God be the one to act on *His* anger. His anger is always perfectly fair and is motivated by deep love and justice. So don't try to take matters into your own hands. Let God be the one to repay the wrongs others do to you.

Leviticus 19:18 (NKJV) says, "You shall not take vengeance, nor bear any grudge. . .but you shall love your neighbor as yourself." People who bear grudges invariably plot revenge. A grudge is slow, simmering anger. It's anger on a back burner, stewing on a low flame, but it's anger just the same.

When you seek revenge, you're desiring to do violence to someone, except, instead of acting in the sudden heat of angry passion, you're acting in cold, calculating malice. The end result, however, is the same.

Instead of hating your enemies and plotting to harm them, you are to "love your enemies" (Matthew 5:44 KJV). Pray that God changes their hearts and has mercy upon them.

HANDLING ANGER PROPERLY

*"In your anger do not sin": Do not let the sun
go down while you are still angry.*
EPHESIANS 4:26 NIV

If you grew up in a home where you were exposed to constant angry outbursts, you might have difficulty believing that there's *ever* an acceptable time to express anger. Some Christians even doubt that believers should feel *sad*. But like happiness, anger and sorrow are valid emotions. "To every thing there is a season. . .a time to weep, and a time to laugh; a time to mourn" (Ecclesiastes 3:1, 4 KJV).

In certain circumstances, anger is an appropriate response. Paul knew that all believers would experience it at times; he just wanted to be sure that they handled it properly. So his first advice was, "In your anger do not sin." Don't get carried away with rage. Godly anger is a catalyst for change, but human temper tantrums don't accomplish God's purposes (James 1:20).

Paul's second piece of advice was: "Do not let the sun go down while you are still angry." Deal with the situation. Express your anger, work through the issues, then let your anger go. Don't let it continue smoldering inside for months or years—even if all the issues aren't resolved immediately. God often needs time to work things out.

ANGER AND HELLFIRE

*"But I say to you that whoever is angry with
his brother without a cause shall be in danger
of the judgment. . . . But whoever says, 'You fool!'
shall be in danger of hell fire."*
MATTHEW 5:22 NKJV

Like most people, you've heard your share of curses and
name-calling. Some people, when upset, demand that
God damn people to hell. They say it so often and so
freely that it loses its ability to shock—but this is truly
a terrible thing to utter. As a Christian, you might not
say such things, but you may be guilty of related sins.

Jesus said that anyone who is angry with his brother
will be subject to judgment. He then said if you even
call anyone "fool," you're in danger of hell. The danger
of losing your temper is that you often utter ill-advised
words, and Jesus warned, "The words you say will either
acquit you or condemn you" (Matthew 12:37 NLT). James
adds that "the tongue is a fire, a world of iniquity. The
tongue. . .is set on fire by hell" (James 3:6 NKJV).

You can wound people deeply with words spoken
in anger, and the best way to avoid doing this is to not
give in to wrath in the first place. Guard your tongue.
You'll be glad you did.

Day 1

UNLOCKING HUMILITY

*Humble yourselves in the presence
of the Lord, and He will exalt you.*
JAMES 4:10 NASB

Humility is the gateway to God's grace. Pride, however, is the lock that keeps you from entering. Where God could rightfully demand total obedience from you as His creation, He instead gave you free will, so that you could choose to love Him. Faced with that choice, though, you may think, as Satan once did, that you know better than your Creator. But rather than leave you to your just deserts—sin's fatal wages—God stooped, reaching down to you and making a way back to Him.

You can do nothing to patch things up with Him—it's not in your nature—so He did everything. The one thing He requires, though, is enough humility to see that you are a sinner, that you have fallen and there is no way you can rise on your own merits. Small and great, poor and rich, everyone is on the same footing before God.

And while it would be enough to surrender your pride and trade your condemnation for His salvation, He offers you more. When you humble yourself, placing Him first and loving others more highly than yourself, He will lift you up. Let God cut the lock of pride off and open the floodgates of peace and blessing.

TRUE INFLUENCE

Be of the same mind toward one another; do not
be haughty in mind, but associate with the lowly.
Do not be wise in your own estimation.

ROMANS 12:16 NASB

———————

Humility involves a great paradox: you gain influence through serving others. If you're like most people, you want your life to count, to make a difference and have an impact in some way. But whether you want to do so globally or locally, true impact starts with influence, and true influence begins with love.

True love requires putting someone else's interests ahead of your own, ahead of your feelings for and about them. You have to listen and discern and be ready to wade through the muck and mire of difficult choices. You have to be ready to learn before you can teach. In short, love requires humility.

Nothing derails humility more than pride. If you're just for yourself, others will know. But when someone else discovers that you are for *them*, it makes all the difference. Empathy is a huge tool in building relationships, but even where you don't have shared experiences to draw on, you can share the comfort of knowing that most people just want their lives to carry meaning and purpose. Few things are more Jesus-like than getting down into the nitty-gritty of life with others.

SHIFT YOUR MINDSET

*The LORD says: "Let not the wise boast of their
wisdom or the strong boast of their strength
or the rich boast of their riches."*
JEREMIAH 9:23 NIV

---·•◆•·---

Even under the grace of the cross, you still have to
adjust your mindset. The things that once served as
markers of your strength and self-sufficiency—your
accomplishments, education, wealth, or status—now
serve as signposts along the wider path of destruction
that you have abandoned to walk the narrow way of
Christ.

Too often, even after they've been saved, people put
their trust in money and possessions: the investment
portfolio that secures their present or the retirement account that secures their future. But it doesn't take much
to turn things upside down—the loss of a job, a market
decline or crash, a lengthy illness—and there it all goes.

In contrast, what God has to offer never loses its
value, never wavers with society's changing tides,
because of the One who guarantees His promise: "Let
the one who boasts boast about this: that they have the
understanding to know me, that I am the LORD, who
exercises kindness, justice and righteousness on earth,
for in these I delight" (Jeremiah 9:24 NIV). Humility
means you shift your thinking from what you have
done to what God has done.

Day 4

PREPARATION AGAINST PRIDE

Clothe yourselves with humility toward one another,
because, "God opposes the proud but shows favor
to the humble." Humble yourselves, therefore,
under God's mighty hand, that he
may lift you up in due time.

1 PETER 5:5–6 NIV

———— ◆ ————

There are many good reasons not to go out naked: culturally, you avoid embarrassment; practically, you avoid sunburn or frostbite; and spiritually, you avoid vulnerability. If you're not careful to arm yourself each day with prayer and the knowledge of God's Word, you're heading onto a battlefield in your Skivvies. And of all the enemies that await you, your own pride may be the most dangerous.

Pride keeps you from putting others first, from serving wholeheartedly, from being willing to go unrecognized, and from seeing that you're not always right. To be clothed with humility is to be approachable, to listen well, and to curtail complaint.

Humility is deliberate preparation to put things in perspective: you are a saved sinner, going out into a world of lost souls, whom God wants to reach, possibly through you. Your agenda, whatever it may be, comes second. Be ready to do what you need to do today—at work, with the family, juggling activities—but keep God's priorities first. Determine to be an instrument of God's grace, and you will find yourself a recipient, too.

Day 5

THE BLESSING OF SPIRITUAL BANKRUPTCY

"Blessed are the poor in spirit,
for theirs is the kingdom of heaven."
MATTHEW 5:3 NASB

Bankruptcy is a scary word financially but a huge blessing spiritually. When Jesus said "poor in spirit," He was referring to humility. Spiritually speaking, you have nothing to offer God; you are bankrupt before Him. There is nothing you can do to enrich Him or to pay the price for your sin.

Your spiritual debt actually dwarfs any physical debt you might have. No one can afford the arrogance of thinking prosperity or possessions will impress God or relieve them from the responsibility of using what He has given them—no matter how small or great—in the service of building His kingdom.

In fact, just as financial bankruptcy can be a tremendous relief from the pressures of trying to catch up and climb out of a debt-dug hole, acknowledging your spiritual insolvency before God is a healthy, pressure-relieving measure. Of course, just as you must avoid any of the irresponsibility that might have contributed to your monetary debt, you have to be careful to keep walking humbly before God. Comparatively, it's a small matter to turn all you are and have over to God, secure in the assurance of your salvation and the work to which He wants you to commit.

POWER UNDER CONTROL

And being found in appearance as a man,
He humbled Himself and became obedient to
the point of death, even the death of the cross.
Therefore God also has highly exalted Him and
given Him the name which is above every name.

PHILIPPIANS 2:8–9 NKJV

———— •◆• ————

There's a fine line between pride and humility. It centers on the idea of meekness, which is often misunderstood to mean being a doormat. In the ancient world, meekness was seen as a vice, not a virtue—associated with people deemed unfit for proper society.

God turned that notion on its head, making it one of those great paradoxes of faith: to be great in God's eyes, you have to humble yourself. If "humble yourself" sounds like a deliberate act, it is. *Meekness* captures the idea of a mustang broken to be bridled. The horse has lost none of its power or majesty; it could break out any time but instead has submitted to the will of another.

There is no finer example of meekness than Jesus Christ. The one who could have forced every knee to bow (and one day will!) instead focused on the mission at hand, accomplishing the will of the Father at the cross. As His child, you have access to His power, both to submit to and do His will.

Day 7

THE COMFORT OF CONTRITION

This is what the high and exalted One says—
he who lives forever, whose name is holy: "I live in
a high and holy place, but also with the one who
is contrite and lowly in spirit, to revive the spirit of
the lowly and to revive the heart of the contrite."

ISAIAH 57:15 NIV

Humility requires an act of submission—a desire to keep the focus on others rather than yourself. God's very interest in mankind is your example. That He who is perfect and complete all by Himself should show such deep interest in your well-being is humbling enough, but that He rewards you for following His lead is even better.

Because of God's generosity, when you humble yourself—prioritizing and contending for others' best interests—He promises to be with you. It's a good promise because it's not natural to be unselfish, and it can even put you in a vulnerable position with coworkers or family members who don't share your commitment to God.

Take comfort in knowing that your desire to be humble draws God's approval and His presence. That includes confessing the times when your pride gets in the way. He will lift your spirits and rejuvenate your heart, just because He loves that you're trying to be like Him.

THE FINEST MOMENT

*For to this you were called, because Christ also
suffered for us, leaving us an example, that you
should follow His steps: "Who committed no sin,
nor was deceit found in His mouth"; who, when
He was reviled, did not revile in return; when
He suffered, He did not threaten, but committed
Himself to Him who judges righteously.*

1 PETER 2:21–23 NKJV

Jeff Bloemberg spent most of his hockey career during
the 1980s in the minor leagues. He did finally get a shot
with the New York Rangers, where he saw action in
forty-three games over four seasons. But he's probably
most remembered for something he didn't do.

The *New York Times* chronicled the events of a playoff
game in 1990 in which an opposing player (referred to
in the article as "a brawler on skates") went looking for
a fight, and he found Bloemberg. Instead of fighting
back, though, Bloemberg hunkered down and took a
flurry of punches to his head and body.

The article quotes him as saying he was a born-
again Christian and he wanted to let his light shine.
The *Times* called it the "finest moment" of the opening
round of the playoffs. As such, his self-control is a living
example of 1 Peter 2:21–23. How would you react in
such a situation?

Week 27 ◆ SELF-CONTROL

AN IMPERISHABLE CROWN

*Everyone who competes in the games goes into
strict training. They do it to get a crown that
will not last, but we do it to get a
crown that will last forever.*

1 CORINTHIANS 9:25 NIV

After failing to qualify for the 2012 Summer Olympics in
the heptathlon (a contest that includes seven different
events), Heather Miller-Koch scaled back her schedule
as a full-time nurse so she could train for the 2016
Summer Olympics in Rio. For the year leading up to
the games, she trained full-time.

Her efforts paid off. She finished second at the
Olympic trials, securing her spot on Team USA. She
was set to compete in the Rio games and considered
her many hours of training to be well worth it. And
she should be proud of her accomplishment, even
though she never went on to win a medal. Very few
people are talented and disciplined enough to even
qualify for the Olympics.

If she was willing to undergo such a strict training
and nutrition regimen to compete for a perishable
crown, how much more ought the Christian be willing
to train for an imperishable crown? How about you?
What are you willing to abstain from in order that the
Gospel message might prevail in your life?

DEVOTED TO GOD

*And we are instructed to turn from godless living
and sinful pleasures. We should live in this
evil world with wisdom, righteousness,
and devotion to God.*

TITUS 2:12 NLT

If you became a Christian later in life, then you can remember how it feels to live without any regard for God. Before Christ, you never gave your vices much thought. You simply engaged in them because they were pleasurable. After Christ, a battle ensued. You felt empowered to reject those activities, and you desired to do so because you'd rather please God than yourself.

Sadly, though, you may have returned to your vices when the stresses of life came and justified your actions, saying that you deserve some happiness. We've all been there. So, what's the antidote? Paul offers it in the second half of today's verse: to live with wisdom, righteousness, and devotion to God.

Wisdom comes from scripture, from the insights of pastors/teachers, and from fellow believers. Don't be shy about asking for help. Righteousness, in this context, refers to properly performing your duties as a Christian. When you live out your faith, you strengthen it. And devotion to God comes by surrendering your desires for self-pleasure in favor of pleasing God.

Day 4

MODERATION IN EVERYTHING

*Do you like honey? Don't eat too much,
or it will make you sick!*
PROVERBS 25:16 NLT

Judea was known for its abundance of honey. First Samuel 14:24–25 says Saul's men, who were pressed to exhaustion from a lack of food, even found honeycomb on the ground in the forest. And, of course, the Promised Land was often described in scripture as a land flowing with milk and honey.

Honey, which was in no short supply, was sweet and invigorating, and it provided a boost of energy. It was a good thing—a resource provided by God. But too much of it would make a person sick. This is a clear metaphor for the pleasures of this world. Many are accessible, fulfilling, and even allowable—in moderation—but excess is never a good idea. They will make your soul sick.

Which worldly pleasures have you yet to master? Food? Drink? Sport? Hobby? Television? Some other form of entertainment? Whatever it is, be willing to name it and then put parameters on it which you will stick to in the future. Seek an accountability partner. Or be publicly accountable on social media. Exhibit self-control and your soul will benefit. The sheep who willingly follows God lacks for nothing (Psalm 23:1).

SELF-CONTROL ♦ *Week 27*

A TIME FOR SILENCE

Then Pilate said to Him, "Do You not hear how
many things they testify against You?" And He
did not answer him with regard to even a single
charge, so the governor was quite amazed.

MATTHEW 27:13–14 NASB

———◆———

The person who lacks self-control is quick to defend himself. Jesus, on the other hand, was the model of self-control when He was arrested and faced accusations by the chief priests and the elders. They accused Him of stirring up people to revolt against civil authority, but He didn't respond to these false accusations. Pilate was incredulous. Why wouldn't Jesus defend Himself?

And does His action set a precedent for His followers? Is the Christian always to remain silent?

Let's answer the last question first. Paul didn't remain silent when charges were brought against him by the Jews (Acts 22). He respectfully laid out his case. Stephen spoke up at his own trial, also doing so in a respectful manner (Acts 7). So, there's a time to speak up and a time to be silent. But in all cases, it should be done respectfully and with a complete exhibition of self-control.

How do you typically respond when you're accused of something—either justly or unjustly? Do you need to improve in this area?

Day 6

CORAM DEO

Let your gentle spirit be known to all men.
The Lord is near.
PHILIPPIANS 4:5 NASB

———— ● ————

Gentleness is easier for some personality types than others. But that has no bearing on Paul's command to the Philippian church. He wanted them to let their gentle spirit be known to *all* men—and it probably didn't come naturally for some of them. But how's the world supposed to believe that the Gospel contains any power unless they see it in the church?

What might a "gentle spirit" look like in your life? How might you live that out in front of the world? Maybe it will include a tamer tongue, a less critical spirit, a more generous ear, an even temper, or a willingness to care less about who gets the credit and more about the final result. Whatever the case, how might committing your weakness to prayer change things in your office, your church, or your home?

Coram Deo means "in the presence of God." The Lord's return is near, as Paul points out in today's verse, and it should reorient the way you live today. Theologian R. C. Sproul words it this way in a recent blog post: "To live coram Deo is to live one's entire life in the presence of God, under the authority of God, to the glory of God."

Day 7

BE ALERT

*So then, let us not be like others, who are asleep,
but let us be awake and sober. For those who
sleep, sleep at night, and those who get
drunk, get drunk at night.*

1 THESSALONIANS 5:6–7 NIV

———— • ◆ • ————

Jesus' disciples often struggled to understand basic spiritual concepts, such as living water, the bread of life, and being born again. They were constantly attempting to understand them through the physical, rather than the spiritual. But eventually, they caught on. The Peter of the Gospels sees the world much differently in the book of Acts and in his later epistles.

In today's verse, Paul spoke to the Thessalonian church about not sleeping like others do. Of course, he was asking them to be aware that Jesus was sitting on His throne and might return at any moment. Thus, living in any other way than being alert and self-controlled is a dangerous state—because you know better.

Some of your coworkers and neighbors are sleeping. They're living as if nothing is at stake, other than the next moment of fun. They're heading for a cliff and have no idea how close it is. You, on the other hand, are fully aware of its proximity. How can that not change the way you live today or prompt you to warn them?

CHOOSING COURAGE

*So be strong and courageous,
all you who put your hope in the L*ORD*!*
PSALM 31:24 NLT

When you're facing a threat, you may pray for God to give you courage, and He may supply it—but that's not always the way He works. He doesn't necessarily give you a download of bravery before you even face the enemy. Instead He commands *you*, "Be strong and courageous, all you who put your hope in the LORD!" Initially, the onus is on you to *choose* to trust the Lord and be courageous.

Focusing on trusting Him makes you aware of the Lord's great power and of the fact that He will defend you. As God told one king, "Do not be afraid nor dismayed because of this great multitude, for the battle is not yours, but God's" (2 Chronicles 20:15 NKJV). God *first* commanded His people to master their fear, and they were able to do so because they trusted in Him.

If God is on your side, you're well able to overcome your enemies. Ask yourself this: "If God is for us, who can be against us?" (Romans 8:31 NKJV). You can safely choose to be courageous, and then as you step out, God anoints you with extra courage and boldness. He will be with you and empower you.

REMEMBER GOD AND FIGHT

*"Do not be afraid of them; remember the Lord
who is great and awesome, and fight for your
brothers, your sons, your daughters,
your wives and your houses."*

NEHEMIAH 4:14 NASB

———— ⋄ ⬩ ⋄ ————

It's a natural human tendency—when confronted by overwhelming force, or something startling or dangerous—to experience fear, to want to simply give up and hide in some hole. That's why, throughout the Bible, God constantly commanded people, "Fear not" (Luke 1:13, 30; 2:10; 5:10 KJV).

Frequently the enemy tries to get you to back down and run away with nothing more than threats and empty words. He often doesn't even need to attack you to cause you to experience anxiety. But God commands, "Do not be afraid because of the words that you have heard" (2 Kings 19:6 NASB).

You need to not only remember that God is great and has tremendous power, but you must remember your loved ones who are depending on you to protect them. Though it may be difficult, you must stand up and fight for their sakes. You won't have to do it alone. God has repeatedly promised to give you strength and to shield you from evil, so count on Him to be with you. If you will do this, God *will* be with you and help you overcome.

WHEN YOU'RE AFRAID

Whenever I am afraid, I will trust in You.
PSALM 56:3 NKJV

King David didn't say, "I shall never fear," but confessed that he *did* fear at times, saying, "Whenever I am afraid. . . ." He was an outstanding warrior, mighty in battle, and very courageous, but even he frequently got in over his head. When circumstances looked bleak and death seemed imminent, David, too, knew fear.

But he also knew what to *do* in such times. He focused on God and determined to trust in Him. He did this each time that fears threatened to overwhelm him. That's how he found peace. "Thou wilt keep him in perfect peace, whose mind is stayed on thee: because he trusteth in thee" (Isaiah 26:3 KJV).

Whenever you fear, make it a habit to turn to God—and *keep* your eyes fixed on Him. As you look steadfastly His way, you bathe your spirit in the light of His presence and partake of His strength. "They looked unto him, and were lightened" (Psalm 34:5 KJV).

But you must make a conscious effort to trust, even if your circumstances don't change for a while and your emotions are still being blasted by the storm. Fears can be very powerful and often are only calmed after a sustained determination to trust God.

Day 4

STRENGTHENED BY COURAGE

Wait on the LORD: be of good courage, and he shall strengthen thine heart: wait, I say, on the LORD.
PSALM 27:14 KJV

———— • ◆ • ————

Sometimes when you desperately need God's help, it doesn't seem like He's coming through for you. You appear to be out in the open, unprotected, facing adversity or enemies by yourself. You wonder where God is. After all, didn't He promise to be there for you? The Bible has one clear piece of advice for you during such times—*wait on the Lord.* God says it twice in this one verse.

If you make the effort to "be of good courage," God will come alongside you, well up within you, and strengthen your heart. It's a promise. Give Him time, and He will strengthen you. A beautiful companion promise, found in the New Testament, says: "The Lord is faithful, and he will strengthen you and protect you from the evil one" (2 Thessalonians 3:3 NIV).

There may be special times of testing, often in lonely, discouraged hours when you feel beaten down and people have abandoned you, that you will be attacked by the forces of evil. At such times, you have to resolve to stand firm. God will then show up, make His presence known, work within you, and strengthen you.

NOT FEARING MAN

We say with confidence, "The Lord is my helper;
I will not be afraid. What can mere
mortals do to me?"
HEBREWS 13:6 NIV

————— ♦ —————

When you ask yourself, *What can man do to me?* you might think, *Lots. People can do plenty to bring grief and fear and pain into my life.* That's often enough true. The Bible even says, "Many are the afflictions of the righteous" (Psalm 34:19 KJV). But it goes *on* to promise, "But the Lord delivereth him out of them *all*" (emphasis added).

The point is: The Lord Almighty is your helper. He's on your side. He may permit enemies to attack you—why, you can't understand—but He will always get the upper hand in the end and bring you through to victory, one way or another.

Jesus said, "My friends, do not be afraid of those who kill the body, and after that have no more that they can do" (Luke 12:4 NKJV). Jesus taught a Gospel where the meek, the weak, the poor, and the downtrodden are truly blessed, despite the fact that they're beaten down, because in the end they will be truly victorious.

You may not always be victorious in this world, but your true home and treasure aren't in this life but in the coming kingdom of God.

HOW TO CAST OUT FEAR

*There is no fear in love; but perfect love casts out
fear, because fear involves punishment, and the
one who fears is not perfected in love.*

1 JOHN 4:18 NASB

———•◆•———

This is a powerful promise: "Perfect love casts out fear."
Two verses previously, the Bible declared, "God is love"
(v. 16). This means that if you live in God and He lives
in you, you're filled with love and "perfected in love."
The result is that you'll have "confidence in the day
of judgment" (v. 17).

When you're filled with God's love, you no longer
fear being rejected by Him. You can be confident that
He's on your side; you no longer need fear that you'll
be punished for your sins. This confidence then fills
you with the courage and positive attitude you need
to face life's many problems.

In the beginning, the apostle Peter was very
conscious of his sins. After Jesus did a great miracle
in his presence, Peter cried out, "Depart from me; for
I am a sinful man, O Lord" (Luke 5:8 KJV). But instead
of rejecting and punishing Peter, Jesus put His Spirit
on him and made him one of His closest followers.

Be filled with God's perfect love today, and it will
cast all fear from your heart!

COURAGE AND FEAR

The wicked flee though no one pursues,
but the righteous are as bold as a lion.
PROVERBS 28:1 NIV

After God did miracles to bring the Israelites into Canaan, Rahab told the two spies, "When we heard of it, our hearts melted in fear and everyone's courage failed because of you" (Joshua 2:11 NIV). God had removed their spiritual defenses, and "their protection [had] departed from them" (Numbers 14:9 NKJV).

The wicked also fear because they have a troubled conscience: "The sound of a shaken leaf shall cause them to flee; they shall flee as though fleeing from a sword, and they shall fall when no one pursues" (Leviticus 26:36 NKJV). "There were they in great fear, where no fear was" (Psalm 53:5 KJV). Today it's called paranoia.

The situation is just the opposite for the righteous. God strengthens their spiritual defenses and they're as bold as a lion. The Lord can anoint you with supernatural confidence and courage. After the early Christians were filled with the Holy Spirit, they preached the Gospel with great boldness (Acts 4:31).

If you lack courage and confidence, ask God to give you the confidence to step out. And *keep* praying! It may not happen right away, but don't give up. Even though it takes a while, God is able to transform you.

Week 28 ♦ COURAGE

Day 1

IN EVERY SEASON

*Then He took the cup, and gave thanks, and gave
it to them, saying, "Drink from it, all of you."*
MATTHEW 26:27 NKJV

During the Last Supper, Jesus followed the standard
protocol for blessings—one over the bread and another
over the wine. But this time, when He gave thanks, it
wasn't a typical premeal gesture of gratitude for the
food. It was loaded with significance, as Jesus knew
that He was headed to the cross—the painful, bloody
fulfillment of His mission on earth.

And yet He gave thanks.

It's easy to be grateful when things are going well,
when you're gainfully employed, well fed, and healthy.
But to thank God when the horizon is dark with
peril, when the future is unclear, is to show a heart
committed to trusting God.

It's good to thank God for all the ways He provides
on a daily basis, especially over a meal as you prepare
to enjoy both the food and the fellowship that comes
with it. It's crucial, though, to do so when things aren't
going well—in the midst of illness, loss, or doubt.
The promise of Jesus' cup is that God can use all your
suffering to good ends, to help you grow, to demonstrate
His grace to others, or to check your priorities. God is
good in every season.

HEART SONGS

*Singing a song of thanksgiving
and telling of all your wonders.*
PSALM 26:7 NLT

———◆———

When was the last time you got a good song stuck in your head? There's something comforting about a familiar melody humming on your lips as you go about your day, like a tether anchoring you to good memories or a pleasant moment.

When David wrote a psalm, the words and harmonies tied him to his relationship with God, often giving him a lens through which to view God's faithfulness throughout his life. In both the good and bad times, David turned his heart toward God, commemorating His love, vowing his trust, confessing his sins, and declaring his commitment to follow. It was such a habit to put God first, to involve Him in every part of his life, that David couldn't help but put it in song.

What would it mean to worship God like that— not to compartmentalize His songs into the musical portion of a church service or a radio playing in the background, but to let the music of His work resonate every day, in every moment? It might be a familiar tune that's striking a chord at a particular moment, or it might be a new song, something coming from your heart alone, thoughts and words of gratitude and praise for your good God.

TRUSTWORTHY

*"Blessed be the Lord, who has given rest to His
people Israel, according to all that He promised.
There has not failed one word of all His good
promise, which He promised through
His servant Moses."*

1 Kings 8:56 NKJV

People let you down. They may not want to or mean
to. . .or they may not care about how you're affected
at all. But as God is pushed further out of society, a
promise means less and less. What used to be a typical
expectation is more and more a shot in the dark. You
want to trust others, but it feels risky, especially once
you've been burned.

What that also means is that someone who *keeps* a
promise has impact. Being trustworthy used to be pretty
standard, but these days it's a distinct characteristic.
Everyone has been let down by a broken word, so much
so that the assumption is that people *should* probably
be honest but they probably *won't* be.

God, however, keeps His promises, and He expects
you to as well. A promise kept is a reflection of the Great
Promise Keeper Himself. It breaks through cynicism,
creating unexpected bonds based purely on trust. It
enables you to reach people you've never met in ways
you'd never anticipate, which is at the heart of the
Gospel itself.

ALWAYS MEANS "ALWAYS"

Giving thanks always for all things to God the Father in the name of our Lord Jesus Christ.
EPHESIANS 5:20 NKJV

To give thanks all the time in every situation is something that most Christians agree with more in principle than in practice. It's easy to see why—when you've suffered a shock or a sudden loss, it's hard to say, "Thanks for the cancer, God," or "I'm so grateful to get fired."

Those words Paul used for "always" and "all things" actually mean "always" and "all things"! But that's impossible, right? Yes. . .unless you have faith. Unless you truly believe that God is in control, that nothing happens to you except what He allows, and that He loves you and wants what is best for you. Otherwise, you can't be thankful for adversity.

Remember, often all you can see is the problem in front of you—the tragedy or pain or hardship. But God has the broadest, most comprehensive perspective imaginable, and that's where you put your trust. When you thank Him in the midst of suffering, it's not the illness or joblessness or uncertainty you're thankful for. It's the belief that God is bigger than any of it and that, no matter what, He can work things out.

AN ATTITUDE OF GRATITUDE

*"I thank and praise you, God of my ancestors,
for you have given me wisdom and strength.
You have told me what we asked of you and
revealed to us what the king demanded."*

DANIEL 2:23 NLT

Prayer so often begins with gratitude, and gratitude often begins with awareness. How many things will God do for you today? Some of them are lasting and ongoing, like salvation and sanctification.

Others are more in the moment, that "daily bread" that helped you pay a bill or meet a need, or those small but crucial encounters that God has in store for you on any given day—a chance meeting at the grocery store or in the hallway at work where God wants you to be available to listen, to speak an inspired word, to share a laugh, or to commiserate a loss. Just to be a part of what God is doing beyond your life, using you to help or touch others' hearts, is humbling and fulfilling.

Set your day on a path of gratitude. Paul wrote, "Devote yourselves to prayer, keeping alert in it with an attitude of thanksgiving" (Colossians 4:2 NASB). Take a moment to appreciate God's provision in your life, and then ask Him to prepare you for a day of divine appointments.

PULL OVER AND PRAY

*It is good to praise the LORD and make music to
your name, O Most High, proclaiming your love
in the morning and your faithfulness at night.*
PSALM 92:1–2 NIV

When was the last time you stopped and counted your
blessings? Daily life is a lot like Germany's autobahn—
eighty miles an hour, all the time, a constant race
of pass or be passed, full of noise and pollution and
emergency phone calls. If you manage to squeeze in
a prayer on your way to whatever's next, it feels like
a small miracle.

At that pace, your time with God gets left at the
roadside, lost in all of the busyness of everyday life.
You lose more than devotional time, though; you lose
perspective. God's faithfulness, His daily mercies, go
whizzing by, till it's easy to take them for granted.
Then, when you're running on fumes, you wonder
where God is.

Make a habit of gassing up spiritually before you go
out each day. Carve out a few minutes in the morning
to thank your heavenly Father for the blessings He daily
provides, for His presence in the work you have ahead
of you, for the unknown opportunities to be about His
business—that amazing work of being His ambassador to
the world, that unique privilege you have as His child.

Day 7

A THANKFUL HEART TRUMPS A NERVOUS MOMENT

*Be anxious for nothing, but in everything by
prayer and supplication, with thanksgiving,
let your requests be made known to God.*

PHILIPPIANS 4:6 NKJV

———•◆•———

Telling someone not to be anxious about a nerve-racking situation is similar to telling someone not to look down from a high place. It's almost impossible to avoid, especially when you're aware of the situation—a presentation or a deadline, or a conversation that might potentially become a confrontation.

And what if God doesn't work things out the way you thought He might or the way you want Him to? That feeling in your stomach can become a hand over your eyes, blocking your view of God. Two little words, smack-dab in the middle of this familiar verse, can break anxiety's grip and point you to God's peace: "With thanksgiving."

When you're stressed out, it's hard to think of being thankful—but it's essential. No matter what you're facing, God will still be God, sovereign and unchanging—and that means you will still be His beloved child, still the subject of thousands of good thoughts, still the precious heart He gave His Son to win back. So, when you face anxiety, thank God for who He is in the midst of it and who you are to Him.

Day 1

GENEROSITY—MORE OR LESS

*[Those who fear the Lord] share freely and give
generously to those in need. Their good deeds
will be remembered forever. They will
have influence and honor.*

PSALM 112:9 NLT

It's easy to succumb to selfishness. As a child you refused to share your treasures, and if you don't change, that attitude can follow you to the grave. You have and want more. You may borrow to get and then spend most of your life working to untangle your future from past debt.

While wrapped up in such an attitude of selfishness you might come face-to-face with someone in need and find yourself crippled by a resistance to share your *more* with those who have *less*. You might even be reluctant to give to God and come up with plenty of excuses why you shouldn't.

Generosity is less about your ability and more about bringing godly character to life using the resources and talents God has given you. The issue is never about the money. It's always about the way you respond to God's commands to live generously.

God's promises to supply *all* your needs are lavish and generous (Philippians 4:19). By understanding His love and care for others as well, you can begin to practice generosity with the awe and willingness to share that God always intended.

THE GIVING MOTIVE

*"When you give to someone in need, don't do as the
hypocrites do—blowing trumpets in the synagogues
and streets to call attention to their acts of charity!
I tell you the truth, they have received all the
reward they will ever get. But when you give to
someone in need, don't let your left hand know
what your right hand is doing. Give your gifts
in private, and your Father, who sees
everything, will reward you."*

MATTHEW 6:2–4 NLT

When God is generous, you know it. A gift comes from
an unanticipated source. An unexpected check arrives
in the mail. Relief is perfectly timed. Your conclusion?
Your help came from the generous hand of God. James
1:17 (NKJV) says, "Every good gift and every perfect gift
is from above, and comes down from the Father."

Did someone have to announce the news? Did God
use social media to let others know He was generous?
Were letters sent to family and friends announcing the
blessing? No, He quietly provided for your need and
invited you to get in touch.

God is generosity's best example. Give, expecting
nothing in return, in order to help where help is most
needed. Share, without drawing attention to the gift,
because God is the only one who needs to know what
was done, and He already does.

A WIDOW'S FAITH

*[Jesus] saw also a certain poor widow putting
in two mites. So He said, "Truly I say to you that
this poor widow has put in more than all;
for all these out of their abundance have put
in offerings for God, but she out of her poverty
put in all the livelihood that she had."*

LUKE 21:2–4 NKJV

God wants you to be generous, but He also wants you
to pay attention to your motives for giving. Today's
verses demonstrate how Jesus reacted to one incredible
act of faith and generosity.

Imagine this widow coming to the temple. She
doesn't own much. She can't earn much. Her current
bank account? Two small coins. She isn't drawing
attention to herself, but Jesus notices. He describes
her gift as "more than all." Why?

There were people at the temple who gave *much*
larger gifts, but she gave in great faith. All the money
the widow had was two small copper coins—and she
gave them *both*. Her future then rested in the hands
of God. If He didn't provide, the widow wouldn't eat.

One small monetary gift was singled out for the
message it sent about faith, and Christians today still
pay attention. It's good to give from a generous heart; it's
even better when that heart is overflowing with faith.

A HEART OF CHEER

*Each of you should give what you have decided
in your heart to give, not reluctantly or under
compulsion, for God loves a cheerful giver.*
2 CORINTHIANS 9:7 NIV

God promised to meet the needs of His people, but
He's asked His people to be generous. In scripture
we're told that giving to the needs of the church is a
priority with God, but He's looking for cheerful givers,
not duty-bound supporters.

True, churches can use the money whatever people's
motives for giving, but the difference is in the heart
of the giver. One who is reluctant or gives under
compulsion may view the *joy of giving* as a mistitled
obligation.

When you're generous because you view sharing as
an act of worship to God, there is a spiritual bonus.
Giving will actually bring joy instead of a dread that
looks at what could have been purchased if the gift
hadn't been given.

God doesn't want you to experience regret when
you give. Perhaps that's why He wants you to focus on
giving in order to see His ability to provide. Giving
brings you in line with God's will, exposes you to His
work, and brings you to the observation deck of His
heart. When you connect with this journey, you come
face-to-face with your own *cheerful* heart.

Day 5

DON'T MISS THE POINT

*"Give, and it will be given to you: good measure,
pressed down, shaken together, and running over
will be put into your bosom. For with the
same measure that you use, it will be
measured back to you."*

LUKE 6:38 NKJV

————— • ◆ • —————

God has never been the originator of the *get-rich-quick*
scheme. However, it could be inferred that this verse
is suggesting that when you give $100 to God then He
is going to give you at least $100 in return, but read
carefully. There's more to it.

Whenever God provides a gift, it's always the gift you
really need. When you give as an act of worship to God,
He could return a gift of a blessing, like encouragement
from a friend, the help of a neighbor, or the restoration
of a relationship. These items are only a few examples of
the gifts God might give to those with a generous spirit.

The *measure* you use might very well be the *cheerful*
nature of your giving or the sense of *obligation* felt when
you offer a gift. Money could be the least valuable gift
God could offer back to you when He offers a gift of
"good measure, pressed down, shaken together, and
running over."

When you *give to get*, you miss the point of generosity.

Day 6

LENDING TO JESUS

*If you help the poor, you are lending
to the LORD—and he will repay you!*
PROVERBS 19:17 NLT

———— ✦ ————

Jesus said that one day when His disciples saw Him
enthroned in heaven, He'd tell them, "I was hungry and
you gave Me food; I was thirsty and you gave Me drink;
I was a stranger and you took Me in; I was naked and
you clothed Me; I was sick and you visited Me; I was in
prison and you came to Me" (Matthew 25:35–36 NKJV).

This statement would confuse many disciples in
that day because they wouldn't be able to recall Jesus
having need for clothing or health care. They certainly
hadn't heard that He had served time in prison. They
may have known Him to have been thirsty or hungry,
but that was about it.

Then Jesus said that He'd explain that anytime
they'd been generous to those in need it was as if they
were generous to Him personally. His disciples would
have recalled a similar thought from the writings of
Solomon: "If you help the poor, you are lending to
the LORD—and he will repay you!" (Proverbs 19:17 NLT).

Jesus wanted His disciples to be identified by their
generosity, love, and compassion. So He made it clear
that He Himself is always the object of your generosity.

Week 30 ✦ GENEROSITY

TRUE LIFE GENEROSITY

*Teach those who are rich in this world not to be
proud and not to trust in their money, which is
so unreliable. Their trust should be in God,
who richly gives us all we need for our enjoyment.
Tell them to use their money to do good.
They should be rich in good works and generous
to those in need, always being ready to share
with others. By doing this they will be storing
up their treasure as a good foundation for the
future so that they may experience true life.*

1 TIMOTHY 6:17–19 NLT

Economies collapse, markets crash, and currencies tumble. Yet people keep reaching for enough money to help navigate troubled times. Yes, saving is biblical. Managing money is, too. You're asked to be wise, but money is not God, and God is not defined by money.

Your faith isn't to be anchored to cash reserves but in the God who owns everything.

No amount of money can buy a sunset, the miracle of life, or the love of a spouse. God's best gifts are extremely lavish and can't be bought. The demonstration of your gratitude is linked to a generous heart. You're hospitable because generosity is relational. You're kind because generosity isn't defined by anything but love. You give because generosity is part of living "true life."

WILLING OR WHINING?

Be still in the presence of the LORD, and wait patiently for him to act. Don't worry about evil people who prosper or fret about their wicked schemes. Stop being angry! Turn from your rage! Do not lose your temper—it only leads to harm. For the wicked will be destroyed, but those who trust in the LORD will possess the land.

PSALM 37:7–9 NLT

A hungry child has to practice patience if Mom says he can't have a snack right before supper. Whether he likes the rule or not, he can choose to wait for food quietly and peacefully until mealtime (plus maybe earn a treat for good behavior), or he can choose to mope around the kitchen whining, "I'm *soooo* hungry." If you've been around young children much, you know they often choose the latter response.

God doesn't want childish bad attitudes while you wait. That's not true patience. The above passage says to "*be still* in the presence of the LORD, and wait patiently for him." And another well-known scripture says, "Be still, and know that I am God" (Psalm 46:10 NLT).

Being still in times of waiting means you have a chance to listen to what God wants to teach you during the downtime. So don't whine; rather, be pleasantly willing to wait.

Day 2

WE ALL WAIT

For whatever things were written before were written for our learning, that we through the patience and comfort of the Scriptures might have hope. Now may the God of patience and comfort grant you to be like-minded toward one another, according to Christ Jesus.

ROMANS 15:4–5 NKJV

Hardship and waiting—no one escapes these, no matter what walk of life you come from. Are you waiting for a hardship to end or be resolved? Or waiting and working toward a new goal? Or waiting on God to answer a prayer? As a believer, you're always waiting and watching for a world dominated by sin and death to end with Jesus' return and the establishment of God's eternal and perfect kingdom.

Through any type of pain and need of endurance, God gives hope through His Word and through His presence. He is the God of patience and comfort, and He offers them in all your circumstances. He calls you to wait patiently on Him while at the same time caring patiently for others. This week, may you be encouraged as you learn about God's promises regarding the patience He desires from you and gives you. May your prayer be, "I wait for the LORD, my soul waits, and in His word I do hope. My soul waits for the Lord" (Psalm 130:5–6 NKJV).

PATIENT FRUIT

"But the ones that fell on the good ground are those
who, having heard the word with a noble and good
heart, keep it and bear fruit with patience."

LUKE 8:15 NKJV

————•◆•————

Have you encountered people who proclaim to know
Jesus and are gung ho about their faith. . .for a little
while? Then when they don't feel blessed enough with
prosperity or resolution to their problems, they turn
away from following Christ? The parable of the sower
talks about all the different kinds of folks who hear
the Word of God. The ones who succeed are those
who hear the Word with good hearts, keep it, and
bear fruit *with patience.*

Jesus truly is a quick fix for the problem of sin—
because the moment anyone genuinely repents, He
wipes their sins out, changing them from scarlet to
white. He is able to do this because He triumphed over
sin and death on the cross. However, a relationship with
Jesus is not always a quick fix for all the consequences of
sin. Sincere relationships with Jesus take patience, not
demanding instant results and immediate miraculous
interventions.

God certainly can do all things, and He promises
to work all things for good for those who love Him
(Romans 8:28), but He will work according to His own
perfect timing. True believers must patiently trust His
direction and schedule.

PATIENT SUFFERING

*Of course, you get no credit for being patient if
you are beaten for doing wrong. But if you suffer
for doing good and endure it patiently,
God is pleased with you.*

1 PETER 2:20 NLT

This scripture doesn't mince words. If a person does the crime, he pays the time, and there's no honor in patiently enduring it. But patiently suffering through punishment or a trial that was in no way warranted shows God you know the real meaning of patience, and He's pleased.

The Christian life offers no guarantee that you won't suffer in this life. Quite the contrary. You will suffer, and the Bible says to rejoice in your sufferings because God builds your character through them (Romans 5).

But the Bible does guarantee God's constant presence with you, no matter what trial you're facing or pain you're feeling. Isaiah 43:2–3 (NIV) says, "When you pass through the waters, I will be with you. . . .When you walk through the fire, you will not be burned; the flames will not set you ablaze. For I am the LORD your God, the Holy One of Israel, your Savior." (Notice that these verses say *when*, not *if*.)

Whatever your lot, wait patiently on God to deliver you from it, because He absolutely will, if not in this world then in His perfect kingdom to come.

SUPERNATURAL PATIENCE

*And we urge you, brothers and sisters,
warn those who are idle and disruptive,
encourage the disheartened, help the weak,
be patient with everyone.*

1 THESSALONIANS 5:14 NIV

———— • ◆ • ————

Be patient with *everyone*? Seriously? You might be thinking, *God, You know my coworkers, right?* Or *what about my neighbor and his ever-barking dogs?* But yes, God wants your patience with *everyone*. Ephesians 4:2 (NIV) says, "Be completely humble and gentle; be patient, bearing with one another in love." It sounds so utterly impossible to be patient with all the different types of people in the world. And it really is impossible for you alone. But as God's Word promises, all things are possible with Him (Matthew 19:26).

Second Thessalonians 3:5 (NLT) says, "May the Lord lead your hearts into a full understanding and expression of the love of God and the patient endurance that comes from Christ." Make sure you catch that it "comes from *Christ*." You can't have patient endurance without His help. God doesn't expect it from you in your own sinful human nature. Consistent patience with others is a supernatural phenomenon, truly a miracle from God in your life.

Depend on Him for patience with people He has placed around you, sharing His love with them and offering compassion and a listening ear, and encouragement when needed. Then just watch and see how God works!

WAIT ON GOD'S JUSTICE

*Better is the end of a thing than the beginning
thereof: and the patient in spirit is better than
the proud in spirit. Be not hasty in thy spirit to
be angry: for anger resteth in the bosom of fools.*

ECCLESIASTES 7:8–9 KJV

Are you naturally hot-tempered or more easygoing?
Whatever the case, this world is full of anger-inducing
topics and experiences. Even if you're the most laid-back
person on the planet, there's bound to be something
that eventually pushes all your buttons. This scripture
in Ecclesiastes reminds you not to be quick to anger, as
do many other scriptures. (Check out Proverbs 14:29;
15:18; 16:32; 29:11; James 1:19–20; to name a few.)

For the minor offenses and the major ones, it's
God's job to bring them all to justice, not yours.
Romans 12:17–19 (NIV) says, "Do not repay anyone
evil for evil. . . Do not take revenge, my dear friends,
but leave room for God's wrath, for it is written: 'It is
mine to avenge; I will repay,' says the Lord."

Remember every day that "a person's wisdom yields
patience; it is to one's glory to overlook an offense"
(Proverbs 19:11 NIV). Don't let anger overtake you; rather,
let God's supernatural patience overwhelm you in the
times you're upset.

Day 7

PERSPECTIVE ON PATIENCE

Therefore be patient, brethren, until the coming of
the Lord. The farmer waits for the precious produce
of the soil, being patient about it, until it gets the
early and late rains. You too be patient; strengthen
your hearts, for the coming of the Lord is near.

JAMES 5:7–8 NASB

———— ◆ ————

Jesus _is_ coming, fellow believer! You must keep faith
in that, even when the world gets you so discouraged
and you wonder, _How long, Lord?_

It's essential to remember that God's timing and
His perspective are so much bigger than yours. There's
much more to His plans and purposes than you will
ever be able to know on this side of heaven (Isaiah
55:8–9; 1 Corinthians 13:12–13).

Take some time to read all of 2 Peter 3 and especially
note verses 8–9 (NIV): "But do not forget this one thing,
dear friends: with the Lord a day is like a thousand
years, and a thousand years are like a day. The Lord is
not slow in keeping his promise, as some understand
slowness. Instead he is patient with you, not wanting
anyone to perish, but everyone to come to repentance."

It's hard to wait on Him. (No kidding!) But He is
good. He is patient with you. He wants _everyone_ to
come to repentance. And He goes with you on every
step of your journey through life.

IF YOU HAVE FAITH

*"You can pray for anything,
and if you have faith, you will receive it."*
MATTHEW 21:22 NLT

———— ·◆· ————

When you pray, do your words rise from a foundation of firm faith? Do you *know* that God will hear and answer? Or do you just *hope* He'll answer?

The scriptures are overflowing with heavenly promises—promises that God hears, that He answers, that He provides, that He cares. As your petitions align with your Father's perfect will, you will begin to experience a faith that blooms in heavenly harmony with your trust in His promises. Meditate on these scriptures, and let their truths refresh your spirit:

God hears: "We are confident that he hears us whenever you ask for anything that pleases him" (1 John 5:14 NLT).

God answers: "Ask and it will be given to you; seek and you will find; knock and the door will be opened to you" (Matthew 7:7 NIV).

God provides: "This same God who takes care of me will supply all your needs from his glorious riches" (Philippians 4:19 NLT).

God cares: "Cast all your anxiety on him because he cares for you" (1 Peter 5:7 NIV).

Believe without doubting that you will receive good things from your heavenly Father. You won't be disappointed. He never fails to keep a promise!

Day 2

SECURITY IN TIMES OF TROUBLE

"He shall call upon Me, and I will answer him;
I will be with him in trouble; I will
deliver him and honor him."

PSALM 91:15 NKJV

When you're struggling with a troublesome issue, what kind of feelings do you encounter? It's likely you experience sadness, depression, doubt, anger, loneliness, fear, or anxiety (to name a few), and whether it's just one or a combination of many, you know how difficult it is to overcome those negative feelings.

It may seem near impossible to crawl out of the dark hole you've dug yourself into—until you see the light and you remember God's promise to you and *all* believers: "Have I not commanded you? Be strong and courageous. Do not be afraid; do not be discouraged, for the LORD your God will be with you wherever you go" (Joshua 1:9 NIV).

Cry out to your heavenly Father, the one who listens, the one who hears your every prayer, the one who is always there. He will replace your anxious feelings with peace, hope, joy, and the calm assurance that everything is going to be just fine. It really will be okay, because God works *all things* together *for good* (Romans 8:28).

Praise Him for His unending love and care, for the peaceful assurance He gives His children, today.

REFOCUS!

*Be anxious for nothing, but in everything by prayer
and supplication with thanksgiving let your
requests be made known to God. And the peace of
God, which surpasses all comprehension, will guard
your hearts and your minds in Christ Jesus.*

PHILIPPIANS 4:6–7 NASB

Worry distracts you from God. And when you're distracted from your relationship with Him, it's easy to forget that He alone is in control of everything. Then your mind becomes bogged down with anxious thoughts. You mistakenly begin to believe you must be in control, which only creates additional anxiety—and more insecurity—in your life.

When you become distracted in your faith, it's time to refocus. Whether you're facing a crushing disappointment, a scary diagnosis, or fear of the future, spend time in prayer and reflection. Your quiet conversation with God will redirect your thoughts and your feelings to Him—in whom there is complete security and trust. The result? Your heart and your mind will do an about-face.

As His peace becomes your peace, you'll want to shout from the rooftops that you've experienced the unexplainable goodness and grace of God. You will become a light to others, who will want to experience a worry-free life in Christ as well. "Let your light shine before others, that they may. . .glorify your Father in heaven" (Matthew 5:16 NIV).

Day 4

WHEN YOU CAN'T
FIND THE WORDS

In the same way the Spirit also helps our weakness;
for we do not know how to pray as we should,
but the Spirit Himself intercedes for us
with groanings too deep for words.
ROMANS 8:26 NASB

———————

Have you ever felt a need to pray, a profound longing deep within your soul, yet you couldn't find the words to talk to God? Maybe you have struggled with praying for a friend who has received a daunting health diagnosis.

Or maybe you have personally experienced a difficult life circumstance—financial turmoil, divorce, death of a loved one, job loss—and for some reason, every time you fall to your knees, you feel nothing but utter weakness. You feel incapable of producing any kind of meaningful communication between your heart and your heavenly Father.

When you feel weak, rest in the holy promise of Romans 8:26, knowing that when you don't have the words, you have a heavenly intercessor, the Holy Spirit. And the Spirit knows your heart. As God's Word says: "When my spirit grows faint within me, it is you who watch over my way" (Psalm 142:3 NIV). The Spirit will bring you and God closer together, even in your weakness. When you can't find the words, the Spirit Himself will intercede on your behalf—every single time!

Week 39 ♦ PRAYER – PART 2

CONFIDENT PRAYER

And this is the confidence that we have in him,
that, if we ask any thing according to his will,
he heareth us: and if we know that he hear us,
whatsoever we ask, we know that we have
the petitions that we desired of him.
1 JOHN 5:14–15 KJV

If you're ever thirsting for assurance—to know with 100 percent confidence—that God is attentive to you, His child, repeat aloud this promise from 1 John 5. Let the words sink deep into your soul. Then quiet your heart and send this prayer heavenward:

Father God, do You hear me when I pray? Not just hear, but listen to every word? Sometimes I experience uncertainty, wondering if You will answer my prayers. Help me to know, God, that I can pray confidently. Because I am Yours, Father, You will never fail to hear, to listen, to answer, to care. . .to love. I pray for Your will to be done in my life, today and always. In Jesus' name I pray. Amen.

God desires for your heart to be overflowing with faith, for His Word says, "Without faith it is impossible to please God, because anyone who comes to him must believe that he exists and that he rewards those who earnestly seek him" (Hebrews 11:6 NIV). Believe, and pray confidently today!

Day 6

RESULTS

Confess your sins to each other and pray for each other so that you may be healed. The earnest prayer of a righteous person has great power and produces wonderful results.

JAMES 5:16 NLT

—————•◦•—————

As a Christ follower, you know prayer is important. It's a necessary line of communication between your heart and God's that helps you maintain a growing, thriving relationship with the heavenly Creator. However, it's easy to fall into a routine where you breeze through your prayers. . .never fully thinking about the impact of your words or the powerful potential packed in just one single prayer.

So much good can be accomplished through prayer. The Bible says that the prayers of the righteous produce results—in fact, James 5 calls them "*wonderful* results." Those positive outcomes include:

- a right standing with God (1 John 1:9)
- wisdom (James 1:5)
- a changed life (James 4:2)
- peace beyond all understanding (Philippians 4:6–7)
- increased faith (Matthew 21:21–22)
- less stress (Psalm 55:22)
- forgiveness (James 5:15)
- healing (James 5:16)

If there is power in one single prayer, imagine how much power there is when *many* prayers are being sent heavenward on your or another's behalf!

HE IS NEAR

*The LORD is nigh unto all them that call upon
him, to all that call upon him in truth.*
PSALM 145:18 KJV

———— ◆ ————

Some days God seems so very far away, doesn't He?

When life isn't quite going as planned. . .

When you've reached the end of your rope. . .

When you're convinced that things are never going
to get any better. . .

When you're completely exhausted from trying to
control, well, *everything*. . .

It sometimes feels as though God has made Himself
scarce, and you're on your own—drowning as wave after
wave of despair comes crashing down upon you and
you're left gasping for air.

In trying times, it's tempting to just give up hope.
But in life's difficult moments it's more important than
ever to keep praying. Keep reaching above the waves for
the hand of your heavenly Father, the only one who is
able to rescue you. "Be strong and of a good courage. . .for
the LORD thy God is with thee whithersoever thou goest"
(Joshua 1:9 KJV). "Fear thou not; for I am with thee. . .I will
uphold thee with the right hand of my righteousness"
(Isaiah 41:10 KJV).

Call out to God. And like David, in Psalm 145, feel
His nearness. He is never more than a prayer away.

Day 1

PROOF THAT GOD LOVES YOU

"I correct and discipline everyone I love.
So be diligent and turn from your indifference."
REVELATION 3:19 NLT

———— ◆ ————

You probably wish that God hadn't *made* a promise like this. He assures you, "I correct and discipline everyone I love." You may think this sounds more like a threat than a promise. But it *is* a promise.

If you're like most believers, you long to experience God's love, but your default assumption is that if God feels tender compassion for you, He will manifest it by blessing you with health, abundant financial provision, and joy-filled personal relationships. So when you suffer sickness, lack, and trying times instead, you doubt that God loves you. You feel He must hate you and be angrily judging you for your sins.

But know this: God's discipline in your life is *proof* that He loves you. It's simply a wise, loving Father correcting your errant behavior, pointing out your need to return to Him, and keeping you on a short leash. He cares enough about you to discipline you and bring you closer to Him. It's where you're truly blessed.

This promise might not bring you much comfort at first glance, but when you truly grasp what it's saying, it has the power to give you great strength and reassurance during troubled times.

PAINFUL BEATITUDES

"Blessed is the one whom God corrects;
so do not despise the discipline of the Almighty.
For he wounds, but he also binds up;
he injures, but his hands also heal."
JOB 5:17–18 NIV

On a flower-festooned hillside in Galilee, Jesus preached difficult teachings such as, "Blessed are those who mourn, for they shall be comforted" (Matthew 5:4 NKJV). Two thousand years earlier, in the neighboring land of Uz, one of Job's counselors stated a similar beatitude: "Blessed is the one whom God corrects."

Blessed to mourn? Blessed to be poor? Blessed to be persecuted? Blessed to be corrected by God—often with pain and grief? It surely doesn't *seem* like this is how a loving God would deal with His children, does it? Nevertheless, it's how you frequently experience His presence in your life.

You must be able to see beyond the discomfort and gaze into the Father's heart of love that moves Him to take such corrective measures. Yes, He wounds you—and wounds usually involve pain—but He's often operating to remove the darts and thorns of the enemy. Yes, He temporarily injures, but His motive in doing so is so that His tender hands can bring healing to festering wounds.

Have faith. Don't despise the difficult process God puts you through.

THE PROCESS OF PRUNING

*"My Father is the gardener. He cuts off every branch
in me that bears no fruit, while every branch
that does bear fruit he prunes so that
it will be even more fruitful."*

JOHN 15:1–2 NIV

In the parable of the vine, Jesus described the process
of pruning. Pruning is quite a bit more involved than
simply lopping off an entire branch. Pruning involves
selectively cutting useless, dead wood, leaving the
productive, fruitful parts of the branch. If a branch
could feel pain, it would experience a great deal of it
when pruned.

Unlike a branch, you *do* feel pain, anguish, and grief
as God cuts dead wood from your life. He demands you
surrender sinful habits and unproductive activities and
pastimes to Him. You're often passionate about them,
and they consume much of your time and energy, but
they bear no fruit for eternity. So God determines to
snip them off—while you often fight to spare them
from His shears.

God accomplishes most of His pruning in your
life by discipline and scourging. He frustrates your
wayward plans and brings your errant dreams to
nothing. He often forcibly removes things from your
tightly clutching fingers. You wonder why God isn't
giving you the desires of *your* heart? He has a higher
good in mind.

A FATHER'S DISCIPLINE

*Know then in your heart that as a man disciplines
his son, so the LORD your God disciplines you.*

DEUTERONOMY 8:5 NIV

Sometimes when you're undergoing God's discipline,
you mistakenly think that He's angry with you, judging
you, and about to thrust you out of His kingdom. How
quickly you forget that you're a born-again child of God
whom He has promised to never abandon or cast out
(John 6:37; Hebrews 13:5).

The heat of God's rebukes can be intense. "When
with rebukes You correct man for iniquity, You make
his beauty melt away like a moth" (Psalm 39:11 NKJV).
But He's rebuking you *because* you're His child. It
doesn't mean that He's done with you. It's proof that
He's dedicated to you and loves you—in fact, that He
delights in you. "For whom the LORD loves He corrects,
just as a father the son in whom he delights" (Proverbs
3:12 NKJV).

You may know this fact but easily forget it. That's
why the Bible tells you to know it *in your heart*.

It pays to meditate on the depth of love that God
has for even His wayward children. Remember the
prodigal son, and how the father longed for him and
welcomed him back. He had never ceased to be a son
of the father.

BLESSED BUT HARD DISCIPLINE

Blessed is the man whom You chasten, O Lord,
and whom You teach out of Your law; that You
may grant him relief from the days of adversity.

PSALM 94:12–13 NASB

God often sends you "days of adversity" which last for
months. Why does He allow unpleasant circumstances
to come into your life and go on and on? Because that's
often what it takes to teach you deep lessons. When
you've learned what He wants to teach you, He turns
off the heat and grants you relief.

"We give great honor to those who endure under
suffering. For instance, you know about Job, a man of
great endurance. You can see how the Lord was kind to
him at the end, for the Lord is full of tenderness and
mercy" (James 5:11 NLT). God allowed Job to experience
intense suffering but afterward gave him relief and
turned his situation around.

The Lord teaches you from His Word during
chastening, reminding you of passages that relate to
what you're going through. These are the lessons you
desperately need to grasp, and you're blessed if God
puts you through this difficult school. You probably
don't *feel* blessed when you're in the middle of being
chastised, but that's the end result, just the same.

NECESSARY DISCIPLINE

No discipline is enjoyable while it is happening—
it's painful! But afterward there will be a
peaceful harvest of right living for
those who are trained in this way.
HEBREWS 12:11 NLT

There's a beautiful worship song, popular some years ago, called "Refiner's Fire," which states the audience's desire to be made holy, purified, and drawn near to God. It's not sung too much these days, not because it went out of style, but because when it dawned on people that they were praying for God to put them through the *fire*, they hesitated to sing it.

If you ask God to purify and chastise you, He will do exactly that. It will make you a better person, but the process can be quite painful. It's worth it though. You might not care to repeat the experience, but if you're honest, you're thankful for when you went through such things. You learned lessons you wouldn't have learned otherwise.

This verse talks about "those who are trained in this way." The Bible even says of Jesus, "Though he were a Son, yet learned he obedience by the things which he suffered" (Hebrews 5:8 KJV). If Jesus Himself learned deep lessons of obedience through suffering, you should expect God to work the same way in your life.

Day 7

SEVERE CHASTENING

The LORD has chastened me severely,
but he has not given me over to death.
PSALM 118:18 NIV

———— ◆ ————

This is a promise you may have occasion to quote at some point in your life. You almost hope not, but there are times when God leads you through deep, dark valleys and you feel like you're almost dying. At times like these, cast yourself upon the mercy of God. When David realized that he had seriously sinned, he prayed, "O LORD, do not rebuke me in Your anger, nor chasten me in Your hot displeasure" (Psalm 6:1 NKJV).

Sometimes you, too, will need to be chastised, and it won't be something you can avoid. God knows when discipline is necessary, but He does it in mercy and with great restraint. . .even though you're "sick almost unto death" (Philippians 2:27 NKJV). God told His people, "I will correct you in justice, and will not let you go altogether unpunished" (Jeremiah 30:11 NKJV).

God doesn't want to take you home before your time, but wants you to live a full life. Learn your lesson quickly so that He can bring the chastening to an end. Ask God to search your heart, convict you of sin, and lead you to repentance.

Even the deepest, darkest experiences have bright sides.

UNDERSTANDING THE LORD'S WILL

Therefore do not be foolish,
but understand what the Lord's will is.
EPHESIANS 5:17 NIV

In a report about television and health, California State University cites these statistics: "According to the A.C. Nielsen Co., the average American watches more than 4 hours of TV each day (or 28 hours/week, or 2 months of nonstop TV-watching per year). In a 65-year life, that person will have spent 9 years glued to the tube."

Meanwhile, *Christianity Today* cited a study by the Evangelical Alliance recently that said: "The average length of time [for evangelicals] spent studying the Bible was between 10 and 20 minutes per session, and over half (57 per cent) said they spent time reflecting on what preachers or speakers have said."

Don't draw the wrong conclusions here, though. TV isn't necessarily foolish. It can be educational and even spiritually edifying, depending on the program. But much of what is available probably *does* indeed fall into the foolish category, doesn't it? And watching television is often a passive activity.

Understanding the Lord and His will, on the other hand, only happens when you're actively seeking Him, much like knowing your spouse only occurs when you spend time in conversation with him or her. What are you doing today to go deeper with God to understand His will?

GLORY IN UNDERSTANDING

*But let him that glorieth glory in this, that he
understandeth and knoweth me, that I am the
LORD which exercise lovingkindness, judgment,
and righteousness, in the earth: for in these
things I delight, saith the LORD.*
JEREMIAH 9:24 KJV

For too long, God's people boasted (gloried) in their
wisdom, their might, or their riches (v. 23)—all of which
are indicators that they had more faith in their own
abilities than they did in Him. In today's verse, the Lord
says that if people "boast"—that is, publicly and firmly
claim ability in some area—they should do so in their
right understanding of Him and the way He exercises
lovingkindness, judgment, and righteousness on earth.

"To glory in a thing is to depend on it as the means
or cause of procuring happiness," wrote Adam Clarke
in his commentary. "But there can be no happiness
but in being experimentally acquainted with that
God who exercises loving-kindness, judgment, and
righteousness in the earth."

To be able to "boast" that you truly know God, you
will first have to go through the fires of testing, walk
through dark valleys of "the shadow of death," and
battle through raging floodwaters that seek to drown
you. You will then walk closely in God's presence. That
is something truly worth boasting about.

HIDING FROM JUDGMENT

A prudent man foreseeth the evil, and hideth himself: but the simple pass on, and are punished.
PROVERBS 22:3 KJV

A careful believer can see sin on his horizon and he changes course, even going so far as to hide for a season, when necessary. It is far better to flee and hide than to face judgment for engaging in the evil of sin.

You'll find many evidences of this in scripture, from Noah, to Joseph, to Abraham and Lot, to God telling His people to flee Babylon because He was about to send a destroying wind (Jeremiah 51:1–6), to the church in Corinth whose members were engaged in sexual immorality (1 Corinthians 6:18).

In so doing, none of these people necessarily experienced physical protection, although there certainly was an element of protection on them as they fled. Instead, they were saving themselves from the judgment that was due to those who continue in sin. Only the wise take such action.

What are you doing to hide yourself from judgment while still engaging the culture around you? Knowing when to do what can be difficult to discern. If you need help, seek out a mature Christian to aid you in working through your circumstances. And take what he or she says to heart.

Day 4

BECOMING PRUDENT

*The simple believe anything, but the
prudent give thought to their steps.*
PROVERBS 14:15 NIV

————•◆•————

When people refer to someone today as a "simple man,"
they mean someone who has simple tastes and a clear
focus in his life. He doesn't need riches or fame. He only
needs dreams, love, and a strong work ethic. That's *not*
what the writer of today's verse meant.

The Hebrew word for "simple" means: silly, seducible,
foolish. On the periphery, a simple man in this context
is one who believes in wild conspiracy theories because
they appeal to his fears or worldview. But anyone can
fall for a falsehood if he isn't prudent. Being prudent
includes having good judgment. Having good judgment
includes a willingness to investigate, question, and
search out the truth.

As it relates to matters of faith, a prudent man
listens to others intently but then sets out to examine
the scriptures for himself. He asks himself whether this
doctrine is consistent with the totality of scripture,
whether it is shallow or strange, whether it appeals
to the spirit or the flesh, and whether it glorifies man
or God.

How are you doing in this area? How are you
showing prudence for the doctrines you believe? Can
you defend your beliefs from scripture? If so, you're
on the right track.

STRENGTHEN THY BRETHREN

*I will instruct thee and teach thee in the way which
thou shalt go: I will guide thee with mine eye.*
PSALM 32:8 KJV

When a sinner becomes penitent, the next step is
often for him or her to teach other sinners to walk
in the way of the Lord. Psalm 32 describes this very
scenario for David. His bones grew old (v. 3) because
of his unconfessed sin. God's hand was heavy on him
(v. 4). But when he acknowledged his sin, he found
forgiveness (v. 5) and God became his hiding place (v. 7).

But David didn't stop there. In verse 8, he promised
to teach others in the way they should go, much like
he promised to do in Psalm 51:13 after repenting of
sin. Solomon did the same thing, referring to himself
as a preacher in Ecclesiastes 1:1. Jesus instructed
Peter likewise, saying: "And when thou art converted,
strengthen thy brethren" (Luke 22:32 KJV).

Who has been your teacher in your faith walk?
If you haven't found one, seek someone out. Who
have you mentored in the faith? In both cases, the
relationship doesn't have to be a formal one. The key
is to either receive or convey godly wisdom that is
rooted in a repentant heart.

STAYING WISE

But everyone knows that you are obedient to the Lord. This makes me very happy. I want you to be wise in doing right and to stay innocent of any wrong.
ROMANS 16:19 NLT

In this day and age, individual churches are sometimes known more for pastors who have fallen or for ugly splits than for their obedience to the Lord—especially in the opinion of a watching world. The same could be said even among the brethren. How many churches can you name in your local area that have a reputation in which "everyone" knows about their obedience to the Lord?

And yet, the church in Rome had this reputation. As important as this was, Paul didn't want them to rest on their reputation. He wanted them to watch out for people who caused divisions—especially those who taught doctrine that was contrary to what they had originally been taught (vv. 17–18). They needed to stay wise in doing right, and one of the ways they were to do so was to stay true to orthodox teaching.

Can this be said about your faith tradition or the church where you're a member? Are you, as a member of that church, submitting yourself to quality teaching and then passing it along to others?

THE FOUNTAIN OF LIFE

The law of the wise is a fountain of life, to turn one away from the snares of death. Good understanding gains favor, but the way of the unfaithful is hard.

PROVERBS 13:14–15 NKJV

The law of the wise (biblical truth) is a fountain of life, bringing renewal, much like water revives a dying plant. One Bible commentator, Dr. John Gill, says doctrinal truth is a means for quickening dead sinners and of refreshing the souls of weary saints.

You've experienced such refreshing in your own life—first at your conversion and multiple times afterward as the Word spoke to your soul. The wise person is never far from biblical truth. He or she drinks of it daily, speaks of it among friends, and meditates on it during good times and bad. When the storms come, these wise people are firmly rooted and unbending. Yes, the winds blow and often cause damage, but the wise spiritually prosper anyway. To travel any other path is far more difficult, especially if the believer has to journey alone.

Would the Christians in your life consider you wise based on what they see and hear from you? Do they hear you citing biblical promises during the storms of your life? Do they find comfort when you offer such promises during their storms?

THE LAW OF KIND WORDS

She opens her mouth with wisdom,
and on her tongue is the law of kindness.
PROVERBS 31:26 NKJV

———◆———

One of the most prominent and important ways you show kindness is by your speech. Words carry power. They can harm or heal, help or hurt; indeed, "the tongue can bring death or life" (Proverbs 18:21 NLT). If you want to live a godly life, taming your tongue is one of your top priorities. As Jesus noted, "By your words you will be acquitted, and by your words you will be condemned" (Matthew 12:37 NIV). The kindness of your speech may be the difference for others, too—particularly unbelievers—in whether or not they see Christ in you.

Some people are naturally kind. For perhaps up to half of the people you encounter, being courteous, respectful, and gentle in their speech and manner is wired into them to some degree. But for the other half of the population, kindness requires discipline. This is where the "law of kindness" comes in. The best way to acquaint yourself with its precepts is to look in God's Word.

David hit on a key concept: "May these words of my mouth and the meditation of my heart be pleasing in your sight, LORD" (Psalm 19:14 NIV). When you internalize God's Word, kindness will govern your tongue.

Day 2

THE KINDNESS OF FORGIVENESS

*Be kind to one another, tenderhearted, forgiving one
another, even as God in Christ forgave you.*
EPHESIANS 4:32 NKJV

Forgiveness is one of mankind's greatest needs. When you recognize that you've wronged someone, the desire to make things right burns within you. However, when you ask someone to forgive you, you give them the power. The ball is now in their court and you can do nothing until they return your volley—if they choose to. It's nerve-racking but oh-so-necessary.

It's different than telling someone you're sorry; *I'm sorry* just means you regret that it happened, but it's not a full acknowledgment that you're responsible for hurting that person. But if that person grants your request to be forgiven, that load is lifted. You can then begin to do what you must to make things right, to restore that relationship.

God's very heart is forgiveness, because He loves you and wants to have a close relationship with you. God is patient and long-suffering and wants to shower you with blessings. His kindness is one of a kind, and until you embrace your desperate need to be forgiven, you can't fully experience it. But once you have, your life changes, and forgiveness gradually becomes a habit—an extension of the great kindness God gave you.

FRIENDLY FILTERS

Do not forget to show hospitality to strangers,
for by so doing some people have shown
hospitality to angels without knowing it.

HEBREWS 13:2 NIV

———— ·◆· ————

It's mildly amusing to think of serving angels dinner: "You guys eat, right? How about some more angel-hair pasta? And you'll never guess what we've got for dessert!" The idea is that you would do a better job of hosting angels than you would someone you've never met, whom you might or might not like. However, even though angels are on a higher plane of existence than you are, they are not the pinnacle of God's creation—people are.

It's hard to think of that woman with the cardboard sign that you gave a bottle of water and five bucks to this morning as the pinnacle of anything, or your unemployed brother-in-law who sleeps on your couch and eats all your leftovers, for that matter. But that's because you're still learning to see them through God's lens.

God uses some pretty serious filters looking at you; the best ones show you washed white by Christ's blood. He sees all people as potential royalty—sons and daughters of the kingdom—and that's how He wants you to see them, too. The promise of salvation is often kept because of a believer's kindness to strangers.

LOVE ONE ANOTHER

We must not just please ourselves.
We should help others do what is right
and build them up in the Lord.
ROMANS 15:1–2 NLT

There's no one like a fellow Christian to drive you completely nuts. It's funny how people labor under the assumption that a bunch of former sinners struggling daily with the battle of the flesh are supposed to have it together all the time. When they don't, it feels even worse than if an unbeliever had done the exact same thing. *"I'd expect that from a pagan—they don't know any better! But you, brother, are supposed to be the spitting image of Christ at all times!"* It's an unrealistic expectation.

Aside from the obvious need to extend forgiveness and grace, we need to recognize that different believers are at different points in their walk with Christ, with differing levels of spiritual maturity. Jesus told you to love one another (John 13:34), so that everyone would know that you are His. Quick, harsh, cynical judgment inside the church is unattractive to those outside. They can get that anywhere.

But if they see you building others up, gently correcting mistakes, offering support through hardships, patiently praying with and for others, and even enjoying others' company, that's going to look different, both inside the body of Christ and out.

MINISTERS OF EMPATHY

*He can have compassion on those who are
ignorant and going astray, since he himself
is also subject to weakness.*

HEBREWS 5:2 NKJV

In ancient Israel, the high priest was, ideally, an empathetic mediator between God and men. Now, however, because of the work of Jesus Christ, your Great High Priest, you no longer need that intermediary. You as a believer have been made a priest also (1 Peter 2:9), chosen by God to pray for others and to represent Christ to those who don't know Him.

One of the most important ways you can do that is by being kind. It was God's kindness, after all, that led you to repentance (Romans 2:4)—His desire to show you that He grasped your struggles and wanted to help—and *could* help because Jesus was fully man and fully God.

In Christ's example, you see that great, life-changing kindness can come from understanding what it is to be tempted, to struggle, and to almost not make it, but it's not automatic. In fact, people often criticize most harshly those whose sins are most like their own. The scope of your ministry is different: when someone stumbles, you should "gently and humbly help that person back onto the right path. And be careful not to fall into the same temptation yourself" (Galatians 6:1 NLT). Forgiven sinners should be forgiving.

DEEP-HEARTED DECENCY

Never let loyalty and kindness leave you!
Tie them around your neck as a reminder.
Write them deep within your heart.

PROVERBS 3:3 NLT

———•———

Following ancient biblical tradition, observant Jewish men wear small boxes filled with Bible verses, called *tefillin*, strapped to their forehead and hand as they pray. The idea is that they keep God's Word on their minds and obey it in their deeds (Deuteronomy 11:18).

Of course, without internalizing such concepts, you run the risk of a superficial brand of service to Christ—the appearance of kindness without any deep concern for someone's spiritual health. But before you can truly invest in someone else's welfare, you have to spend time writing God's love deep within your own heart. Jesus said, "The mouth speaks what the heart is full of" (Luke 6:45 NIV). If God's words are in your heart, they will come out in your speech—discerning, life-giving, useful words "fitly spoken. . .like apples of gold in settings of silver" (Proverbs 25:11 NKJV).

Use sticky notes to post favorite verses around the house, where they can easily be seen. God wants to write His Word on your heart, and He will if you let Him. If you begin with loyalty and kindness, you'll be off to a good start, able to get along with both men and God.

Day 7

CHANGE THE GAME

*"Love your enemies, and do good, and lend,
expecting nothing in return; and your reward will
be great, and you will be sons of the Most High;
for He Himself is kind to ungrateful and evil men."*

LUKE 6:35 NASB

———•◆•———

True kindness often comes with a cost—there's nothing simple or easy about loving your enemy or being decent to someone who has treated you badly. But that's what Jesus has called you to do. Talk about a tough task! Even if you aren't vengeful by nature, you wouldn't naturally want to have anything to do with someone who had stolen from you or lied about you.

But remember: Even if you're the world's biggest sweetheart, you still need God's forgiveness. When Jesus said that God is kind to ungrateful, wicked people, He wasn't just talking about thieves and murderers; He meant everyone. Everyone needs forgiveness; everyone needs salvation.

Some of the greatest impacts you could ever have for God's glory could be in the way you treat those who have wronged you. That's how you show the difference Jesus has made in your life. When you love someone unlovable or give to someone who is insolvent, you're showing the kind of mercy God showed at the cross—and that's a game changer.

Week 35 ◆ KINDNESS

HONEST AND TRUE

And in their mouth was found no deceit, for they are without fault before the throne of God.

REVELATION 14:5 NKJV

———— •◆• ————

No deceit. Ponder those words for a moment. Have you ever known a human being incapable of deceit? Even the finest person occasionally fails. It's tough to be honest 100 percent of the time.

Don't think so? What do you say when your best friend asks your opinion of her new (over-the-top/crazy) hairdo? If you're like most, you fumble around for something kind (but wholly untrue) to say.

There's a fine line between kindness and sincerity, isn't there? Somehow, you have to find that place. God calls you to be sincere, which means you're called to honesty. That means you have to "speak the truth in love" (Ephesians 4:15 NLT). It's never easy, but honesty is always the best policy.

What does this have to do with your spiritual walk? God has called you to be genuine. You're a representation of Him, after all. When you walk in sincerity (free from hypocrisy), then you're the witness He has called you to be. Today, take some time to ask the Lord to shine His spotlight on areas of your heart that might be deceitful. Time to clean out those cobwebs!

SINCERITY ◆ Week 36

Day 2

A HOLY LONGING

*Like newborn babies, long for the pure milk
of the word, so that by it you may grow
in respect to salvation.*

1 PETER 2:2 NASB

———◆———

You've likely heard the expression "Fake it till you make it." Many times this flies in the face of what God expects from you. There's no "faking it" in His plan. He longs for your actions to be rooted in sincerity and honesty. He wants your trust in Him to be real, deep, and abiding.

Where does this type of sincerity come from? It begins with a genuine holy longing for the Lord. If you're going through the motions of reading your Bible and praying, if sincerity isn't the driving force, then you need to re-examine your core beliefs.

Have you made Jesus the Lord of your life? Does He sit on the throne of your heart? If not, then make things right today. When you come to Him with a sincere heart, genuinely longing for His presence, His touch, His Word, He's free to act on your behalf. His promises become more than possibilities; they are yours for the taking.

So, begin again. Like a babe, let your pure longing for the Lord drive you into His arms for a heart transformation you'll never forget.

Day 3

FROM THE HEART

*For we are not, as so many, peddling the word
of God; but as of sincerity, but as from God,
we speak in the sight of God in Christ.*
2 CORINTHIANS 2:17 NKJV

———— ◆ ————

Likely you've come in contact with a con man or two
over the years. These frauds often peddle religion in an
attempt to snag your money. They have a clever scheme,
one rooted in evil, but they spend most of their time
pulling the wool over people's eyes. There's nothing
sincere about them. Their acting skills are stellar, well
rehearsed, but time usually gives them away.

Contrast these not-to-be-trusted folks with a believer
who would give his life for those he loves. He's the real
deal, one who genuinely cares about others. That's what
God is looking for. Either you're truly in—100 percent
committed to the Lord and His call on your life—or
you're not. God sees the heart and knows when you're
not being genuine.

Today, take a little time to examine your *real deal*
level. Are you putting on a show, hoping to convince
others that you've got it all together? If so, draw near to
God and do business with Him so that He can purify
your heart and set you on a path of sincerity.

Day 4

CHILDREN OF THE DAY

But let us, who are of the day, be sober,
putting on the breastplate of faith and love;
and for an helmet, the hope of salvation.

1 THESSALONIANS 5:8 KJV

———————— •◆• ————————

Remember that old saying "Nothing good happens after midnight"? While that may not be completely accurate, there is a nugget of truth at the core of the expression. Under the covering of darkness, in the depth of the shadows, bad things can be hidden away, out of view. The enemy gets away with his schemes in the dark. Thieves don't usually sneak into your home at noon, after all. They wait until midnight and slip in beneath the shadows.

Good things happen in the light—at least that's the perception. God has called you to be a child of the light (the day). Everything is out in the open. You're not hiding secrets. You're not covering up sin. You're an open book, one who is willing to deal with heart issues in a sincere way. How does a child of the day live? Honestly. Legitimately.

Take the time to analyze your faith walk today. Is anything hiding in the shadows? If so, let God sweep it away.

Day 5

A CLEAR CONSCIENCE

*We can say with confidence and a clear conscience
that we have lived with a God-given holiness and
sincerity in all our dealings. We have depended
on God's grace, not on our own human wisdom.
That is how we have conducted ourselves before
the world, and especially toward you.*

2 CORINTHIANS 1:12 NLT

Remember that feeling you would get as a child whenever you'd done something naughty? You couldn't control the feelings of guilt and shame. They swept over you. God created you to live in holiness and sincerity. It's in your spiritual DNA.

That's why conviction sweeps over you whenever you slip into illegitimate living. The Lord wants your life to be free from care, filled with His promises. A seared conscience isn't part of His plan. He wants your life to be peaceful and filled with joy. The path to such a life is rooted in complete truth. Where do you find truth? In relationship with your heavenly Father.

Sure, you can fool some of the people some of the time, but if you want true peace (freedom from guilt and shame), you have to *be* the person you *say* you are. Your conscience will be completely clear when you're living out your faith day by day, placing your sins at the feet of Jesus.

Day 6

A BLAMELESS LIFE

*For I want you to understand what really matters,
so that you may live pure and blameless
lives until the day of Christ's return.*
PHILIPPIANS 1:10 NLT

If someone asked you to make a top ten list of the things that really mattered in your life, what would you write down? Your family? Your friends? Your job? Your church? Your talents? Your material possessions?

It's good to take inventory of the things that matter the most so that you can check your heart's motivations to make sure they're pure and blameless. (Sometimes you do the right things, but for the wrong reasons.) God wants you to understand what really, truly matters. Sure, He's concerned about your job, your relationships, and your possessions, but He's mostly interested in making sure you're motivated to live for Him and to share His love with others.

Take that job, for instance. God wants you to work hard, but not just to bring home a paycheck. He longs for you to share His love with your coworkers. Take another look at today's scripture. There's a promise buried within its words. If you understand what really matters, then you can live a pure and blameless life. Understanding what matters is key to seeing that amazing promise fulfilled.

GOD PLEASERS

For our exhortation was not of deceit, nor of uncleanness, nor in guile: but as we were allowed of God to be put in trust with the gospel, even so we speak; not as pleasing men, but God, which trieth our hearts. For neither at any time used we flattering words, as ye know, nor a cloke of covetousness; God is witness.

1 Thessalonians 2:3–5 kjv

You've tried so hard not to be a people pleaser. In fact, you've gone out of your way to make sure your motivations are pure. But here you are, struggling once again. You're tempted to do something, or say something, because you're feeling intimidated. You could kick yourself for feeling this way. You're guarded, fearful. If only you had the courage to speak God's words in the situation instead of stumbling your way through.

It's time to take inventory, friend. Make a list of people in your life who bring out the people pleaser in you. Give those names to the Lord. Ask for His help. He will show you how to redirect your focus so that your aim is to please Him, not them.

Sure, you want people to like you. That's important. But at what cost? Put God in His rightful place and watch those relationships shift in a new, holy season.

WHAT DO YOU NEED?

*And my God shall supply all your need according
to His riches in glory by Christ Jesus.*
PHILIPPIANS 4:19 NKJV

———— •◆• ————

What do you need? It's an important question. Some
things on your list will be *needs* and some are *wants*.
One can often be mistaken for the other, but you may
assume that God should take care of both.

You may *need* a car, but may *want* a specific
manufacture, model, and options package. You *need*
food, but may *want* a specific type. You *need* water,
but may *want* a brand that comes from exotic springs
flowing from ancient mountains.

If God doesn't seem to be supplying your needs, it's
time to determine what your needs actually are. If you
need food and water, God can supply the need, but it
may not be the brand or type you want. That doesn't
mean God didn't supply. It might mean that what He
supplied didn't match your want, even though it fully
met your need.

Do you struggle with this? Everyone does. You
could be convinced that when you pray God has to
answer your prayers with a "yes" response. But more
than anyone, God knows what you need. He knows
better than you do. Giving you something you don't
need fails to truly meet your need.

THE 20/20 BENEFIT

Once I was young, and now I am old.
Yet I have never seen the godly abandoned
or their children begging for bread.
PSALM 37:25 NLT

It's been said hindsight is 20/20. When you look back, you have a clearer picture of what was true and what was false. You have greater insight, understanding, and wisdom.

The psalmist speaks from the perspective of one who's been there, done that. He makes two conclusions, powerful in their implications: (1) the godly have never been abandoned; (2) the children of the godly have never had to beg for bread.

These are the observations of a psalmist. The two lessons are from his experience over many years. The overarching conclusion is that *God provides.* He takes care of His family. His love is demonstrated repeatedly as He continues to meet your needs.

When you draw close to God, you begin to learn His will (those things He wants you to do). You can be confident that when God gives you a task He also gives everything you need to complete the task. He doesn't ask you to do something without also making it possible to do what He asks.

He will supply your needs. He does have a plan. This is the part where you walk by faith.

Week 37

♦

GOD'S PROVISION

BE GOD RICH

*Charge them that are rich in this world,
that they be not highminded, nor trust in
uncertain riches, but in the living God,
who giveth us richly all things to enjoy.*

1 TIMOTHY 6:17 KJV

If God gives you everything you need but not everything you want, how could you possibly be considered rich? Doesn't most of what you want *cost* something? Wouldn't it make more sense to have *more* if you're to be considered rich?

Just as there's a difference in the mind of God between a need and a want, there's also a difference between rich and poor. Today's verse points out that those who are rich according to society's standards may place their trust in what they own and not in the God who provided everything.

No one could ever own more than God. No one but God could provide the majesty of a lightning storm in summer, the rush of a waterfall, the splendor of a canyon. These are riches you can enjoy due to God's generosity. But it doesn't end there. You might enjoy conversation with an aging relative, the laughter of a baby, or late-night conversations with your spouse. These, too, are incredible riches.

Do you trust in money or the God who gives blessings money could never buy?

Day 4

GOD KNOWS—NO WORRIES

*"Your heavenly Father knows that you need all
these things. But seek first His kingdom and
His righteousness, and all these things
will be added to you."*
MATTHEW 6:32–33 NASB

For Christians, worry can be described as a lack of faith.
The verses that come right before today's passage talk
about birds, flowers, and grass. They're all taken care of
by God and are perfect examples demonstrating that
He can be trusted to provide.

You worry about so many things and act as if
worrying is the only logical answer to controlling
whatever it is you worry about. God says worry can't
add time to your life, and science says it may actually
decrease your life span. God says life is more than what
you wear and what you eat. While you throw out the
leftovers and drop off last year's fashions to the second-
hand shop, you should remember that God provided
what you're getting rid of while you worry about what
you *don't* have.

Because God knows what you need, He asks you
to seek Him first, above everything else. He puts His
spotlight on relationship. If you seek Him above the
worry, hoarding, and gathering, He will be free to take
care of all the things you've tried to take care of alone.

WHAT YOU SEEK

The lions may grow weak and hungry,
but those who seek the LORD lack no good thing.
PSALM 34:10 NIV

————•◆•————

God doesn't have to borrow from the bank, ask you to wait until He gets paid, or sell some of His creation to take care of your need. He is lavish, needs no additional help, and only asks you to wait if it's in your best interest to wait.

The psalmist in this verse describes hungry lions. He's pointing out that lions who are predatory by nature can't always provide for themselves if there's no prey to be found. On the other hand, you get to go straight to the source of need fulfillment—God.

If your thinking can be transformed, you can begin to see that in God's economy money is only a tool and His blessings often don't arrive in the form of cash.

He promises that if you seek Him you will lack *no good thing.* Is it possible the lions in this verse describe those who only rely on their personal strength, wisdom, and skill? Is it possible that the psalmist is saying actions that don't include dependence on God lead to spiritual hunger and weakness? If that's true, how should this change what you seek?

CONTENT AND SATISFIED

Keep your lives free from the love of money and be content with what you have, because God has said, "Never will I leave you; never will I forsake you."

HEBREWS 13:5 NIV

God's provision works in cooperative partnership with your personal contentment. When you love money more than God, you will *not* experience contentment and you *will* rely on yourself more than God.

It's ironic that when you're discontent you'll choose money over God's provision. You want what you don't have and sidestep God in an effort to crave more, get more, and take more. When you're chained to money, you'll be dissatisfied in your bondage.

Contentment believes that when God promised He would never leave or forsake you, He meant it. You can be satisfied in knowing that God's gifts can't be bought, earned, sold, or transferred. You could offer God every dollar the world has ever known and it wouldn't be enough to buy a single gift from His hands. He would be offended if you tried to buy what He offers at no cost. His gifts are free, and His currency of choice has never been money.

If you can think of God's provision in terms of something *more* than money, you'll take enormous strides toward a contentment that's designed to satisfy.

Day 7

THE SHEPHERD PROVIDES

*The LORD is my shepherd, I shall not want.
He makes me lie down in green pastures;
He leads me beside quiet waters. He restores
my soul; He guides me in the paths of
righteousness for His name's sake.*

PSALM 23:1–3 NASB

———◆———

Sheep often wander from their shepherd. One particular sheep was of a variety known for rich and thick wool. This sheep avoided capture many times over several years. He faced a self-imposed death sentence because his wool then grew so thick it created numerous health challenges that couldn't be overcome on their own. And the sheep couldn't shave himself. The shepherd ordered a drastic measure to save it. Once sheared, the sheep's health improved and, if he stays with the shepherd, he'll live happily ever after.

God compares believers to sheep and calls Himself the Shepherd. They're given the benefits of His leadership. He prepares the way, gives them confidence when facing opposition, and refreshes their innermost being. Oh, there's one more benefit—*they lack nothing.*

God takes care of His people's needs in the same way a shepherd cares for his sheep. He understands the fear in their hearts, questions in their minds, and pressing needs of each moment. That's where He meets them—and it's just where they need to be met.

Day 1

ABOUNDING IN FAITHFULNESS

*The LORD passed in front of Moses, calling out,
"Yahweh! The LORD! The God of compassion
and mercy! I am slow to anger and filled
with unfailing love and faithfulness."*

EXODUS 34:6 NLT

———— ◆ ————

As the Lord passed before Moses, He introduced Himself in a way that revealed His very nature. This is such a beautiful declaration that it bears a closer look. The Lord said that He was "the God of compassion and mercy" and "slow to anger." These are very attractive attributes, because humans make frequent mistakes and require compassion, mercy, and patience.

The Lord is also "filled with unfailing love and faithfulness." Think of it: God is filled to overflowing with love. It colors and drives everything He thinks, says, and does. That's why 1 John 4:8 (KJV) says, "God *is* love" (emphasis added). And He's also filled with faithfulness; He's the very essence of dependability and trustworthiness.

Do you sometimes question whether God actually is utterly loving in His attitude toward you? Do you wonder if you can always depend on God or whether He will zone out during your times of trouble? Not a chance. He's watching over you constantly and has your back.

Even when it *seems* as if God has failed, a deeper gaze into His eternal purposes will reveal that He never stopped loving you.

Day 2

GOD IS UTTERLY FAITHFUL

Let us hold fast the confession of our hope without
wavering, for He who promised is faithful.
HEBREWS 10:23 NASB

———— ·◆· ————

This is one of the most powerful, beautiful promises in
the Bible. In it, the unknown writer of Hebrews urges
you to tightly grasp your Christian faith and refuse to
let go, to cling to it without doubting or becoming
anxious. The reason he can so confidently tell you to
do this is because "He who promised is faithful." God,
who made so many promises, can be counted on to
do what He has said.

For example, God promised, "Whosoever shall call
upon the name of the Lord shall be saved" (Romans
10:13 KJV), and since He's utterly faithful to stick to
what He has sworn He would do, God will be certain
to save you if you have sincerely cried out to Him.

In the same way, God will be sure to look after
your financial needs. Philippians 4:19 (NKJV) promises
that "God shall supply all your need according to His
riches in glory." And in Philippians 4:13 (NKJV), the
Bible states, "I can do all things through Christ who
strengthens me."

These are all promises that you can confidently
lay hold of and claim that the Lord will fulfill. Why?
Because He's faithful, unchanging, and constant.

Day 3

GOD CAN NOT—DOES NOT—LIE

God is faithful, through whom you were called into fellowship with His Son, Jesus Christ our Lord.

1 CORINTHIANS 1:9 NASB

This verse opens with the profound statement: "God is faithful." According to the dictionary, to be "faithful" is to be loyal, constant, steadfast, and unswerving. If there was any room for doubt, if God were capricious, you'd never be certain if you had firm footing to stand on. But God is the solid Rock that you can confidently base your life upon.

"God is faithful," and because He has called you into a spiritual relationship with His Son, Jesus, you can count on the fact that He will perfect the work He has begun in you and safely bring you into His heavenly kingdom. He "will also confirm you to the end, blameless" (v. 8 NASB).

Paul spoke "in the hope of eternal life, which God, who cannot lie, promised long ages ago" (Titus 1:2 NASB). The devil, who is the ultimate deceiver, often likes to try to get you to doubt that God is faithful. But remember, Satan "is a liar and the father of lies" (John 8:44 NASB), whereas "God. . .cannot lie."

God is not constantly changing His mind. He won't mislead you or pull the rug out from under your feet. Trust Him.

GOD WILL MAKE IT GOOD

*"God is not a man, that He should lie, nor a son
of man, that He should repent. Has He said,
and will He not do? Or has He spoken,
and will He not make it good?"*
NUMBERS 23:19 NKJV

———— • ◆ • ————

Men often *intend* to do good, but fall short. They lie, recant on good intentions, back out of commitments, and change their minds. They say they'll do something, but in the end often wind up *not* doing it. They make promises, but frequently fail to follow through on them.

The expression "make it good" means to fulfill a promise. It's not heard too much these days, but it has a clear, unchanging meaning. Once God says He'll do something, He follows through on His promise. That's because He's faithful. He doesn't have second thoughts or suddenly come across new information that forces Him to change His mind. God is all-knowing, and nothing surprises Him.

If God has *said* He will do something, He will *do* it. Of course, you have to be certain that He was actually saying what you thought He was, otherwise you're setting yourself up for a disappointment. But once you're convinced that God intends to do something for you, or do a miracle in your life, don't let go of your faith.

Day 5

GOD'S UN-NULLIFIABLE FAITHFULNESS

What if some were unfaithful? Will their
unfaithfulness nullify God's faithfulness?
Not at all! Let God be true,
and every human being a liar.
ROMANS 3:3–4 NIV

———— ••• ————

Paul was discussing how God had chosen Israel to be His special people and planned to save them, and this led to a discussion of the fact that the majority of Jews down through history had been unfaithful. So Paul asked if their disobedience ruined God's plans. Did God give up and cease to uphold *His* end of the covenant because His people had failed to live up to their part?

Paul responded, "Not at all! Let God be true, and every human being a liar." God was still faithful to do what He *said* He would do, human failings notwithstanding. God still brought His stated purpose about. "All Israel will be saved" as God had promised (Romans 11:26 NIV), but He clarified that "not all who are descended from Israel are Israel" (Romans 9:6 NIV).

God is faithful. He has clear, unalterable purposes for the nation of Israel—and for you as well—and He's determined to bring those plans to fruition. But how much *you* enjoy the fulfillment of God's plans depends on your own faithfulness.

Every human being can lie and mess up, but God will still be true.

UNFAILING LOVE AND FAITHFULNESS

"I am not worthy of all the unfailing love and faithfulness you have shown to me, your servant."

GENESIS 32:10 NLT

———— ⋅ ◆ ⋅ ————

As Jacob was returning from Haran to Canaan, he told God, "I am not worthy of all the unfailing love and faithfulness you have shown to me." He reminded God that twenty years earlier, he had left Canaan with only his staff in his hand, but while in Haran, God had blessed him as He had promised and made Jacob fabulously rich.

Despite declaring that he wasn't worthy of God's faithfulness, Jacob was desperate for the Lord to help him now. So he reminded God that He'd told him to return to Canaan—where he now faced imminent danger—and prayed, "You promised me, 'I will surely treat you kindly, and I will multiply your descendants'" (v. 12 NLT). For that promise to be fulfilled, Jacob and his family had to survive. So Jacob asked God to *remain* faithful and keep *this* promise, too.

God was faithful to Jacob, and He still shows His unfailing love and faithfulness to you today. Like Jacob, you may feel utterly unworthy, but your desperate need overrides all else, and so you cry out to God for Him to love and be faithful to you as well. Trust Him and He will.

A TRULY FAITHFUL GOD

"He is the Rock; his deeds are perfect. Everything he does is just and fair. He is a faithful God who does no wrong; how just and upright he is!"

DEUTERONOMY 32:4 NLT

The verse above makes several strong, positive statements about God's nature, but perhaps in a discouraged moment you might feel like disputing them. For example, the phrase: "He is a faithful God who does no wrong." Sometimes when you've desperately prayed for finances—claiming Philippians 4:19 (NIV), "My God will meet all your needs"—and the money doesn't arrive, you may feel like God *hasn't* been faithful.

It takes great faith in times when it appears that God has fallen down on the job to continue to say, "His deeds are perfect. Everything he does is just and fair." But while it looks from your limited viewpoint that God *hasn't* been faithful, remember that He's looking down on things from a much higher vantage point.

With your limited understanding, all you're able to understand is simple equations like $2 + 2 = 4$, but when things don't work out that simply, you protest that they "don't add up." But God, by comparison, is working with quantum equations that you can never comprehend, with far more complex factors to consider. . .and He's not finished yet.

THINK THE TRUTH, SPEAK THE TRUTH

*Who may dwell in Your holy hill? He who
walks uprightly, and works righteousness,
and speaks the truth in his heart.*

PSALM 15:1–2 NKJV

———— • ◆ • ————

Honesty is a habit, and like most habits, it begins in
the mind. Thought determines action, which sounds
simple enough until you have to do it. Each day brings
opportunities for dishonesty—not because you're a
malicious fraud but simply because you're human.
As a human, you fall under Paul's blanket statement:
"All have sinned and fall short of the glory of God"
(Romans 3:23 NKJV).

You're prone to putting your own interests above
what you know is right. Whether it's fudging your
taxes or filtering your social media posts, you want to
give the impression that you have it all together. But
you know you don't. And God knows that.

He knows everything about you, including those
paper clips you "borrowed" and those "accomplishments"
on your résumé that aren't actually yours. An upright
walk and righteous works began with speaking truth
in your heart. God wants you to walk and talk the
holiness He purchased for you. Keep doing what you're
doing right now—spending time in His Word, learning
it, and speaking its truth in your heart—and His truth
will become a habit in all you think, say, and do.

SELF-PROTECTION THROUGH GROUP INTERVENTION

*Pray for us; for we are confident that we have
a good conscience, in all things
desiring to live honorably.*

HEBREWS 13:18 NKJV

Sometimes, accountability gets a bad rap, reduced to the level of a trend or eye-rolling Christianese, when really it's a crucial tool in an honest life. When you spend too much time trapped in your own head, it becomes frighteningly easy to stumble. Either your own concerns overwhelm you to the detriment of losing perspective or the weeds of sin grow unfettered by concerned eyes and hearts.

God will honor your desire to serve Him with honesty and integrity, but one of the reasons you are to stay in fellowship with other believers (Hebrews 10:25) is to be encouraged to honor God with an honest assessment of your conscience and behavior.

Without someone to pray for you—an individual or small group—you're susceptible to your heart's own brand of honesty, which, frankly, is subject to decay. "The human heart is the most deceitful of all things, and desperately wicked. Who really knows how bad it is?" (Jeremiah 17:9 NLT).

When you bring someone into your life, letting them know your desires and troubles and habits, you're safeguarding your honesty in an effort to live honorably.

Day 3

LACK OF COMMUNICATION

Be of the same mind one toward another. . . .
Recompense to no man evil for evil.
Provide things honest in the sight of all men.
ROMANS 12:16–17 KJV

One of the most challenging things for a Christian is being open and honest with other Christians. People in the church are quick on the draw when it comes to any sense of unbiblical behavior among the brethren. On the one hand, the Bible tells disciples to be vigilant when it comes to false teaching and false teachers and to hold each other accountable to the truth.

At the same time, Christians put on a good front on Sundays, if only because they don't want to get kicked out of the club. The downside of that is they lack honesty in simple things, like the struggles they're facing in their marriages, with their kids, at work, or with old ghosts from their pre-Christian days that have resurfaced.

God's children need less fear of excommunication and more fear of the separation that comes from lack of communication. The battle between the spirit and the flesh is hard. When they encourage and strengthen a fellow believer, they respect the entire body of Christ, caring for that particular representation of it that God has placed in their path.

Week 39 ♦ HONESTY

277

ATTAINING INTEGRITY

For we are taking pains to do what is right,
not only in the eyes of the Lord but
also in the eyes of man.
2 CORINTHIANS 8:21 NIV

Ben Franklin said, "Honesty is the best policy," but Paul would tell you it's not necessarily the easiest. However, he did suggest it's the most worthwhile, because honest habits and words carry weight with both God and men. Above all else, he strove to be God's man in every situation, whether he was teaching in the synagogue or making tents.

It didn't matter to Paul whether he was speaking with dignitaries or ditchdiggers, the message was on point: "I resolved to know nothing while I was with you except Jesus Christ and him crucified" (1 Corinthians 2:2 NIV). You may think, *Okay, that's Paul; he was pretty radical*—and you'd be right. But what made him that way was his unwavering commitment to know Christ and to represent Him in all that he did.

Paul probably didn't miss many chances to share the Gospel, but he earned a ready audience because he was also a good tent maker and a good neighbor, and a leader who challenged and supported his fellow believers. Those things aren't uncomplicated, but they are necessary in living a day-in-day-out commitment to Jesus.

HONEST IN EVERY WAY

*Even corrupt tax collectors came to be baptized
and asked, "Teacher, what should we do?"
He replied, "Collect no more taxes
than the government requires."*
LUKE 3:12–13 NLT

———— • ◆ • ————

John the Baptist shot straight with the crowds who came to be baptized: "Prove by the way you live that you have repented of your sins and turned to God" (Luke 3:8 NLT). John's no-nonsense, no-holds-barred message presaged the deep honesty of Christ's coming—the undeniable truth of what God was willing to do in order to make you a way home to Him.

Our response to that great salvation is to live honorable lives with the added bonus of doing kingdom work: sharing with others about Jesus, His great love and work, and how He has changed you.

It's a message that resonates in the most unexpected ways with the unlikeliest of people—much as John's call to repentance struck a chord with tax collectors. Jews in Rome's employ, they were hated for their corrupt ways, increasing burdens to fatten their own wallets. But John called them to do their work honestly as a reflection of God's call to be holy—set apart, different— from the world around them. More than anything, honesty sets you apart and gives you the chance to tell others why it matters.

Day 6

CLEAN HEART, CLEAN HANDS

He that hath clean hands, and a pure heart;
who hath not lifted up his soul unto
vanity, nor sworn deceitfully.

PSALM 24:4 KJV

———————

When Jesus taught, He went straight to the heart of a matter. Looking lustfully at someone is the same as committing adultery with them, and wishing evil on someone is the same as killing them. While legally there's a big difference between a thought and an act, with God, there's none.

That shouldn't surprise you; after all, as far back as David, God made it clear that, while people look at appearances, He looks at the heart (1 Samuel 16:7). What is in the heart influences behavior. Regarding bad deeds, Jesus said, "But those things which proceed out of the mouth come from the heart, and they defile a man" (Matthew 15:18 NKJV).

Literal dirt on your hands isn't a source of spiritual uncleanness, but the dirt in your heart is fertile ground for the worst things imaginable. Fortunately, the heart can also be a fount of good behavior. With Christ as the source, supported by prayer and time in the Word, living water can fill your heart, flowing through you, cleansing the bad habits, and replacing them with godly wisdom, perspectives, and action.

HONESTY ◆ Week 39

KEEP YOUR EYE ON THE BALL

*"My righteousness I hold fast, and will not let it go;
my heart shall not reproach me as long as I live."*
JOB 27:6 NKJV

———•◆•———

If, in a moment of decision, you have to decide whether or not to be honest, you've already got two strikes against you: one, that you know the truth and are still considering a lie, and two, that you fear men more than God. One of the reasons God singled out Job as a man of integrity (Job 2:3) is that when he stepped up to the plate, he already knew what pitches he was going to swing at. He understood that God was the source of his blessings and character, not himself.

Anything that looked like temptation, Job was ready to back off and let it pass without a second look—affairs, self-righteousness, hardships. He wasn't disconnected from life, just prepared. His honesty came from a place of preparation and obedient practice of what God said was right.

He "maintained his righteousness" the way a ballplayer works the batting cage: learning from opponents' tendencies, perfecting technique, and trusting in preparation come game time. Job's statement wasn't a brag but a declaration: he followed God in every way he could think of, and God gave him peace and comfort in the trials of life.

Nick 39 ◆ HONESTY

MOTIVATING LOVE

*Let us think of ways to motivate one another to acts
of love and good works. And let us not neglect our
meeting together, as some people do, but encourage
one another, especially now that the day
of his return is drawing near.*

HEBREWS 10:24–25 NLT

You can encourage others who are in a season of
need; that's an obvious way to show love. Sometimes
overlooked is the fact that you can encourage others,
especially those who are in a season of plenty, to join
you in acts of love and good works.

Christians should constantly be thinking of
ways to motivate themselves and fellow believers to
help others. One of the best ways to do so is to be a
dedicated member of a solid Christian fellowship. If
your church is truly Bible believing, it cannot help but
be actively meeting needs of people in its community
and encouraging its members to work hand in hand
in loving service.

The author of Hebrews urges believers not to give
up meeting together. Gathering for church each week
is immensely important and not to be neglected or
done just when the mood strikes you or there's nothing
better to do. Hearing the Word preached, worshipping,
and serving others together are excellent ways to show
encouragement and love.

Week 40 ♦ LOVE FOR OTHERS – PART 2

Day 2

LAVISH LOVE

*"Can a mother forget the baby at her breast and
have no compassion on the child she has borne?
Though she may forget, I will not forget you!"*

ISAIAH 49:15 NIV

Early one morning over breakfast, a four-year-old girl
said sincerely to her mom, "I don't like it when my
sister gets in trouble. I love her." The mother smiled
and asked, "Then why do you tattle on her sometimes,
trying to get her in trouble?" The little girl replied
tearfully, "Sometimes I forget my love."

You will forget your love for others at times, too.
Everyone does. Thankfully, your heavenly Father never
forgets His love for you! And because His love for you,
and mindfulness of you, never fails, He reminds you
of His love constantly, calls you to it, and urges you
to share it with others.

First John 3:1 (NIV) says, "See what great love the
Father has lavished on us, that we should be called
children of God! And that is what we are!" Though
Christians still might act like selfish children at times,
first and foremost they are children of a heavenly Father
who lavishes His love on His people. That cannot help
but fill up your life and overflow to the people He has
placed around you.

Day 3

FREE TO LOVE

*Be careful so that your freedom does not cause others
with a weaker conscience to stumble. For if others
see you—with your "superior knowledge"—eating
in the temple of an idol, won't they be encouraged
to violate their conscience by eating food that has
been offered to an idol? So because of your superior
knowledge, a weak believer for whom Christ died
will be destroyed. And when you sin against other
believers by encouraging them to do something they
believe is wrong, you are sinning against Christ.
So if what I eat causes another believer to sin,
I will never eat meat again as long as I live—
for I don't want to cause another
believer to stumble.*

1 CORINTHIANS 8:9–13 NLT

Tripping someone to make them fall definitely isn't a
loving thing to do. At best, it's a thoughtless prank; at
worst, it can cause injury. One important way Christians
can love others is by not causing them to stumble
spiritually, as that can cause harm to their soul and
even destruction. You are called to freedom and you
are covered in God's grace, yet as Galatians 5:13–14
(NLT) says, "For you have been called to live in freedom,
my brothers and sisters. But don't use your freedom to
satisfy your sinful nature. Instead, use your freedom to
serve one another in love."

LOVING ENEMIES

"You have heard that it was said, 'You shall love your neighbor and hate your enemy.' But I say to you, love your enemies, bless those who curse you, do good to those who hate you, and pray for those who spitefully use you and persecute you, that you may be sons of your Father in heaven; for He makes His sun rise on the evil and on the good, and sends rain on the just and on the unjust."

MATTHEW 5:43–45 NKJV

⸺•◆•⸺

Does anyone actually *like* this passage of scripture? The Bible surely isn't a feel-good self-help book but is "sharper than any two-edged sword, piercing even to the division of soul and spirit, and of joints and marrow, and is a discerner of the thoughts and intents of the heart" (Hebrews 4:12 NKJV).

God's holy Word will convict and make you uncomfortable. It's hard to think of anything more uncomfortable than showing love to, blessing, doing good to, and praying for those who curse and hate you. Yet that's exactly what Jesus Himself instructs in this passage.

You might wonder how on earth to even *start* showing love to your enemies. Begin by asking for God's help and by sincerely praying for them. Then read Proverbs 25:21–22 and do likewise.

Day 5

LOVE LETS GO

*Thou shalt not avenge, nor bear any grudge against
the children of thy people, but thou shalt love
thy neighbour as thyself: I am the Lord.*

LEVITICUS 19:18 KJV

———— • ◆ • ————

Have you ever been guilty of offending someone, sincerely apologized, but then had that mistake held against you despite your repentance? It's disheartening to say the least. Thankfully, your heavenly Father never acts that way toward you. First John 1:9 (NKJV) promises, "If we confess our sins, He is faithful and just to forgive us our sins and to cleanse us from all unrighteousness."

Now, have *you* ever been the one to hold a grudge against someone? If your holy God forgives you so fully, how can you hold anything against someone who comes to you in repentance? No, you are to love like 1 Corinthians 13:4–5 (NIV) describes: "Love is patient, love is kind. It does not envy, it does not boast, it is not proud. It does not dishonor others, it is not self-seeking, it is not easily angered, it keeps no record of wrongs."

Did you catch that last part? It keeps *no record* of wrongs.

Let the God who sees all and knows all and loves all be the one to judge each person according to their actions. *You* are called to forgive and love and leave justice in God's hands.

Day 6

FERVENT LOVE

*Since you have in obedience to the truth purified
your souls for a sincere love of the brethren,
fervently love one another from the heart.*

1 PETER 1:22 NASB

———————

To "fervently love" means to do so intensely, zealously,
with very strong feelings. That's how Peter states
Christians should love one another. In a later chapter
he says, "Finally, all of you be of one mind, having
compassion for one another; love as brothers, be
tenderhearted, be courteous" (1 Peter 3:8 NKJV). And
in 1 Peter 4:8 (NIV), he concludes, "Above all, love each
other *deeply*, because love covers over a multitude of
sins" (emphasis added).

Peter isn't describing a surface-level kind of love for
one another; he's talking about profound, rich, and
abiding love among believers. How do you experience
this? Pray for more love! Be a student of the believers
God has placed around you and ask Him to help you
know how best to love them. Listen earnestly to others
when they need someone to talk to. Truly care about
others, "rejoice with those who rejoice; mourn with
those who mourn" (Romans 12:15 NIV). And "bear one
another's burdens, and so fulfill the law of Christ"
(Galatians 6:2 NKJV).

Day 7

LET LOVE GROW

*And this I pray, that your love may abound still
more and more in knowledge and all discernment.*
PHILIPPIANS 1:9 NKJV

The longer you walk with God and mature in your
relationship with Him through Christ and the work
of the Holy Spirit, the greater and better your love will
grow. Your obedience to the Great Commandment
will increase.

When asked what was the greatest commandment
in the Law, Jesus replied, "'Love the Lord your God with
all your heart and with all your soul and with all your
mind.' This is the first and greatest commandment. And
the second is like it: 'Love your neighbor as yourself.'
All the Law and the Prophets hang on these two
commandments" (Matthew 22:36–40 NIV).

You will have more knowledge of love and more
wisdom to determine God's will for you in sharing
His love.

So let love grow. Don't let anything hinder your
walk with God. When temptation comes your way,
reject it and draw closer to your Savior. Fill your mind
up with scripture, and then "do not merely listen to
the word, and so deceive yourselves. Do what it says"
(James 1:22 NIV).

A MIGHTY PROTECTOR

For You are my rock and my fortress; therefore,
for Your name's sake, lead me and guide me.

PSALM 31:3 NKJV

When you need protection from life's storms, you can *always* find safety in the One who is a rock and fortress. Throughout the scriptures you'll find several references to God as "my rock," "my fortress," "my deliverer," "my shield," "my stronghold," and "my salvation." God is a mighty protector. For starters, check out these verses:

Psalm 18:2 (NLT)—"The LORD is my rock, my fortress, and my savior; my God is my rock, in whom I find protection. He is my shield, the power that saves me, and my place of safety."

Psalm 62:2 (NLT)—"He alone is my rock and my salvation, my fortress where I will never be shaken."

Psalm 94:22 (NLT)—"But the LORD is my fortress; my God is the mighty rock where I hide."

Second Samuel 22:2 (NKJV)—"The LORD is my rock and my fortress and my deliverer."

Reach out to God. Seek refuge in the one who waits, ready to rescue you. No matter how strong, how confident, how secure in faith you are, you can never do any better than to give yourself over to God, who will help you safely navigate through life's storms—today and for all time.

Week 41 ◆ PROTECTION

WHEN TROUBLES COME

*God is our refuge and strength,
an ever-present help in trouble.*
PSALM 46:1 NIV

—————•◦•—————

You don't need to invite trouble into your life. If you've lived any number of years, you understand and know with 100 percent certainty that hard times will come whether you want them to or not. John 16:33 (NIV) states, "In this world you will have trouble." Not *might* have trouble. . .but *will*.

No matter how hard you push or pull, your will is no match against unsettling life events. You can't close your eyes and make them disappear. And, quite unfortunately, there's no avoiding them.

Sickness. Job loss. Infertility. Divorce. Death of a loved one. Just to name a few hard things. You've likely experienced at least one—maybe even all—of these difficult life circumstances. So where do you choose to run when troubles come and you're deep in the mire of despair?

Jesus says, "Take heart! I have overcome the world" (John 16:33 NIV). With a power like that on your side, you need to fear nothing in this world. Your Savior is powerful. He is sovereign. There isn't one hardship—no matter how insurmountable it may seem—that He can't help you overcome. You can rest secure in your heavenly Father, who's *always* present (Psalm 139:7–10).

Day 3

YOUR BURDEN BEARER

Cast your burden upon the LORD and He
will sustain you; He will never allow
the righteous to be shaken.
PSALM 55:22 NASB

Worry is an overwhelming, often suffocating, cumbersome companion. If you allow worry to seep into your soul, it's difficult to break free from its strong grasp.

What burdens you most? The unknown? A persistent barrage of what-ifs that plagues your thoughts? Whatever it is, there's hope. You don't need to carry it alone. In fact, Jesus promises to give you rest from the afflictions that weigh you down: "Come to me, all you who are weary and burdened, and I will give you rest" (Matthew 11:28 NIV). You can flee to Him when your thoughts become too much to handle, when life becomes oppressive. . .because He cares for you: "Cast all your anxiety on him because he cares for you" (1 Peter 5:7 NIV).

Whatever burden you're carrying today, give it to the ultimate Burden Bearer. He will carry the load for you. If you feel weighted down with worries and cares, scripture has a beautiful promise. Read this verse aloud and commit it to memory: "And my God will meet all your needs according to the riches of his glory in Christ Jesus" (Philippians 4:19 NIV). You won't be disappointed!

Day 4

CONFIDENT GUARANTEE

*In the fear of the LORD there is strong confidence,
and his children will have refuge.*
PROVERBS 14:26 NASB

———————

Has insecurity ever threatened to rip away your very last shred of confidence? Doubt is a crippling enemy that can leave you feeling uncertain, weak, and fearful.

If you've ever, for even a moment, doubted your heavenly Father's promises, spend time bolstering your faith—right now. Begin fortifying your heart with the hopeful promise of Proverbs 14:26. If you trust and obey the Lord, He'll provide all the confidence you'll ever need. You will always find a safe haven with Him. "God is our refuge and strength, a very present help in trouble" (Psalm 46:1 KJV).

The benefits to those who fear the Lord are many: "Blessed be the Lord, who daily loadeth us with benefits, even the God of our salvation" (Psalm 68:19 KJV). He offers peace, guidance, grace, love, salvation, and so much more! Just one of the benefits He provides to His children is this confident guarantee: the heavenly Protector will equip your spirit with courage while providing a peaceful refuge.

Today, set your soul free to soar with the assurance of God's promises. . .even if you're feeling insecure. For when you're weak, there you will find strength (2 Corinthians 12:10). Praise the Lord for His faithfulness!

Day 5

HEAVENLY ARSENAL

Above all, taking the shield of faith,
wherewith ye shall be able to quench all
the fiery darts of the wicked.
EPHESIANS 6:16 KJV

When evil threatens your soul, God wants you to know that you have a heavenly arsenal at your disposal: "Put on the full armor of God, so that you can take your stand against the devil's schemes" (Ephesians 6:11 NIV). According to Ephesians 6, you can stand firm against evil and arm yourself with protection like:

The belt of truth (v. 14)

The breastplate of righteousness (v. 14)

Feet fitted with the readiness that comes from the gospel of peace (v. 15)

The shield of faith (v. 16)

The helmet of salvation (v. 17)

The sword of the Spirit (v. 17)

Prayer—on all occasions (v. 18)

Ask God to give you the courage and the weapons you need to win against the enemy. When you arm yourself with His spiritual protection, you'll be living according to His best plan for you, and your faith will be resolute.

There's no need to cower in fear and weakness when the devil comes knocking. Stand tall. Stand confident. Stand strong. "Be strong in the Lord and in his mighty power" (Ephesians 6:10 NIV). The protection of almighty God is there for you; He has your back.

EVERY STEP OF THE WAY

*"When you pass through the waters, I will be
with you; and when you pass through the rivers,
they will not sweep over you. When you walk
through the fire, you will not be burned;
the flames will not set you ablaze."*

ISAIAH 43:2 NIV

Can you imagine stepping into a raging river and not
getting swept away by its current? Or walking through a
blazing inferno and suffering not even one minor burn?
Impossible, right? However, that's exactly the kind of
protection your heavenly Father offers His children.

Think back to the story of Shadrach, Meshach, and
Abednego in Daniel 3. King Nebuchadnezzar had the
trio thrown into the fiery furnace when they refused
to bow down to his image. When he looked into the
blazing furnace, the king saw a fourth man walking
around with Shadrach, Meshach, and Abednego—and
all appeared alive and well! "Look!" Nebuchadnezzar
shouted. "I see four men, unbound, walking around in
the fire unharmed! And the fourth looks like a god!"
(Daniel 3:25 NLT).

Remember, God is with you through every challenge
you'll ever face. He always has your best in mind. And
although He doesn't promise you won't have to deal
with hard things, He does promise to be with you *every
single step* of the way.

Day 7

A FIRM FOUNDATION

*The LORD is good, a strong hold in the day of
trouble; and he knoweth them that trust in him.*
NAHUM 1:7 KJV

———— • ◉ • ————

You know that God's Word promises guidance for daily
living. But did you know that God's Word is a great
source of comfort, too—especially for those who put
their trust and faith in Him?

No doubt about it, it's human nature to attempt to
escape life's troubles. Whether your escape hatch leads
to outright denial or drowning your worries and cares
in some kind of addiction (alcohol, drugs, overwork)
or other unhealthy habits, when you choose to take
matters into your own hands rather than handing
them over to Jesus, the outcome is always the same. *You
really can't fix anything on your own.* However, you do
tend to create more of a jumbled mess out of your life.

When troubles come—and they will—seek the
comfort your soul craves in the above verse from the
book of Nahum. Meditate on the promise of God's
goodness and protection. Rest your troubled soul in the
peace that can only come from your heavenly Father.
He *alone* is the firm foundation you need.

Instead of running away from your troubles, run
into the open arms of Jesus. There you will find safety
and protection.

Week 41 ◆ PROTECTION

Day 1

SEEKING WISE COUNSEL

*A wise man will hear and increase in learning,
and a man of understanding will
acquire wise counsel.*

If you're an understanding person, you value other people's opinions. As a result, you make a concerted effort to seek out their counsel and generally *get* the information you're looking for. And when you get it, you listen to it carefully. That's precisely why the Bible says that a wise man "will acquire wise counsel" and "will hear and increase in learning."

It's all so easy and the benefits so enormous, you wonder why anybody would *not* seek out good counsel. The problem sometimes is pride: you're ashamed to admit that you don't know something, and rather than humble yourself and learn, you try to muddle through on your own.

Or you may be too impatient. You want to get going immediately and don't want to take the time to sift through people's varying opinions and decide on the best course of action.

Often, you avoid seeking advice because you already know others will caution you that your plan won't work—and you don't want to hear any opposing views. But that isn't wise. Take the time to seek out godly, informed counsel and you'll make decisions that are safer and more likely to succeed.

THE ULTIMATE COUNSELOR

*For a child will be born to us, a son will be given to
us; and the government will rest on His shoulders;
and His name will be called Wonderful Counselor,
Mighty God, Eternal Father, Prince of Peace.*

ISAIAH 9:6 NASB

———— • ❖ • ————

We so often think of Jesus as the helpless baby born in
a stable in Bethlehem, or of the flesh-and-blood man
who went to the cross at Golgotha to die for our sins.
But Jesus' many exalted titles—"Mighty God, Eternal
Father, Prince of Peace"—reveal that although He was
a mortal man, He is also the divine, eternal Son of
God. As the Nicene Creed states, He is "very God of
very God. . .being of one substance with the Father."

Among Jesus' magnificent titles is this one:
"Wonderful Counselor." Kings and rulers in ancient
times habitually sought the advice of the very wisest
counselors when making important decisions. Jesus
is the best possible counselor. Because He is one with
God the Father, "His understanding is infinite" (Psalm
147:5 NKJV). He is "perfect in knowledge" (Job 37:16 NKJV).

When you need divine wisdom and supernatural
insight, look to "Christ, in whom are hidden all the
treasures of wisdom and knowledge" (Colossians 2:2–3
NKJV). He has the answers you so desperately need for
every situation.

Day 3

A DIVINE COUNSELOR

When he, the Spirit of truth, is come, he will guide
you into all truth: for he shall not speak of himself;
but whatsoever he shall hear, that shall he speak:
and he will shew you things to come.

JOHN 16:13 KJV

The Holy Spirit, the Spirit of truth, is also called "the Spirit of Christ" (Romans 8:9 KJV), so since Jesus Christ is the Wonderful Counselor, the Spirit is also. In fact, it's through His Spirit living in your heart that God speaks to you. How does He counsel you? He "[guides] you into *all* truth." Whatever you need to know about, literally *everything*, the Spirit can reveal truth to you about it.

Sometimes He will whisper the precise answer into your heart in a supernatural revelation, speaking to you in "a still small voice" (1 Kings 19:12 KJV) that only you can hear. Other times He will guide you through a set of seemingly natural circumstances that gradually lead you to the right conclusion.

The Bible describes the Spirit in John 14:16 (KJV) as the "Comforter," but while the Greek word certainly means "Comforter," it also means "Advocate, Encourager, or Counselor." Allow the Spirit of Christ to counsel you. He longs to speak to you, to show you the truth. Listen to His voice today.

LISTENING TO COUNSEL

The way of a fool is right in his own eyes,
but he who heeds counsel is wise.
PROVERBS 12:15 NKJV

Everyone gets into headstrong moods at times and becomes so convinced that they're right that they refuse to listen to counsel from others. It's understandable if this happens once or twice, but when it's a recurring attitude, this is very foolish. It's what the Bible is talking about when it says, "The way of a fool is right in his own eyes."

If you want to be wise and spare yourself a great deal of trouble, heed the counsel that mature Christians give you. They truly care for you and have your best interests at heart. "Get all the advice and instruction you can, so you will be wise the rest of your life" (Proverbs 19:20 NLT).

God will often give you wise advice through ordinary people, but if you're fired up about an idea, you may ignore them and ride roughshod over them—and this is especially true if you have a dominant or persuasive personality and are used to getting your way.

Remember, as a disciple of Jesus, you are to love the Lord, yield your plans to Him, and be willing to change them if He counsels a better course of action.

INSTRUCTION AND LEARNING

*Give instruction to a wise man and he will
be still wiser, teach a righteous man
and he will increase his learning.*
PROVERBS 9:9 NASB

It's frustrating to give advice to someone who gets irritated when you try to point things out, who constantly cuts you off with, "Yeah, yeah, I already know. You don't need to tell me." Then you watch them continue blithely on their way, run into the very problem you tried to warn them about, and suffer the consequences.

And even more frustrating is when they refuse to learn their lesson from that. They *continue* to refuse to listen, and run into similar trouble *again*.

It's much more rewarding to give instructions to a wise-hearted individual who isn't too stubborn or proud or impatient to listen. It pays big dividends to be humble enough to admit that you don't know everything and to listen. If you give instruction to such a man, he will become wiser. If you teach a righteous man—a man who isn't proud and full of himself—he will increase his learning.

Does this describe you? You may not think of yourself as wise in the sense of being highly educated and knowledgeable, but true wisdom is often simply having a humble spirit and being patient enough to listen to others.

Day 6

HEARTFELT COUNSEL

The heartfelt counsel of a friend
is as sweet as perfume and incense.
PROVERBS 27:9 NLT

———— • ◉ • ————

Wisdom is more than simply being able to quote applicable information, refer to pertinent facts and figures, or pass on valuable life lessons. While all of these are essential elements of imparting wisdom, there's another facet to it: You must *love* the person you're reaching out to. In the best scenario, it's genuine love—not a critical attitude or a know-it-all spirit—that motivates you to communicate advice to others.

Having a genuine concern for people's welfare is what motivates you to make yourself vulnerable and share from your heart. Love inspires you to humble yourself and disclose your own past mistakes for the benefit of others. It's what makes sharing heartfelt counsel so sweet.

When others sense that you truly care for them, they're far more apt to take what you say and put it into practice. And long after that incident has passed, they'll remember the loving way you shared and the compassion in your face and voice.

That's why the Bible says, "The heartfelt counsel of a *friend* is as sweet as perfume and incense." A true friend gives you advice and counsel because they genuinely care for you. And love is what motivates you to do the same for others.

Day 7

COUNSELING WITH MANY PEOPLE

Where no counsel is, the people fall:
but in the multitude of counsellors there is safety.
PROVERBS 11:14 KJV

———◆◆◆———

When you insist on doing detective work and trying to figure out problems all by yourself, you frequently arrive at a skewed conclusion. That's because, being human, you often start with a mistaken presumption, so you screen out certain facts. But it can be very insightful to ask others their opinion. They might just be in possession of key pieces of information, details that will make all the difference in what you plan to do or say.

An autocrat is convinced that he knows everything and thinks he needn't run his decisions past any other person, and while some people *are* naturally good at decision-making, this management style often leads to collapses—and rather spectacular ones at that: "Where no counsel is, the people fall."

You've heard the expression "Get a second opinion." But in the Bible, that's the bare minimum. God's Word advises you to get as many opinions as possible, stating that "in the *multitude* of counsellors there is safety." Do you *really* want to play it safe? Talk with as many counselors as you can. It pays to carefully research and base important decisions upon a broad range of life experiences and perspectives.

COUNSEL ◆ Week 44

YOU KNOW HIM

*"The world cannot accept [the Spirit of truth],
because it neither sees him nor knows him.
But you know him, for he lives with
you and will be in you."*
JOHN 14:17 NIV

The unconverted look for truth in science, experience, and sometimes even gut feelings. The problem with all of these is that they're not necessarily objective or comprehensive. You've listened to a friend, coworker, or even a foe dance around the topic when you brought it up. Maybe that person even studied religion in college, but he or she never actually met the Truth, so it remained elusive.

Bible commentator Albert Barnes said it this way in *Notes on the Bible*: "The men of the world are under the influence of the senses. They walk by sight, and not by faith. Hence, what they cannot perceive by their senses, what does not gratify their sight, or taste, or feeling, makes no impression on them."

The Christian, on the other hand, acknowledges his or her senses but is not governed by them. For you know that truth is found in the person of the Holy Spirit, who lives in you. He is the promised Comforter who offers guidance and direction as you submit yourself to the reading and preaching of the Word.

GOD, THE ROCK

"The Rock! His work is perfect, for all His ways are just; a God of faithfulness and without injustice, righteous and upright is He."
DEUTERONOMY 32:4 NASB

Rodney King. O. J. Simpson. Ferguson. Charlotte.

Regardless of where you stand on those issues, nothing incites anger and unrest more than injustice, or sometimes even just a perceived injustice, due to skin color, social status, gender, or belief system.

You grew up with the expectation, or at least the hope, of being treated fairly. You wanted the same size piece of pie as your sister. You anticipated receiving a fair wage for your first job as well as after your most recent promotion. And you have every expectation of being treated fairly under the law. But injustice often wins the day in this world. Thanks be to God, that won't always be the case.

God is a rock. In John Wesley's commentary, he referred to God as being stable, invincible, and immutable "in his counsels and promises and ways." So take heart. God is faithful and just, righteous and upright in all His ways. He will administer ultimate justice in due time. In fact, He's in the process even now through the redeeming power of Christ.

Work for truth and justice in the here and now, but count on *God's* righteousness and justice.

LOVELY THOUGHTS

Finally, brothers and sisters, whatever is true,
whatever is noble, whatever is right, whatever is
pure, whatever is lovely, whatever is admirable—
if anything is excellent or praiseworthy—
think about such things.

PHILIPPIANS 4:8 NIV

Whatever you think about, you eventually act on. If you're thinking about the promises of God and about whatever is pure and lovely, then you'll feel peace, security, and hope. You'll want to be the hands and feet of Christ to those who are hurting and lonely.

If you're thinking about the falsehoods that Satan whispers into your ear and about whatever is impure and unlovely, then you'll feel anxious, insecure, and hopeless. You'll want to withdraw from everybody, where you'll remain ineffective for the kingdom of God.

You won't always be able to control your thoughts. Satan is on the prowl, seeking those whom he can kill and destroy, so he won't give up while you still have breath in your lungs. But you can reject him and his ways in favor of truth and love.

Do a quick inventory of your actions this past week. Which category do they most closely align with? Did you actively seek to minister to others, or were you withdrawn? How can you change your thought pattern this week by focusing on truth?

Week 43 ◆ TRUTH

Day 4

SPEAK THE TRUTH

*"These are the things you are to do:
Speak the truth to each other, and render
true and sound judgment in your courts."*
ZECHARIAH 8:16 NIV

After a period of judgment, God wanted His remnant to know that they shouldn't fear because He had "determined to do good again to Jerusalem and Judah" (Zechariah 8:15 NIV). Following His promise, He told them how they were to treat one another: speaking truth to each other and rendering true and sound judgments in court.

You might bristle at the idea of fellow Christians speaking truth to you because you had a bad experience with believers who were harsh or jumped to conclusions about your actions in the past. But just as God tells His people to issue sound judgment in court, He wants the same for His people when they are in fellowship. Believers are to stir up one another in truth.

Are you engaging in deep conversations with fellow believers on a weekly basis? Are you speaking truth to others? Are you growing as a result? While it's not always easy to find a safe place to have such conversations, never stop looking.

Invite somebody from church to dinner this week. Be honest about your faith walk. And be willing to give and receive truth.

TRUTH PERSONIFIED

*Jesus saith unto him, I am the way, the truth,
and the life: no man cometh unto
the Father, but by me.*
JOHN 14:6 KJV

After Jesus promised His disciples that He was going to prepare a place for them in heaven and then return for them, Thomas queried, "Lord, we know not whither thou goest; and how can we know the way?" (John 14:5 KJV). Jesus explained that He was the way, the truth, and the life; He was and is *the* way to the Father.

Two thousand years later, in an age in which the very notion of truth is questioned, Jesus is still truth personified. His ways, His words, and His thoughts are truth. He revealed characteristics of the Father for you so you would know how to live. He loved His enemies. He cared for the poor. He healed the sick. He taught the spiritually ignorant. And He spent time alone with the Father.

Does your life look like this? Or do you spend more time arguing about the truth? If you really want to see truth advance, then love your enemies, help the poor, nurse the sick back to health, disciple new converts, and spend ample time in prayer with the Father each day. For these are the acts of truth.

BUY THE TRUTH

*Buy the truth, and do not sell it, also wisdom
and instruction and understanding.*
PROVERBS 23:23 NKJV

———•◆•———

Your grandparents or great-grandparents probably never dreamed of buying a car on credit. Instead, they scrimped and saved until they had enough to pay cash for it. Then they carefully selected the vehicle that would best serve their needs for the long haul, since they wouldn't be buying one again anytime soon. Once they brought the vehicle home, they valued it—maintaining it to the best of their ability.

This is the word-picture that the writer of today's verse paints for readers regarding truth. When you work hard to save for a significant purchase, you value the product once you get it home. You would never consider abandoning it.

Are you putting in the effort to "buy the truth" from God's Word? Are you scrimping and saving truth as you find it? Are you investing time and energy to dig into commentaries? Are you listening to sermons? Are you taking notes about your truth findings? Or are you simply taking free samples?

Christianity isn't a religion for the reluctant. While your salvation is established and secure through Christ's efforts, your sanctification only comes as you learn and submit to the truth, at the leading of the Holy Spirit.

FROM GENERATION
TO GENERATION

*For the LORD is good. His unfailing love continues
forever, and his faithfulness continues
to each generation.*

PSALM 100:5 NLT

———— • ◆ • ————

God has been at work in your bloodline since long
before you were born, no matter how far previous
generations in your family strayed from Him.

King Josiah's family is a great example. His father,
King Amon, "did what was evil in the LORD's sight,
just as his father, Manasseh, had done" (2 Kings 21:20
NLT). Manasseh worshipped idols, abandoned the Lord,
and refused to follow Him (vv. 21–22), and his son did
likewise. But King Josiah's *great*-grandfather Hezekiah
"did what was pleasing in the LORD's sight, just as
his ancestor David had done. He removed the pagan
shrines, smashed the sacred pillars, and cut down the
Asherah poles" (2 Kings 18:3–4 NLT).

Each generation in Josiah's family had a chance to
serve the Lord. Some chose to do so and others turned
their back on Him. But the Lord was still faithful, and
Josiah's own reforms rank him as one of the greatest
kings in Judah's history.

Regardless of how wayward previous generations in
your family may have been, you can decide today, this
moment, to serve the Lord. His unfailing love continues
forever. Lean into that promise today.

Day 1

KEEPING WORDS IN CHECK

*We all stumble in many ways. Anyone who is
never at fault in what they say is perfect,
able to keep their whole body in check.*

JAMES 3:2 NIV

People speak to communicate but too often share things
from a skewed perspective, or don't have all the facts,
or say things in an insensitive tone. Misunderstandings
and offenses are the blight of relationships. In their
efforts to share their thoughts, everyone makes mistakes.
But if anyone consistently avoids offending others
because he or she is considerate and speaks carefully,
that person has great self-control.

There's a valuable promise in this verse also. It
states that anyone who habitually refrains from foolish
speech is *also* able to refrain from impulsive, thoughtless
actions, and thus spare themselves much trouble in life.

Proverbs 31:26 (KJV) describes the ideal woman
and gives the key to how to always speak wisely: "She
openeth her mouth with wisdom; and in her tongue
is the law of kindness." Because she determines in her
heart to say only kind and loving words, her actions
display the same gentle consideration and make her
greatly loved.

Pray and ask God to help your tongue be ruled
by the law of kindness. Then, whether you're highly
intelligent and educated or not, your speech will display
profound wisdom.

DANGERS OF IDLE CHATTER

*When there are many words, transgression is
unavoidable, but he who restrains his lips is wise.*
PROVERBS 10:19 NASB

People who incessantly indulge in small talk often
say things they shouldn't. They try to fill the void, so
they end up doing a lot of idle chatter and outright
gossip. Others constantly try to be amusing, but when
they run out of things worth saying, they keep talking,
getting more and more foolish. "The beginning of the
words of his mouth is foolishness: and the end of his
talk is mischievous madness" (Ecclesiastes 10:13 KJV).

They end up chattering like a bird, making a great
deal of noise, but not saying much that's intelligent.
Isaiah described this senseless racket when he said, "Like
a crane or a swallow, so did I chatter" (Isaiah 38:14 KJV).

Much of the time, the saying is true: "Silence is
golden," and a person who refrains from speaking is
wise. Solomon observed, "Even fools are thought wise
when they keep silent; with their mouths shut, they
seem intelligent" (Proverbs 17:28 NLT). Now, it's true that
it can be frequently helpful to have the gift of gab. . .
but more often it pays to be the strong, silent type.

If you're a chatterbox, ask God to help you to
understand the wisdom in restraining your speech.

Day 3

HEALING WORDS

*Gracious words are a honeycomb,
sweet to the soul and healing to the bones.*
PROVERBS 16:24 NIV

———— •◆• ————

Hearing considerate, gracious words is as pleasing to your ear as eating a honeycomb is to your tongue. And kind words are very healing to your spirit. The power of loving words can warm and release deep hurts of the past, like an expert masseur's probing fingers unlocking the stiffness and pain buried deep within cramped muscles.

Contrast this with careless, hate-filled words: "There is one who speaks rashly like the thrusts of a sword, but the tongue of the wise brings healing" (Proverbs 12:18 NASB). When people make cutting remarks intended to inflict pain, they are very much like the thrusts of a sword.

Since God has promised that gentle, Spirit-filled words can bring healing, you ought to strive for your words to relieve pain in people's lives—not add to it. Many people struggle through life, unable to deal with the baggage and hurts of their past, but loving words can bring life to their inner person and cause them to bloom.

God's Word is even more life-giving and healing. As Jesus said, "The words that I speak unto you, they are spirit, and they are life" (John 6:63 KJV). So speak encouraging promises into people's lives today.

EMOTIONAL OUTBURSTS

A fool vents all his feelings,
but a wise man holds them back.
PROVERBS 29:11 NKJV

———— • ✦ • ————

Many people are very emotional, and this has both benefits and drawbacks. When they're *up* and happy, they can be a sheer pleasure to be around. But when they're *down* and moping around, they spread dark clouds of misery. Such people often freely vent their emotions. But they need to be aware that such venting can be very discouraging to others.

This verse is talking about self-absorbed people who don't *care* how they drag others down, but who rage, sulk, and complain loudly when things aren't going their way. They only think about themselves and don't attempt to restrain themselves.

In fact, they *knowingly* engage in angry outbursts to manipulate others. They find it much more effective than reasoned arguments. But these kinds of tactics destroy respect and love and drive friends away, so though they often help people get what they want, they're also very foolish.

All believers, at one time or another, speak emotionally charged words and need to consider the effect their speech is having on others. May God's children cease being guilty of wheedling, whining, manipulating others, and using guilt trips to get their way. There are more honest, mature ways of communicating needs to others.

Day 5

SPEAKING ENCOURAGING WORDS

*"The Lord GOD has given Me the tongue of the
learned, that I should know how to speak
a word in season to him who is weary."*

ISAIAH 50:4 NKJV

———— • ◆ • ————

This is a good promise to claim, because the ability
to encourage others is a valuable gift. Barnabas had it.
He "was a good man, full of the Holy Spirit," and he
"encouraged them all that with purpose of heart they
should continue with the Lord" (Acts 11:23–24 NKJV).

When you love others, you become aware of their
needs and are more eager to reach out to them when
they're going through difficult times. Isaiah said,
"Strengthen the weak hands, and make firm the feeble
knees. Say to those who are fearful-hearted, 'Be strong,
do not fear! Behold, your God will. . .come and save
you'" (Isaiah 35:3–4 NKJV). Often people just need to be
reminded to get their eyes on the Lord and trust Him.

Job had the gift of encouraging speech as well. One
of his friends remarked, "Your words have supported
those who were falling; you encouraged those with
shaky knees" (Job 4:4 NLT). Ask God to give you a wise
tongue, as well, and to teach you to speak the right
words at the right time to those who are weary and
worn out.

Day 6

SPEAKING WITH GRACE

*Let your speech always be with grace. . .so that you
will know how you should respond to each person.*
Colossians 4:6 nasb

It's important to study your Bible and know basic
information about the faith to share with others.
"You must worship Christ as Lord of your life. And if
someone asks about your hope as a believer, always be
ready to explain it" (1 Peter 3:15 NLT). But this doesn't
mean just having pat, memorized explanations. You
need to be able to respond in a nuanced manner to
people to meet their individual needs.

For that, you have to allow the Holy Spirit to give
you wisdom, because only He knows people's hearts
and is aware of exactly what will touch them in a
profound way. If you're constantly striving to walk in
God's Spirit and be in tune with Him, He will give you
the wisdom to know what to say (Matthew 10:19–20).

This doesn't necessarily mean you'll have a perfect
batting score and always know precisely what to
answer, but "the love of God has been poured out in
our hearts by the Holy Spirit who was given to us"
(Romans 5:5 NKJV), so if your heart is filled with Him,
you'll automatically speak in love, and that's the *most*
important thing.

AVOID FOUL LANGUAGE

But now is the time to get rid of. . .malicious behavior, slander, and dirty language.
COLOSSIANS 3:8 NLT

As a believer, you are to avoid foul language, not because it's "not nice," but because it's abusive and demeaning. It's understandable when new believers slip up once in a while, because they're still in the process of leaving their old life behind. The problem comes, however, when someone who has been a disciple for many years habitually uses coarse language.

Some believers like to shock fellow Christians by swearing. They believe that using gutter talk proves that they're more genuine and in touch with reality than "sanctimonious Christians who are too polite to swear."

The New Testament is clear, however, saying: "Don't use foul or abusive language. Let everything you say be good and helpful" (Ephesians 4:29 NLT). A few verses later, Paul adds: "Obscene stories, foolish talk, and coarse jokes—these are not for you" (Ephesians 5:4 NLT). *These are not for you.* God's Word couldn't be much plainer.

By saying, "Now is the time to get rid of. . .dirty language," God makes it clear that you *can* control your tongue. If you determine to obey God and make a conscious effort to refrain from swearing, He will help you.

THE POWER OF HIS MIGHT

*Finally, my brethren, be strong in the Lord,
and in the power of his might.*
EPHESIANS 6:10 KJV

How many times have you felt so weak that you wondered if you could go on? There really are days when pulling the covers over your head seems like a better plan than getting out of bed. But people depend on you, so you put your feet on the floor and get going, even when you don't feel like it. On days like this your inner man might need a shot of vitamin B12, but your outer man has to keep moving, one foot in front of the other. Time to get going.

Oh, but there's good news! You don't have to square your shoulders and pretend to be strong when your knees are wobbly. It's not up to you, anyway. God wants you to be strong in the power of His might. *His,* not yours. Isn't that a relief?

So, go ahead and kick back those covers. Get out of bed. But tell your inner man to get ready, because God is going to do a supernatural, invigorating work to give you the strength you need to face the day. He's going to load you up with holy vitamins to complete the tasks ahead of you.

Day 2

ON BEHALF OF THOSE HE LOVES

*"For the eyes of the LORD run to and fro throughout
the whole earth, to show Himself strong on behalf
of those whose heart is loyal to Him. In this you
have done foolishly; therefore from now
on you shall have wars."*

2 CHRONICLES 16:9 NKJV

Don't you love the image of God's eyes running to and
fro throughout the earth? What a wonderful thought,
that He's ready and willing to show Himself strong on
your behalf. The very moment His eyes land on you,
the work begins. In your moment of greatest weakness,
He's there, eyes fixed on you, His child. He springs into
action, bringing strength.

What a wonderful promise! There's a role you have
to play in this promise, though. Did you catch it? Your
heart must remain loyal to Him. In other words, you
can't be swayed by other things, however tempting.

If you want His strength, you have to stay in His
presence. If you foolishly turn away from Him, however,
you'll lose His strength. The internal and external wars
will be devastating. But God promises to give strength
to those who remain loyal because of His great love.

TRADING WEAKNESS
FOR STRENGTH

*He gives strength to the weary
and increases the power of the weak.*
ISAIAH 40:29 NIV

———— ·◆· ————

Have you ever watched a thermometer inch its way up, up, up? If so, then you've witnessed a genuine transformation. That thermometer is being changed from the inside out as an external force (the heat) serves as trigger. The mercury deep inside the thermometer responds to the external trigger and is nudged upward.

This is similar to what happens when you give God control of your heart. He longs to change you from the inside out. When you're at your weakest (picture that thermometer at its lowest point), the Lord steps in. He gives strength. Your internal/spiritual temperature begins to rise. Your perspective changes. Your desire to do His will kicks in.

Eventually, you're loaded with energy, ready to go. Why? Because God is always in the "increasing" business. The words *weak* and *powerless* don't exist in His vocabulary.

So, brace yourself. He's in "Let's get going!" mode today. Give Him what you have—your exhaustion, your crazy schedule, your pain—and watch as the Lord invigorates you, transforming you from the inside out. Whew! It's getting hot in here!

Day 4

ALL THINGS

I know how to get along with humble means,
and I also know how to live in prosperity; in any
and every circumstance I have learned the secret
of being filled and going hungry, both of having
abundance and suffering need. I can do all
things through Him who strengthens me.

PHILIPPIANS 4:12–13 NASB

Oh, how hard you try to do things in your strength. You muster the courage to put one foot in front of the other, even when you don't feel like it. You press forward, though you're beaten down. But you can't do it. Not in your own strength. So, defeat sets in.

But there's good news today. What you can't do in your own power, God *can* do. He can bolster you from the inside out and make it possible for you to accomplish not just a few things, but all things. Ponder that word: *all*. You can do *all* things through Christ Jesus who gives you strength.

Those things you fear most? You can conquer them in Jesus' name. That person who intimidates you the most? You can face him with courage. You can get through any situation, good or bad. That's a promise you can take to the bank.

WINGS LIKE EAGLES

But those who hope in the LORD will renew their
strength. They will soar on wings like eagles;
they will run and not grow weary,
they will walk and not be faint.

ISAIAH 40:31 NIV

———•—•———

Have you ever renewed something? Your insurance policy, for instance? Your contract with the electric company? Your driver's license? It's impossible to renew something you haven't already taken possession of in the first place. To keep it, you have to acknowledge that you already have it.

That's how it is with God's strength, too. No matter where you are now, no matter how low you might feel, it's possible to once again take hold of what is already yours. But first you have to acknowledge that He's already done the work. God has given you a promise that if you put your hope in Him, then He will renew your strength. All He asks is one thing: actually put your trust in Him, not in your own accomplishments. He will do the rest.

Oh, what an amazing, over-the-top God you serve! His strength will send you soaring above your circumstances. You'll be a witness to others that a daily renewal policy is a terrific idea—one with amazing benefits.

AN ETERNAL PORTION

*My flesh and my heart fail; but God is the strength
of my heart and my portion forever.*
PSALM 73:26 NKJV

———•◆•———

When you think about the word *portion*, what comes
to mind? Perhaps you think about your dinner plate,
filled with carefully portioned selections—a healthy
balance of proteins, vegetables, and grains. A little of
this, a little of that.

Even a carefully portioned meal is just temporary,
though. Once you eat it, it's gone. God's idea of
portioning is just the opposite. His Word says that He
is your portion forever. In other words, He's all you'll
ever need, not just for today, but for tomorrow and all
of eternity. He really gives a generous portion.

No matter what you're walking through today, no
matter how close you are to giving up, God's promise
hasn't changed. He's got an eternal portion of strength
for you. He won't give it and then take it away. So,
lift your eyes to Him. Remind yourself—by speaking
it aloud—that He's enough, not just for the problems
you're facing today, but for all of eternity. Next time
someone remarks that you have a full plate, point to
heaven and say, "Yes, I do."

THE WAITING GAME

*Wait on the L**ORD**; be of good courage, and He shall strengthen your heart; wait, I say, on the L**ORD**!*
P<small>SALM</small> 27:14 NKJV

———— •❖• ————

Patient people have the supernatural ability to accept delays without panicking. They go through struggles without knee-jerking or letting anger get the best of them. Impatient people are often frustrated. They want what they want and they want it now. (Sound like anyone you know?)

Isn't it interesting that the Lord commands His kids to wait on Him? He doesn't want you to get out ahead of Him and mess things up. He asks you to wait to see His promises fulfilled. He also wants you to trust His timetable. If you're waiting for your dreams to come true, you have to recognize the truth: His calendar is perfect. God also wants you to be of good courage while you're waiting.

Talk about a tough request. It's hard enough to wait, but to keep an uplifted heart? Oh, but the payoff is sweet! God will strengthen your heart if you follow His "wait it out" plan. So, where do you stand today? Patient. . .or impatient? The right choice can change the outcome of your situation in a hurry.

Day 1

FINDING WISDOM

*Joyful is the person who finds wisdom, the one who
gains understanding. For wisdom is more profitable
than silver, and her wages are better than gold.
Wisdom is more precious than rubies; nothing
you desire can compare with her.*

PROVERBS 3:13–15 NLT

How different might your life look if you hadn't made
bad choices out of ignorance?

Maybe you quit college, not realizing how much a
lack of education would hinder your career choices,
and you've struggled ever since. Or maybe you entered
a romantic relationship for the wrong reasons and
it turned into a disaster. Whatever it was, finding
wisdom wasn't as high of a priority as your immediate
wants. . .and you paid a price.

Most people spend large portions of their lives
chasing the temporal. They seek a bigger nest egg, an
attractive spouse, nice possessions, and, if they're honest,
power and prestige—with little regard for finding true
wisdom.

Today's verse says wisdom is more profitable than
silver and her wages are better than gold. Nothing you
desire can compare with her. And it says wisdom brings
joy. Do you believe this? If so, how, specifically, are you
seeking wisdom? Proverbs 9:10 (NLT) is a great starting
place: "Fear of the LORD is the foundation of wisdom.
Knowledge of the Holy One results in good judgment."

A FLOOD OF KNOWLEDGE

*They will not hurt or destroy in all My holy
mountain, for the earth will be full of the
knowledge of the LORD as the waters cover the
sea. Then in that day the nations will resort
to the root of Jesse, who will stand as a signal
for the peoples; and His resting
place will be glorious.*

ISAIAH 11:9–10 NASB

———•◆•———

According to the United States Geographical Survey
website (www.usgs.gov), about 71 percent of the
earth's surface is water covered. So, even if you live in
a landlocked part of the country, it's still hard to avoid
water. Drive a few miles one way or another, and you're
bound to encounter a stream, river, lake, or pond.

A day is coming, promises the prophet Isaiah, in
which the earth will be full of the knowledge of the
Lord, just as the waters cover the sea. The nations will
turn to Jesus, as the root of Jesse, who will stand as the
symbol of righteousness for all the people.

If you're discouraged by political events, court
decisions, moral downturns, corruption, or just an
overall lack of biblical understanding around you, take
heart. A day is coming when the knowledge of the Lord
will flood this earth and nobody will be able to miss it.

FORSAKE EVIL

"And this is what he says to all humanity:
'The fear of the Lord is true wisdom;
to forsake evil is real understanding.'"
JOB 28:28 NLT

———— ✦ ————

The world offers all sorts of wisdom. In many ways, it has turned knowledge and wisdom into gods, sitting in judgment of God and His Word. It says God's principles, as found in scripture, are archaic, outdated, out of touch—or, at the very least, not really meant to be taken literally.

Job, on the other hand, said something very different: the fear of the Lord is true wisdom. He had complete faith in what God said and feared Him in the healthiest of ways, knowing that if he forsook God, then he'd pay the price. But his next sentiment in today's verse is most intriguing: "To forsake evil is real understanding."

Doesn't the world today say the exact opposite when it embraces, promotes, and even legislates practices that God calls evil? In so doing, it reveals a lack of real godly understanding.

With that said, are there areas in your life in which you are failing to forsake evil, offering excuses instead of taking action? Be honest with God and in your own heart. Return to the Lord and He will have abundant mercy. You can make things right today.

WISDOM OF THE ANCIENT

*With the ancient is wisdom; and in length of days
understanding. With him is wisdom and strength,
he hath counsel and understanding.*
JOB 12:12–13 KJV

In 2014, there were 45.2 million people in the United
States who were sixty-five years of age and older,
according to the Administration on Aging. And,
amazingly, there were 72,197 people who were at least
one hundred years of age.

Many of these senior citizens lived through the Great
Depression, a world war, and the changing dynamics of
family and society in general. They know a lot about
hardship, sacrifice, honor, and adapting to change. And
yet, too many of them will die with that knowledge
and wisdom inside them because not enough people
cared to ask them about it.

Today's verses say that with the ancient is wisdom,
understanding, and strength. Have you tapped into this
reservoir of wisdom? Or is your first call generally to a
peer? What can you do to begin intentionally availing
yourself of the wisdom of the ancient?

How about asking a grandparent for specific advice
about a situation you face? Or visit a senior citizen
and steer the conversation toward current events so you
can hear him or her put events into a larger historical
context. Reach out and be willing to listen.

BIBLICAL MEDITATION

Make me understand the way of Your precepts;
so shall I meditate on Your wonderful works.
PSALM 119:27 NKJV

In Amos 8:11, God warned His people about a coming day when they would experience a famine of hearing from Him. "They shall wander from sea to sea, and from north to east; they shall run to and fro, seeking the word of the LORD, but shall not find it" (Amos 8:12 NKJV).

As dire as that situation was in Amos's day, it's even worse today. You probably aren't noticing many people wandering from sea to sea seeking a word from the Lord. Instead, the Bible sits on bookshelves, coffee tables, and nightstands without being opened for weeks or months on end.

Many churches and small groups are encouraging Bible reading plans as a way to get people back into God's Word, but today's verse talks about going even deeper. The psalmist asks God to make him *understand* His precepts so he can *meditate* on His wonderful works.

What are you doing to digest and meditate on God's precepts? Some jot down Bible verses on index cards and then refer to them throughout the day. Others text Bible verses back and forth for discussion. And others journal through the scriptures. If you want a solid foundation, meditate on the Word.

Day 6

FADING FOLLY

The mind of the intelligent seeks knowledge,
but the mouth of fools feeds on folly.
PROVERBS 15:14 NASB

———— • ◆ • ————

Supermarket checkout lines are full of folly. They contain one tabloid after another, and each one is trying to outdo the other in their outrageous claims about the lives of celebrities. Christians know this, but their eyes are still frequently drawn to these headlines. They read them and eventually may even repeat them in casual conversation.

"Wickedness is meat and drink to them [those who feed on folly]," wrote John Wesley in his commentary about this verse.

The human mind, when it's not in a constant state of renewal by the Word of God, feeds on folly. This is a by-product of the fall. But there's good news: you can choose to seek knowledge instead. And today's verse indicates that those who have knowledge crave even more.

How are you currently seeking biblical knowledge? Do you have a Bible reading plan in place? Are you keeping up with it? Are you in a Bible study, taking classes at church, or in a small group that reads and discusses the Bible? If not, jump in. You'll find that once you get a taste of the truth, you'll want even more. And the folly of this world will begin to fade.

Week 46 ◆ UNDERSTANDING

Day 7

FEAR THE LORD

*Then shalt thou understand the fear of the Lord,
and find the knowledge of God. For the Lord
giveth wisdom: out of his mouth cometh
knowledge and understanding.*

Proverbs 2:5–6 KJV

If you respect the fast-moving current of a river you plan to navigate, then you learn how to properly operate a canoe. If you respect the height of a mountain you plan to climb, then you learn everything you can about how the harness system works. If you respect the inherent hardships of a hiking trail, then you learn which provisions you need to take.

Respect, even fear, leads to knowledge—at least it should. In Proverbs 2, the writer begins by saying that if people are going to receive wisdom from God, then they will hide God's commandments in their hearts so they can incline their ears to wisdom and apply their hearts to understanding. Their fear of the Lord leads to understanding. They wouldn't dream of navigating a spiritual river, climbing a spiritual mountain, or hiking a spiritual trail apart from such fear because they know that a lack of respect often leads to injury or even death.

How about you? Do you approach difficult circumstances without being spiritually prepared? If so, begin this day by hiding God's commandments in your heart.

THE SCOPE OF GOD'S LOVE

For as high as the heavens are above the earth,
so great is His lovingkindness toward
those who fear Him.
PSALM 103:11 NASB

———— •·•·• ————

God's love is deeper than the roots of your despair, higher than the pinnacle of your best moments, longer than the number of your days, and wider than the sum total of what you see and understand. God's love exceeds your expectations, surpasses your greatest dreams, and informs your response to those around you.

God is love, and His love is kind. His kindness leads you to Him, and when He issues the invitation to be part of His family, the only barriers to accepting His gift are the barriers you erect. God's love pursues, envelops, and offers a better-than-lifetime guarantee. His love outlasts everything you know, outshines the brightest sun, and outgives the most generous philanthropists.

You can break God's heart with your choice to sin, but you can't stop His love. You can reject rescue, but you can't stop Him from offering. You might be better off trying to empty the ocean with a thimble or moving a mountain using a teaspoon than trying to stop God from loving you. *It can't be done.*

God is love—and love is God's gift to you. Go ahead, discover it.

SACRIFICIAL LOVE

*"For this is how God loved the world: He gave his
one and only Son, so that everyone who believes
in him will not perish but have eternal life."*

JOHN 3:16 NLT

———— ·◆· ————

The people of Israel were in the wilderness between the lands of slavery and promise. It had become common for them to break God's law, and as a result, deadly snakes were sent slithering through camp and began biting people. Then the Lord told Moses, "Make a snake and put it up on a pole; anyone who is bitten can look at it and live" (Numbers 21:8 NIV).

God was foreshadowing what it would be like when Jesus was offered as the only way to recover from the deadly bite of sin. God loves all humanity. He sent His only Son to be the healing agent by dying on a cross. The gift of forgiveness was offered, and people need to be intentional about accepting it.

God didn't love you a little and tell you that you had to do some of the work yourself. He loved you completely and Jesus paid the price completely. God hates sin, but His love is never fickle. He can love you wholly because Jesus sacrificed everything. The sacrifice of one brought grace, forgiveness, and life to *all* who believe.

Day 3

FILLED UP—SPILLED OUT

*Beloved, let us love one another, for love is
from God; and everyone who loves is
born of God and knows God.*

1 JOHN 4:7 NASB

———— ◆ ————

Water features are the focus of many gardens, backyards, and interior living spaces. In many of these features a pool fills and then spills onto smaller pools or rocks below. The water continues to fill and overflow. Just so, God's love fills you to overflowing. This is why you should overflow with joy on others.

You've already learned that you can authentically love others because He loved you first. His love teaches you how to love. Love is an intentional choice that proves your family resemblance to God.

The love you share needs to be shown to those who love God and those who aren't quite there yet. No exclusions, conditions, or disclaimers apply. You don't ignore sin, but you also don't ignore the very thing that God said would help identify those who belong to His family—*love*. People who aren't sure about God don't need your condemnation. They need a love and kindness that points to an aspect of God that can redeem anyone from the pawnshop of peddled futures.

God pours His love into your life every day. Are you pouring out to others?

Day 4

NOT JUST A GOOD IDEA

"This is My commandment, that you love one another as I have loved you."

JOHN 15:12 NKJV

---◆---

A command is something that tells your computer what to do. A command is something children are to follow when it's issued by a parent. Likewise, when God does the commanding, you are to obey Him.

God isn't a self-help guru. He doesn't offer an optional five-step plan for believers who desire a happy life. He's less interested in your preferences than He is in transforming your life into what He planned. When you follow His commands, you're agreeing that He's in control. You don't usually follow the command of someone who doesn't have authority. God *does*.

God's command? "Love one another." He didn't say, "You might want to have a few warm fuzzy thoughts about others," or, "It's helpful to let people think you care." His command requires you to do the hard work of actually loving people, and if you need a reason, you're reminded that God loved you first.

Love isn't just a good idea or something you should work toward. God commands you to love. God has loved you freely and commands you to share what He has given to you. Even if it *wasn't* a command, it would still be a great idea—but remember: it *is* a command.

A FAITHFUL AND
STEADFAST LOVE

Thy lovingkindness is before mine eyes:
and I have walked in thy truth.
PSALM 26:3 KJV

———————

The sun rises and sets. Flowers grow and send forth fragrance. Pets become friends. The stars invite you to gaze their way. Birds sing and you notice. Each of these moments are sponsored by God's love for you.

God's love is unshakable, steadfast, and unmovable. It's something you notice in the beauty of nature, the innocence of children, and appreciate seeing in the lives of others. Your journey with Jesus is assured. The God who's given what the world needs to support life is absolutely faithful in His promise to love you.

Today's verse encourages you to keep God's love fixed in your mind by simply noticing the everyday things around you. God's love comes in both the unexpected and common. He cares for you through the lives of others. He shares with you in every breath you take and in everything that takes your breath away.

God's love is never a one-time gift. It's absolutely complete and without equal. It bends the core of your being in His direction. It inspires you to see people the way God sees them. It opens a whole new world that's built on seeking the best for those you love.

EVERY DAY

*The LORD's lovingkindnesses indeed never cease,
for His compassions never fail. They are new
every morning; great is Your faithfulness.*

LAMENTATIONS 3:22–23 NASB

———◆———

This verse picks up where yesterday's thoughts end. Yes, God's love is an immovable rock. It can be counted on, trusted, and shared. Yet, these verses create a sense of anticipation. You can almost visualize the author perpetually looking forward to Christmas morning— every day.

Mercy is described as lovingkindness that's given when it's least deserved. It's personal, intentional, and desperately needed. Mercy is unexpected in a world of justice, yet it's described as a gift from God that has no end.

Faithfulness is always doing what you say you'll do, being absolutely trustworthy and willing to prove the truth of your promise. God's love is like that.

Every morning, without fail, you must make a quick assessment of where you stand with God, and every morning identify God's steadfast love, never-ending mercy, and rock-solid faithfulness.

God doesn't skip a day, take vacations, or change His mind. He loves you, always has, and will never stop. This is observable, assured, but undeserved. And that's the point: God does what you can't. He is love. He is mercy. He is faithful. And He shows you how to do the same. Every day.

PART OF THE FAMILY

*"Are not five sparrows sold for two cents? Yet not
one of them is forgotten before God. Indeed, the very
hairs of your head are all numbered. Do not fear;
you are more valuable than many sparrows."*

LUKE 12:6–7 NASB

You may not pay much attention to sparrows. They flit
from one place to the next with few people pausing to
pay attention. They're rarely complimented for their
looks, and even fewer people keep sparrows for pets,
yet Jesus says they never classify as forgettable to God.

You probably haven't taken the time to catalog,
number, and track the hairs on your head. You may
notice if it seems some hair is changing color or falling
out more than usual, but you probably don't obsess
over numbering your hair. You likely don't give it
much thought.

This is where the contrast to God's love shines
bright. If God cares for the well-being of sparrows and
hair, do you have any real idea how much He cares
for *you*?

Nothing escapes God's notice, and it extends to your
entire life. If God were to be interviewed and asked to
talk about you, He could describe every moment. And
in sharing all the things He loves about you, He could
say, "You know, they're part of My family."

HATE IS SUCH A STRONG WORD

All who fear the LORD will hate evil.
Therefore, I hate pride and arrogance,
corruption and perverse speech.

PROVERBS 8:13 NLT

————•●•————

No question about it: God uses some strong words against pride. It's easy to wonder: *Does God hate it when I feel proud of a job well done? Does God hate it when I feel proud of my children's accomplishments? Does God hate it when I feel proud of my church for the way they have served our community and spread Jesus' love?*

No, that feeling of pleased satisfaction is *not* what the Bible is referring to when it talks about the pride that God hates. God hates the kind of pride that keeps people from realizing their need for Him. He hates it because of how much He wants to give salvation through Jesus Christ to everyone. But if people won't acknowledge and accept Him, He can't save them. So when you read scriptures saying that God hates pride, think of what a loving God He is that He hates what keeps people from receiving His gift of eternal life.

This week, let's gain some perspective on the issue of pride and what God's Word says about it.

Day 2

DON'T PLAY WITH PRIDE

*Pride goes before destruction, and a haughty
spirit before stumbling. It is better to be
humble in spirit with the lowly than
to divide the spoil with the proud.*

PROVERBS 16:18–19 NASB

———— ◆ ————

Scripture warns you that pride is dangerous and not a trifling matter. So you are to strive for humility, which is the opposite of pride. James 4:6 (NIV) says, "God opposes the proud but shows favor to the humble." True humility recognizes the importance of God above all and others above self. If everyone lived in true humility, think of what a wonderful world it would be!

Pride is often an overassurance about status and plans and goals, and it's foolish since you can't even guarantee your next breath, let alone guarantee what you'll do next year or even tomorrow. Consider 1 Corinthians 10:12 (NIV) which says, "So, if you think you are standing firm, be careful that you don't fall!"

Of course, you can make wise plans and goals. It would be silly not to. But believers should always be asking for God's direction in those plans and goals and recognize that "in their hearts humans plan their course, but the LORD establishes their steps" (Proverbs 16:9 NIV).

IN YOUR OWN EYES

Do not be wise in your own eyes;
fear the LORD and shun evil.
PROVERBS 3:7 NIV

———— • ◆ • ————

It's certainly no fun to feel like a fool, so who honestly doesn't want to seem wise in their own eyes? Of *course* you want to sound and seem like you have your wits about you. So, does scripture promote kids shirking their schoolwork or adults never learning something new? Should Christians be ignorant and uneducated in the world so that they never feel satisfaction in what they've learned? No, not at all. There's a big difference between worldly wisdom and knowledge, and there's a healthy balance in fearing the Lord first and letting true knowledge and wisdom result from that.

The Bible says in Proverbs 9:10 (NASB), "The fear of the LORD is the beginning of wisdom, and the knowledge of the Holy One is understanding." God is the very beginning of all wisdom and knowledge. Respecting Him first is the only way to really know anything at all. It makes perfect sense that the source of learning about the world around you is the one who created it all in the first place!

So don't be proud in what you've learned. Be proud of God for giving you the ability to learn, and for who He is, what He has done, and what He reveals to you.

Day 4

FIGHTING PRIDE AND
SELF-PRESERVATION

*"If anyone desires to be first,
he shall be last of all and servant of all."*
MARK 9:35 NKJV

———◆———

Perhaps the hardest part of the Christian life and the most counterculture aspect is the issue of pride and self-preservation. Believers have to fight for a good perspective because you constantly hear the likes of: "Do what feels right for *you*," "Look out for number one," "You can't help others if you don't help yourself first."

Yet many scriptures contradict these statements. Consider these:

"Don't be selfish; don't try to impress others. Be humble, thinking of others as better than yourselves" (Philippians 2:3 NLT).

"Jesus said to his disciples, 'If any of you wants to be my follower, you must give up your own way, take up your cross, and follow me. If you try to hang on to your life, you will lose it. But if you give up your life for my sake, you will save it'" (Matthew 16:24–25 NLT).

"If you want to be my disciple, you must, by comparison, hate everyone else—your father and mother, wife and children, brothers and sisters—yes, even your own life" (Luke 14:26 NLT).

Of course, it's a balance that takes wisdom. Give your life fully to God then constantly pray for His perfect guidance on how He wants you to use it for His glory.

LET YOUR WORDS BE HUMBLE

*"Talk no more so very proudly; let no arrogance
come from your mouth, for the LORD is the God
of knowledge; and by Him actions are weighed."*

1 SAMUEL 2:3 NKJV

Do you struggle to guard your tongue? Is there a human
on the planet who doesn't? All believers spout off with
pride at times. James chapter 3 talks about how boastful
the tongue is and how hard it is to control it. It's a
bittersweet, comforting passage of scripture that lets
you know the struggle is real for absolutely everyone.

Striving to eliminate pride in your life and focusing
on humility before God and others will help you
with your communication and relationships. For good
reason, the Bible instructs you to keep your words
humble. "A gentle answer deflects anger, but harsh
words make tempers flare. The tongue of the wise makes
knowledge appealing, but the mouth of a fool belches
out foolishness" (Proverbs 15:1–2 NLT).

So what's the best thing you can do to control your
tongue and guard it from pride? Keep it so busy with
prayer and praise that it can't do much else. If you
feel like boasting, get pumped up about God. "As the
Scriptures say, 'If you want to boast, boast only about
the LORD'" (2 Corinthians 10:17 NLT).

Day 6

HEALTHY PERSPECTIVE

*For by the grace given me I say to every one of
you: Do not think of yourself more highly than
you ought, but rather think of yourself with
sober judgment, in accordance with the
faith God has distributed to each of you.*

ROMANS 12:3 NIV

———— • ◆ • ————

Scriptures on pride and humility can be misused. God doesn't ever want you to think you're worthless. He thinks you're so valuable that He sent His Son to die to save you, so obviously you have great worth. But a healthy perspective on pride and humility is to realize that *real* and *lasting* self-worth comes from your identity in Christ.

In this world, yes, it's possible to go it alone without Jesus as Lord of your life, but no one can ever be truly fulfilled that way. They can make it look good from the outside, of course, but they'll always be hollow and aimless inside without Jesus. Ultimately, this world will amount to as much as the briefest blink of an eye compared to eternity. So remember that your value and status for eternity are based wholly on Jesus.

How you humbly follow Jesus determines what your eternal future looks like. To sacrificially put others first in the here and now earns unimaginable rewards for you in heaven forever! (See Luke 12:33–34; Luke 18:22; 2 Corinthians 5:10; 1 Timothy 6:17–19.)

Week 48 ◆ PRIDE

HE CARES

*"But it is wrong to say God doesn't listen,
to say the Almighty isn't concerned."*
JOB 35:13 NLT

———— ·•·•· ————

Do you believe God cares about you and listens to you?
Don't let worldly circumstances ever make you doubt
that. Job 35:13 says it's wrong to say He's not listening
or concerned about you. Acting like God doesn't care
about you can be a form of pride.

Some people use the excuse that "God doesn't care
about little old me" to simply fuel their desire for self-
dependence and pride in their own abilities because
"no one *else* is looking out for me anyway." Not true.
Acting like you're not worthy of God's concern or that
you've fallen off His radar contradicts His Word. God
promises that He never leaves or forsakes you and that
nothing can ever separate you from His love.

If you ever feel tempted by false humility in the
attitude of "I'm not worthy, so God must not care,"
read and remember this scripture: "What is the price
of five sparrows—two copper coins? Yet God does not
forget a single one of them. And the very hairs on your
head are all numbered. So don't be afraid; you are
more valuable to God than a whole flock of sparrows"
(Luke 12:6–7 NLT).

Day 1

KEEPING THINGS IN PERSPECTIVE

*For I reckon that the sufferings of this present
time are not worthy to be compared with
the glory which shall be revealed in us.*

ROMANS 8:18 KJV

⸻ ⬦ ⸻

As a Christian, you're destined to suffer for your faith at one time or another, and though you know it's for a truly noble cause, it can still hurt. It can be humiliating, cause you financial loss, or seem downright unjust. And as a result, it can be discouraging.

Contrary to what you may wonder at times, God doesn't enjoy seeing you suffer. "He does not afflict willingly, nor grieve the children of men" (Lamentations 3:33 NKJV). Why then does He allow such unwanted trouble? Why does He permit adversaries to do awful things to His children? Well, believe it or not, God is able to get much good out of what men intend as evil.

And the best news is, the Lord has promised to reward—*greatly* reward—you for suffering for His name. Jesus advised that when people persecute you, "Rejoice in that day and leap for joy! For indeed your reward is great in heaven" (Luke 6:23 NKJV).

Leap for joy? Yes, that's what Jesus said. This tells you heaven must be wonderful beyond your wildest dreams. You may be suffering now, but one day you'll be overjoyed.

Day 2

GOD'S SPIRIT UPON YOU

*If you are reviled for the name of Christ,
you are blessed, because the Spirit of
glory and of God rests on you.*

1 PETER 4:14 NASB

———

When opponents attack you because of your Christian
beliefs or lifestyle, and their anger and scorn are directed
against you, it can be intimidating. It's something you'd
normally try to avoid. But although they're uttering
vitriolic curses against you, you're blessed instead.

This is because when you obey Christ and identify
with Him to the point of suffering for His name, you're
clearly walking in His Spirit. Jesus said, "Abide in me,
and I in you" (John 15:4 KJV). His Spirit abides (dwells)
in your heart, but you in turn must seek to walk so
close to Him that you're in the center of the cloud of
His presence (Exodus 13:21), surrounded by Him.

His presence then envelops you and rests upon
you. "You are blessed, because the Spirit of glory and
of God rests on you." In Psalm 90:17 (KJV) the Israelites
prayed, "Let the beauty of the LORD our God be upon
us," and one of the surest ways for you to have God's
beauty is for you to walk close to Him, in the midst of
His presence, so that His Spirit rests upon you.

ADVERSITY ✦ Week 49

OVERCOMING THE WORLD

*"These things I have spoken to you, that in Me
you may have peace. In the world you will
have tribulation; but be of good cheer,
I have overcome the world."*

JOHN 16:33 NKJV

———•◆•———

This is a beautiful promise, and one you can constantly take to the bank. Perhaps low finances are wearing you down; perhaps you're struggling with illness; perhaps friends are bad-mouthing you; perhaps family members look at you as some kind of "religious weirdo"; or perhaps people are maligning your character in the workplace.

As Jesus promised, "In the world you *will* have tribulation." And Paul added, "All that will live godly in Christ Jesus shall suffer persecution" (2 Timothy 3:12 KJV). It's guaranteed.

But Jesus *also* guarantees that you can have marvelous peace. Despite difficult circumstances, you can be cheerful, knowing that Jesus has overcome the world. All that the world had to throw at your Savior couldn't take Him down. And His Word then promises in turn that you "have overcome them: because greater is he that is in you, than he that is in the world" (1 John 4:4 KJV).

What is the secret to having peace in the midst of such trials? Trusting God. "You will keep him in perfect peace. . .because he trusts in You" (Isaiah 26:3 NKJV).

Day 4

ESTABLISHED BY GOD

*After you have suffered for a little while, the God
of all grace, who called you to His eternal glory
in Christ, will Himself perfect, confirm,
strengthen and establish you.*

1 Peter 5:10 NASB

As much as you would like to, you can't always avoid
trouble. Problems relentlessly assault you, and a number
of them will find a way through your defenses. In
fact, you will experience *many* troubles. But just as
relentlessly, God comes to your aid. The Psalms promise,
"The righteous person faces many troubles, but the
Lord comes to the rescue each time" (Psalm 34:19 NLT).

However, you often have to suffer from life's problems
for a while before God delivers you from them. Like
Jesus, you may at times be "a man of sorrows, and
acquainted with grief" (Isaiah 53:3 KJV). You can forget
that little Sunday school song about being "happy all
the time." Life doesn't work that way, and the Bible
makes no such promises.

But one thing the Bible *does* promise is that after
you have suffered for a while, God will deliver you.
He will personally come alongside you to confirm,
strengthen, and establish you. Yes, He allows you to
be tested by the refiner's fire, but His end goal is not to
destroy you but to purify you and to strengthen you.

SHARING IN
CHRIST'S SUFFERINGS

*Dear friends, do not be surprised at the fiery
ordeal that has come on you to test you, as though
something strange were happening to you. But. . .
you participate in the sufferings of Christ, so that
you may be overjoyed when his glory is revealed.*

1 PETER 4:12–13 NIV

———— • ◆ • ————

You willingly participate in the sufferings of Christ
when you go out of your way to help the less fortunate.
Such sacrifices cost you time and effort, and may even
bring hardship and discomfort upon you. You may
give to the needy when you already have many bills
to pay. Or you may do good to your enemies, only to
be mocked and rebuffed for your efforts.

If you're new at following Christ in self-sacrificial
ways, you may be surprised that He allows you to
suffer for doing good. (Perhaps you expected to be
rewarded instantly instead.) But what's happening
should *not* strike you as strange. You're following in
Jesus' footprints, being rejected as He was rejected and
suffering as He suffered.

Of course this will hurt, but God promises that
when Jesus returns in all His glory, He will amply reward
you. So don't be afraid to take on a little trouble as you
reach out to others. God *will* reward you. . .in the end!

REIGNING IN ETERNITY

If we suffer, we shall also reign with him.
2 TIMOTHY 2:12 KJV

You know God will reward you for suffering for His sake, because Jesus said that when you're persecuted, "great is your reward in heaven" (Matthew 5:12 KJV). Exactly *how* magnificent is your reward? Very great indeed. Paul said, "If we suffer, we shall also reign with him."

When Jesus' kingdom comes upon earth, you who have followed and obeyed Him and suffered for His name will literally rule earth with Him. Jesus personally promised, "To the one who is victorious and does my will to the end, I will give authority over the nations—that one 'will rule them with an iron scepter'" (Revelation 2:26–27 NIV). It also says, "They. . .reigned with Christ a thousand years" (Revelation 20:4 NIV).

You may suffer scorn now, but in that day you'll be highly exalted. God will enjoy rewarding you with tremendous authority and blazing glory, causing all people to greatly honor you.

It's no fun suffering, and sometimes you wonder, *Is it worth it?* It's definitely worth it! God will delight to lavish wonderful things on you in heaven and give you tremendous happiness. So remain faithful to Him now, even during difficult times. You'll be glad that you did.

WALKING AS JESUS WALKED

*For to this you were called, because Christ
also suffered for us, leaving us an example,
that you should follow His steps.*

1 PETER 2:21 NKJV

One of the less-appreciated truths of Christianity is that God frequently calls you to suffer. In the Gospels you see Jesus suffering, and this wasn't just something that He experienced because it was His unique destiny. Jesus was doing it because He was setting an example for His followers. He intended for you to follow His example.

Here's another little-loved truth. Paul declared, "I now rejoice in my sufferings for you, and fill up in my flesh what is lacking in the afflictions of Christ, for. . . the church" (Colossians 1:24 NKJV). Christ's suffering on the cross is all you need to obtain salvation, but preaching the Gospel and living a godly life frequently involve self-sacrifice and privation.

This may not be the comfort zone you were seeking, but remember, Jesus calls you to a self-sacrificial lifestyle. It's wonderful to be blessed and prosperous and lacking nothing, but that isn't always the path to becoming more Christlike. Nor is it usually the path to reaching the world with the Gospel.

God uses adversity to test your faith, teach you patience and perseverance, and refine you and make you pure.

HOLD FIRMLY

*We have come to share in Christ, if indeed we
hold our original conviction firmly to the very end.*
HEBREWS 3:14 NIV

This scripture describes what perseverance in the Christian faith is about—holding firmly to the trust you had when you first accepted Jesus as your Lord and Savior. Do you remember that day? Take a moment to think back to the moment when you surrendered your life to the only one worthy.

Maybe it was years ago, maybe you were very young, or maybe it was more recent. You realized your need for a Savior. You confessed your sin and asked His forgiveness. You believed in His death on the cross as the sacrifice for your sin, and you trusted in His resurrection, His victory over death, and His promise for eternal life. And now you have the Holy Spirit dwelling in you.

Hold fast to all that, friend. Hold tight and don't let go. This world will constantly try to steal your faith. Your enemy the devil relentlessly tries to devour you. Don't let him. Persevere. Actively maintain your faith and live it out even though the world is constantly hostile toward you because of it. Don't let that discourage you. Let the devotions this week encourage you to hold firmly to the confidence you had at the beginning.

PERSEVERANCE ◆ *Week 50*

EYES ON JESUS

*Therefore, since we are surrounded by such a huge
crowd of witnesses to the life of faith, let us strip
off every weight that slows us down, especially the
sin that so easily trips us up. And let us run
with endurance the race God has set before us.
We do this by keeping our eyes on Jesus,
the champion who initiates and perfects our
faith. Because of the joy awaiting him,
he endured the cross, disregarding its
shame. Now he is seated in the
place of honor beside God's throne.*
HEBREWS 12:1–2 NLT

To persevere in the Christian faith you must keep
your eyes on Jesus. As the old hymn says, "Turn your
eyes upon Jesus. Look full in His wonderful face. And
the things of earth will grow strangely dim, in the
light of His glory and grace." Both the triumphs and
the troubles of this world pale in comparison to the
glory and grace of Jesus. He sustains you through any
difficult and trying periods.

Today's scripture reminds you that Jesus "endured
the cross, disregarding its shame" because He had joy
waiting for Him just beyond this life, in heaven. Your
life may be full of trouble, but take heart. You, too,
have eternal joy awaiting you in heaven. Don't give up!

ACTION REQUIRED

*[They strengthened] the souls of the disciples,
encouraging them to continue in the faith,
and saying, "Through many tribulations
we must enter the kingdom of God."*

ACTS 14:22 NASB

———•◆•———

To persevere in your faith, you can't just sit back and relax. Real faith is active. If you let it stagnate, you won't confidently continue in it. If you don't actively work on building your relationship with Jesus Christ, you will falter.

Acts 14:22 says that we will enter the kingdom of God "through many tribulations." That sure doesn't sound like rest and relaxation, but God strengthens you and increases your ability to persevere through many difficulties.

How do you keep your relationship with Jesus thriving in the midst of hardship? By daily personal time in God's Word. By regular fellowship and worship in a Bible-teaching church. By service to others. By discipling someone less mature than you. God uses all these things to increase your perseverance. He strengthens your relationship with Him as He helps you connect with people and encourage one another.

Colossians 1:10 (NLT) says, "Then the way you live will always honor and please the Lord, and your lives will produce every kind of good fruit. All the while, you will grow as you learn to know God better and better." That's the kind of perseverance to strive for.

Day 4

TRIED AND TRUE

*These trials will show that your faith is genuine.
It is being tested as fire tests and purifies gold—
though your faith is far more precious than mere
gold. So when your faith remains strong through
many trials, it will bring you much praise and
glory and honor on the day when Jesus Christ
is revealed to the whole world.*

1 PETER 1:7 NLT

Keeping the faith through adversity is never easy, but it shows God and others that you're for real. No one escapes hard times in this world, but a person's faith in Christ, or lack of it, will determine how he handles them. You have to be willing to go through the heat of the fires to make your faith strong and pure. Then see what happens, as God develops your character to be more like Jesus.

Romans 5:3–5 (NLT) says, "We can rejoice, too, when we run into problems and trials, for we know that they help us develop endurance. And endurance develops strength of character, and character strengthens our confident hope of salvation. And this hope will not lead to disappointment. For we know how dearly God loves us, because he has given us the Holy Spirit to fill our hearts with his love."

CONSTANT PRAYER IS KEY

*With all prayer and petition pray at all times in
the Spirit, and with this in view, be on the alert
with all perseverance and petition for all the saints.*
EPHESIANS 6:18 NASB

———— • ◆ • ————

You absolutely cannot persevere in faith in Jesus Christ
all on your own. It's just not possible. So how, then?
Through constant, endless, diverse prayer. Notice
how many times Ephesians 6:18 uses the word *all*.
And reread this powerful phrase: "With *all* prayer
and petition pray at *all* times. . . ." Paul put a lot of
emphasis on that word *all*, and it shows the kinds of
prayer and times for prayer—all kinds and at all times!
There is no bad topic or request to pray about and no
bad time to do it.

Do like 1 Thessalonians 5:16–18 (NLT) instructs:
"Always be joyful. Never stop praying. Be thankful in
all circumstances, for this is God's will for you who
belong to Christ Jesus."

Many people are looking for God's will in their lives,
and this scripture spells it out clearly. It's God's will
that you be joyful, that you never stop praying, and that
you be thankful in all circumstances. Do these things
and you'll be able to persevere until Christ's return.

SOMETIMES SAY NO

For the grace of God has appeared that offers
salvation to all people. It teaches us to say "No"
to ungodliness and worldly passions, and to live
self-controlled, upright and godly lives in this
present age, while we wait for the blessed hope—
the appearing of the glory of our great
God and Savior, Jesus Christ.

TITUS 2:11–13 NIV

If you've ever overcommitted yourself, you've learned the importance of saying no. In a fallen world, there sure are a lot of bad things to get involved in. But there are also a lot of wonderful things to do, especially in the church. But too many people get the idea that they should commit to *everything* they're asked to do, or be a part of *every* ministry going on, and so on. That can be overwhelming.

Titus 2 talks about saying no to ungodliness and worldly passions. For sure, you must avoid such things. But it's wise to be aware that even the best ministries in your church might be ungodly (in that they're not God's will for you) if you're doing them for the wrong reasons or they're stealing your time from what God *really* wants you to do.

Ask God to help you persevere in the good works He has planned for you. Nothing more, nothing less.

Week 51 ♦ PERSEVERANCE

PERSEVERANCE ◆

THOUGH YOU FALL. . .

Though he fall, he shall not be utterly cast down;
for the LORD upholds him with His hand.
PSALM 37:24 NKJV

———•◆•———

Psalm 37:24 encourages you to persevere, knowing that God never abandons you no matter how bad your circumstances. "Nothing can ever separate us from God's love. Neither death nor life, neither angels nor demons, neither our fears for today nor our worries about tomorrow—not even the powers of hell can separate us from God's love. No power in the sky above or in the earth below—indeed, nothing in all creation will ever be able to separate us from the love of God that is revealed in Christ Jesus our Lord" (Romans 8:38–39 NLT).

Consider heroine of the faith, Corrie ten Boom, who persevered through absolute horror in Hitler's Europe. She learned firsthand that "we are hard pressed on every side, but not crushed; perplexed, but not in despair; persecuted, but not abandoned; struck down, but not destroyed. We always carry around in our body the death of Jesus, so that the life of Jesus may also be revealed in our body" (2 Corinthians 4:8–10 NIV).

Knowing that God's love will never leave you and that faithful ones have preceded you, choose to persevere each new day, confidently hoping in Jesus Christ.

Day 1

THE PROOF IS IN THE PUTTING (OTHERS FIRST)

For this is the love of God, that we keep His
commandments. And His commandments
are not burdensome.

1 JOHN 5:3 NKJV

———— • ◆ • ————

Love is hugely misunderstood in the world. It gets characterized as warm, fuzzy feelings that are strong enough to make two people promise undying loyalty to each other but not strong enough to last a lifetime. Marriages wither and drop when one or both spouses can no longer muster whatever it was they felt when they first dated and fell for each other. Parents harshly criticize children, children disrespect and disobey parents, friends fall out over miscommunication, and grace is nowhere to be found. It gets worse when you love God that way.

That was John's concern, so he cleared up a few misconceptions and laid out love's parameters: As Christians, you know you love God if you obey His commandments, which means loving His children (1 John 5:1–3). When you sacrifice your comfort and self-interest for the welfare of others, you're showing them the kind of love that Jesus showed you.

When you love like that, you're loving God, and you're relieved of the burden of this world's weakened affections. "Every child of God defeats this evil world, and we achieve this victory through our faith" (1 John 5:4 NLT).

Day 2

WAITING ON LOVE

But as it is written, Eye hath not seen, nor ear heard, neither have entered into the heart of man, the things which God hath prepared for them that love him.

1 CORINTHIANS 2:9 KJV

Waiting, as they say, is the hardest part. But for the Christian, it's the best part. Paul quoted the prophet Isaiah, who instead of *love* used the word *wait*: ". . .what [God] hath prepared for him that waiteth for him" (Isaiah 64:4 KJV). Paul's switch indicates that there is something in waiting on God that relates closely to loving Him.

On one hand, waiting on God shows your love for Him, your trust that He has shown you in His Word and by His Spirit all of the amazing and wonderful things He has planned for you. And yet, His best gifts are not hidden from you—abundant life, peace, and salvation—things that no one on earth could give or teach you.

The world can't fathom the wonder of God's Holy Spirit, living in you, guiding and directing you into His truth, and drawing out good fruit: love, joy, peace, long-suffering, kindness, goodness, faithfulness, gentleness, and self-control (Galatians 5:22–23). The gifts that God's people awaited in Isaiah's day became available through Jesus—and people who love Him are part of His work in spreading that good news.

*(Left margin, vertical text):* LOVE OF GOD – PART 2 ◆ Week 51

WHO'S YOUR DADDY?

*Jesus told them, "If God were your Father,
you would love me, because I have come
to you from God. I am not here on
my own, but he sent me."*

JOHN 8:42 NLT

———◆———

Human instinct picks and chooses what version of truth and knowledge best serves its own advantage. It's not natural to be others oriented; in fact, even believers tend to "orient" others for their own purposes, cultivating those relationships that best suit their agenda. They can only break from this propensity by the blood of Christ.

If that sounds harsh, consider the context of the verse. Jesus was engaged in another showdown with the Pharisees, who had gone from just hating His guts to wanting Him dead. They thought they were doing God's work in dealing with this uneducated carpenter and His "blasphemous" claims, but Jesus took a different view, telling them: "You belong to your father, the devil, and you want to carry out your father's desires" (John 8:44 NIV).

His point was that loving God is not just a matter of knowledge but of understanding God's heart—which matches His holiness with grace and His justice with reconciliation. When God is your Father, you will take Him at His word—loving Him first and foremost, but also loving others and seeking to win them to His kingdom.

DESIRE RESTRAINED BY DELIGHT

Take delight in the Lord,
and he will give you your heart's desires.
PSALM 37:4 NLT

Imagine the damage you would do using only the second half of that verse—if God were, in fact, some type of cosmic genie whose sole purpose was to please your heart. Some would take the easy path and turn their lives into pleasure gardens, indulging whims, lusts, and momentary feelings.

Then, there would be those who determined that they knew what was best for everyone else and set about creating a world in their image—from the family all the way up to government, with society, culture, and knowledge all reflecting the maxim: *Do what you want; you know best.*

Both scenarios sound a lot like Satan-approved dystopias, as well as reflections of the world you actually live in. Thankfully, though, God is there, not as a wish machine but as a loving King. When Jesus returns, He will set the world to rights, exercising iron-hard justice against those who have refused to delight in Him.

Until then, you can be thankful that you have a heavenly Father in whom you rejoice, and that the more you seek Him, the more your heart's desires will align with His, and you have a fighting chance to bring His light into your corner of this dark world.

Day 5

LOVE FEARLESSLY

God is love, and all who live in love live in God,
and God lives in them. And as we live in God, our
love grows more perfect. . . . Such love has no fear,
because perfect love expels all fear. If we are afraid,
it is for fear of punishment, and this shows that
we have not fully experienced his perfect love.
We love each other because he loved us first.

1 JOHN 4:16–19 NLT

Have you ever loved someone so completely, so joyfully, that there is no sacrifice you wouldn't make, no humiliation you wouldn't endure, no length to which you wouldn't go in order to ensure that person's best and highest good?

That kind of love is truly remarkable, rare and special in a selfish world—but even so, your love isn't perfect. You know what you want to do and why, but your imperfections keep you from always doing it.

Only God loves perfectly, because only God is perfect. You can rest in His love, knowing He has done everything in Christ to forgive your past, provide for your present, and secure your future. Let His love fill you and flow through you, so that you can also love others fearlessly—loving like Jesus loves you, His special one for whom He gave all.

A SANCTIFIED SPONGE

*Do not love the world or anything in the world.
If anyone loves the world, love for
the Father is not in them.*

1 JOHN 2:15 NIV

———————

You are like a sponge, probably far more than you'd care to admit. You absorb everything that happens, taking in the bad with the good—learning, experiencing, and growing as you go. While sponges are impressively expansive, however, they are not unlimited in capacity. You have to be careful what you take in, because there's only so much room. And if you absorb the wrong things, the good gets squeezed out.

The world pressures you to conform, squeezing you with materialism and relativism, hoping to push God out and fill you with fleeting pleasures and convenient truths that never fully satisfy. The reason Jesus prayed that God would protect you in the world but not take you out of it (John 17:15–16) was so that you might have a godly influence.

Fortunately, you can squeeze out the world and absorb God's love and truth instead. Staying regularly in prayer, Bible study, and Christian fellowship all keep you filled with living water, steeped in God's Spirit and presence. Those practices sanctify you, helping you to love God more and be a conduit of His love to others.

Day 7

STRAIGHT LINES FROM
CROOKED STICKS

*We know that all things work together for good
to them that love God, to them who are the
called according to his purpose.*

ROMANS 8:28 KJV

———————

A medieval saying observed that God makes straight lines with crooked sticks. All of life's mysteries, disappointments, successes, and failures fall under that purview. Romans 8:28 is famous for covering similar territory, but because it's so well-known, it's worth noting a few things this promise is *not*.

For starters, it's not a promise for all people, but just for those who love God, who understand what the Bible says about love—that God *is* love and those who love Him show it by obeying Him and turning their best in life to His service and glory.

Furthermore, it's not because you deserve it, but because He called you. You seldom love God well or enough, and yet He loves you, saving you, adopting you as His child, and making you part of His work on earth.

Finally, it's not about some things, or most things, but *all* things. You can commit with confidence to whatever work He is doing—even if it's one by which you and others are allowed to suffer or fail—because God's grace will "be with all those who love our Lord Jesus Christ in sincerity" (Ephesians 6:24 NKJV).

Day 1

NO MORE SORROW

*The Lamb which is in the midst of the throne
shall feed them, and shall lead them unto living
fountains of waters: and God shall wipe
away all tears from their eyes.*

REVELATION 7:17 KJV

Sometimes life is so difficult that you don't know how you're going to make it another day. Financial pressures, health issues, and family problems can cause tremendous strain on you—physically, mentally, and spiritually. You cry out to God for relief, but He doesn't seem to answer, at least not immediately, nor in the way you wish. And so you cry bitter tears.

You wonder if God has abandoned you. You ask yourself if He even cares about your pain. Yes, He does. The Bible tells you, "In all their affliction he was afflicted" (Isaiah 63:9 KJV). Your God was there feeling your pain every time you suffered. Jesus was "a man of sorrows, and acquainted with grief" (Isaiah 53:3 KJV). He knows every tear that you've cried (Psalm 56:8).

One day Jesus will personally lead you into the transcendently beautiful gardens of heaven, with the fountains of the water of life cascading close by, and God, your Father, will hold you in His loving arms and wipe away all the tears from your eyes. Even now He seeks to comfort you in your sorrows.

TAKING THE LONG VIEW

"Those who love their life in this world will lose it. Those who care nothing for their life in this world will keep it for eternity."

JOHN 12:25 NLT

Many people seek primarily to enjoy the things and the pleasures of this world. They want to live "the abundant life," to have a comfortable, affluent Christianity, and to enjoy the best this world has to offer on a continual basis. They're generally not that interested in sacrificing or suffering for the sake of the Gospel.

It's not a sin to be wealthy, but possessing riches does present constant challenges. Jesus warned, "Take heed and beware of covetousness, for one's life does not consist in the abundance of the things he possesses" (Luke 12:15 NKJV). He also stated that "the deceitfulness of riches, and the desires for other things entering in choke the word" (Mark 4:19 NKJV).

On the other hand, if you live modestly and are willing to share with those in need, you avoid many temptations and snares. Your *true* rewards are in heaven, not on earth. You have to take the long view, the eternal view, to have this mind-set. You must know that you won't receive all your compensations in this life, but trust God to reward you in the next life.

THE CITY OF LIGHT

There will no longer be any night; and they will not have need of the light of a lamp nor the light of the sun, because the Lord God will illumine them.

REVELATION 22:5 NASB

This passage says "they will not have need of the. . . light of the sun," so some Christians conclude that when God creates the new heavens and the new earth there will no longer be a sun. With no star to orbit, Earth will wander aimlessly through space. But that's missing what the verse is saying.

There will still be a sun, and its light will continue to shine on earth, but those who live in God's magnificent city won't *need* its light. God Himself will dwell in the heart of the new Jerusalem and fill it with intense glory. But the regions at the far side of this planet will still need sunlight.

John noted that "the city was pure gold, like clear glass" (Revelation 21:18 NASB). The nature of this material will allow God's light to glow throughout the entire city unimpeded. God's glory will fill every nook and cranny of the new Jerusalem, including the saints who dwell there. In that day, as Jesus said, "your whole body will be full of light" (Matthew 6:22 NIV).

Day 4

ETERNAL LIFE IN JESUS

*"You study the Scriptures diligently because
you think that in them you have eternal life.
These are the very Scriptures that testify about me."*

JOHN 5:39 NIV

———— •◆• ————

The Jews in Jesus' day read, studied, discussed, and memorized the Hebrew scriptures from childhood, seeking to encounter everlasting life. But frequently, despite their in-depth studies, they were still left wondering, "What good thing shall I do, that I may have eternal life?" (Matthew 19:16 KJV).

When Jesus told some Jews to work "for the food which endures to eternal life" (John 6:27 NASB), they asked, "What shall we do, so that we may work the works of God?" Jesus answered, "This is the work of God, that you believe in Him whom He has sent" (vv. 28–29 NASB). Jesus was plainly declaring that the only "work" necessary to acquire endless life was to put their faith in Him.

From the mention of the Prophet whom the people were required to hear and obey (Deuteronomy 18:15–19), to the Suffering Servant who would take on the sins of mankind (Isaiah 53:4–8), to the resurrected Son of God (Psalm 16:8–11), the scriptures gave witness to the coming Savior.

Jesus is the only way God has provided for people to encounter eternal life. Have you received the Spirit of Jesus into your heart?

A NEW, ETERNAL EARTH

*But in keeping with his promise we are looking
forward to a new heaven and a new earth,
where righteousness dwells.*

2 PETER 3:13 NIV

———•◆•———

God promised in 600 BC, "Behold, I create new heavens and a new earth; and the former things will not be remembered" (Isaiah 65:17 NASB).

Right now your mortal body only lives about eighty years, but during the rapture when it's transformed, it will become indestructible and immortal. This physical planet is now temporal as well, but it will go through a transformation also. One day "the heavens shall pass away with a great noise, and the elements shall melt with fervent heat, the earth. . .shall be burned up" (2 Peter 3:10 KJV).

John declared, "Then I saw a new heaven and a new earth; for the first heaven and the first earth passed away" (Revelation 21:1 NASB). The original earth was dissolved (2 Peter 3:11–12), but God promised, "The new heavens and the new earth which I make will endure before Me" (Isaiah 66:22 NASB). They will literally last for all eternity.

Earth will become a global paradise, full of wonderful exotic flora and fauna, lovelier than the garden of Eden. But best of all, from its iron core to its basaltic crust, it will be transformed into eternal materials.

Day 6

WITH THE LAMB FOREVER

*Therefore are they before the throne of God,
and serve him day and night in his temple:
and he that sitteth on the throne
shall dwell among them.*

REVELATION 7:15 KJV

One day you'll be personally with Jesus and spend the rest of eternity in His presence. You'll no longer need to try to imagine what God is like, because you'll gaze upon Him with your own eyes and have direct access to His throne. And you'll see His Son, Jesus, sitting at His right hand.

You'll spend a great deal of time in His heavenly temple—in His presence, in the area immediately surrounding His throne. "One thing I ask from the LORD. . .to gaze on the beauty of the LORD and to seek him in his temple" (Psalm 27:4 NIV).

And God who sits on the throne will live with you. Think of it! God Himself will hold you and comfort you.

Even now, before that day, you have a High Priest—Jesus Christ—who can sympathize with your sins, shortcomings, and weaknesses, because He was tempted on earth just as you are. "Let us therefore come boldly to the throne of grace, that we may obtain mercy and find grace to help in time of need" (Hebrews 4:15–16 NKJV).

Day 7

ABIDING ETERNALLY

And the world is passing away, and the lust of it;
but he who does the will of God abides forever.

1 JOHN 2:17 NKJV

This decrepit world with all its flagrant lust and anti-God agenda seems to be in its heyday, going strong and glorying in its pride and exaltation, but if you know the signs to look for, you can see that it's even now cracking at the seams and teetering off the rails into the deep ditches to join the wreckage of other doomed ideologies and failed philosophies.

The Lord is constantly "casting down. . .every high thing that exalteth itself against the knowledge of God" (2 Corinthians 10:5 KJV), and one day He will bring man's entire corrupt world system to its knees. Then "the meek shall inherit the earth; and shall delight themselves in the abundance of peace" (Psalm 37:11 KJV).

Yes, in that day the righteous shall truly enjoy peace! They'll no longer be a despised minority, persecuted by the immoral majority.

It can be very difficult at times to remain faithful to God's Word when most of the world is aggressively fighting to go in the opposite direction, but take cheer! You'll still be around in the everlasting kingdom of Christ, utterly unopposed, when the wicked have fallen and are no more.

CONTRIBUTORS

Quentin Guy writes from the high desert of New Mexico, to encourage and equip people to know and serve God. He currently works in publishing for Calvary Albuquerque and has cowritten such books as *Weird and Gross Bible Stuff* and *The 2:52 Boys Bible*, both of which are stuck in future classic status. A former middle school teacher, he serves with his wife as marriage prep mentors and trusts God that his children will survive their teenage years. Quentin's devotions appear in weeks 4, 13, 22, 26, 29, 35, 39, and 51.

Glenn A. Hascall is an accomplished writer with credits in more than a hundred books. He is a broadcast veteran and voice actor and is actively involved in writing and producing audio drama. Glenn's devotions appear in weeks 3, 7, 12, 19, 24, 30, 37, and 47.

Kelly McIntosh is a wife, mother of twins, and editor from Ohio. She loves books, the beach, and everything about autumn (but mostly pumpkin spice lattes). Kelly's devotions appear in weeks 6, 11, 32, and 41.

JoAnne Simmons is a writer and editor who's in awe of God's love and the ways He guides and provides. Her favorite things include coffee shops, libraries, the Bible, good grammar, being a wife and mom, dogs, music, Disney World, punctuation, church, the beach, and many dear family and friends—but not in that order. If her family weren't so loving and flexible, she'd be in big trouble; and if God's mercies weren't new every morning, she'd never get out of bed. JoAnne's devotions appear in weeks 8, 14, 18, 23, 31, 40, 48, and 50.

Ed Strauss is a freelance writer living in British Columbia, Canada. He has authored or coauthored more than fifty books for children, tweens, and adults. Ed has a passion for biblical apologetics, and besides writing for Barbour, has been published by Zondervan, Tyndale, Moody, and Focus on the Family. Ed's devotions appear in weeks 1, 9, 15, 21, 25, 28, 33, 38, 42, 44, 49, and 52.

Janice Thompson, who lives in the Houston area, writes novels, nonfiction, magazine articles, and musical comedies for the stage. The mother of four married daughters, she is quickly adding grandchildren to the family mix. Janice's devotions appear in weeks 16, 20, 36, and 45.

Lee Warren is published in such varied venues as *Discipleship Journal*, *Sports Spectrum*, Yahoo! Sports, Crosswalk.com, and ChristianityToday.com. He is also the author of the book *Finishing Well: Living with the End in Mind (A Devotional)*, and he writes regular features for *The Pathway* newspaper and *Living Light News*. Lee makes his home in Omaha, Nebraska. Lee's devotions appear in weeks 2, 5, 10, 17, 27, 34, 43, and 46.

SCRIPTURE INDEX